# A+ Certification
# Test Yourself
# Practice Exams

# A+ Certification
# Test Yourself
# Practice Exams

Syngress Media, Inc.

Osborne McGraw-Hill

Berkeley New York St. Louis San Francisco Auckland Bogotá Hamburg London Madrid Mexico City
Milan Montreal New Delhi Panama City Paris São Paulo Singapore Sydney Tokyo Toronto

Osborne McGraw-Hill
2600 Tenth Street
Berkeley, California 94710
U.S.A.

For information on translations or book distributors outside the U.S.A.,
or to arrange bulk purchase discounts for sales promotions, premiums, or
fund-raisers, please contact Osborne/**McGraw-Hill** at the above address.

A+ Certification Test Yourself Practice Exams Guide

234567890 DOC DOC 901987654321098

ISBN 0-07-211877-6

| | | |
|---|---|---|
| **Publisher**<br>Brandon A. Nordin | **Copy Editor**<br>Kathleen Faughnan | **Series Design**<br>Roberta Steele<br>Arlette Crosland |
| **Editor-in-Chief**<br>Scott Rogers | **Proofreader**<br>Pat Mannion | **Cover Design**<br>Regan Honda |
| **Acquisitions Editor**<br>Gareth Hancock | **Computer Designers**<br>Ann Sellers<br>Mickey Galicia<br>Roberta Steele | **Editorial Management**<br>Syngress Media, Inc. |
| **Project Editor**<br>Jody McKenzie | | |
| **Technical Editor**<br>Darin McGee | **Illustrators**<br>Lance Ravella<br>Brian Wells | |

## From Global Knowledge Network

At Global Knowledge Network we strive to support the multiplicity of learning styles required by our students to achieve success as technical professionals. In this book, it is our intention to offer the reader a valuable tool for successful completion of the A+ exams.

As the world's largest IT training company, Global Knowledge Network is uniquely positioned to offer this book. The expertise gained each year from providing instructor-led training to hundreds of thousands of students worldwide has been captured in book form to enhance your learning experience. We hope that the quality of this book demonstrates our commitment to your lifelong learning success. Whether you choose to learn through the written word, computer-based training, Web delivery, or instructor-led training, Global Knowledge Network is committed to providing you the very best in each of those categories. For those of you who know Global Knowledge Network, or those of you who have just found us for the first time, our goal is to be your lifelong competency partner.

Thank you for the opportunity to serve you. We look forward to serving your needs again in the future.

Warmest regards,

Duncan Anderson
Chief Operating Officer, Global Knowledge Network

# ABOUT SYNGRESS MEDIA

**Syngress Media** creates books and software for Information Technology professionals seeking skill enhancement and career advancement. Its products are designed to comply with vendor and industry standard course curricula, and are optimized for certification exam preparation. You can contact Syngress via the web at www.syngress.com.

# ABOUT THE CONTRIBUTORS

**Cameron Brandon** (A+, MCSE, CNE, CNA, and MCPS: Internet Systems) is a Network Engineer/Administrator in the greater Portland, Oregon, area with Capstone Technology Corporation. His specialty is Windows NT with BackOffice Integration.

Cameron participated in the Intel migration to Windows NT in Oregon, the largest migration of its kind in history. He completed his MCSE, CNE, CNA, MCPS: Internet Systems, and A+ certifications in five months, which shows what you can do if you set your mind to it.

**Ted Hamilton** (A+ Certified Technician) is a systems engineer for Electronic Data Systems. He has been involved with computers since 1979. A graduate of the College of Wooster with a bachelor's degree in Business Economics, he has also completed some work in graduate-level accounting. In addition to writing for this book, he was also a contributor to the *A+ Certification Study Guide* (Osborne/McGraw-Hill).

Recognizing the growing role that computers play in our lives and seeing the huge demand for computer networking engineers, Ted has focused on continually upgrading his computer knowledge, including studying for the MCSE certification. You can reach Ted by email at Tjhtjhtjh@aol.com or reach him on the web at http://homepage.usr.com/h/hamilton/.

**Tom Judge** (A+, MSCE, CNA) is a relatively new IS professional. Prior to his mid-life change of career, he worked in broadcast television for almost 20 years. Having an interest in communications media at an early age, he began his career in the early 1970s as an audio engineer. Tom moved from audio production and engineering to video production and engineering in the mid-1970s.

In 1992 he bought his first PC, a 386 laptop that he took on the road with him while traveling for ABC Sports as a field support engineer on remote productions. Through self-training he studied and passed the necessary exams to achieve his MCSE status in the fall of 1997. He also holds an A+ certification and Novell CNA certification.

Tom owns and operates an ISP under the domain of tgsolutions.com. The company name, T&G Simple Solutions (prompting his favorite motto, "I like to keep it simple wherever possible.") is located in Kinnelon, New Jersey. You can reach Tom at simple@tgsolutions.com or on the web at www.tgsolutions.com.

**Dwight Watt** (A+ Certified Technician) is a Computer Information Systems instructor at the Elbert County Campus of Athens Area Technical Institute in Elberton, Georgia, and is a consultant in Swainsboro, Georgia. He holds an Ed.D. from the University of Georgia, and an MBA and BA from Winthrop University. He is the author of *Structured COBOL for Technical Students*. He has also co-authored several papers. Dwight has worked on computer programming and network design and installation for several organizations. He can be reached at Dwight-Watt@worldnet.att.net.

## Technical Review by:

**Darin McGee** is a Senior Network Engineer under contract with the FCC. He holds the CNP, MCSE + Internet, MCNE, NCIP, and A+ Service Technician certifications. Darin has been working with computers since 1979, when he taught himself the BASIC programming language on a Tandy TRS-80. Darin can be reached at darin@tolder.com.

# ACKNOWLEDGMENTS

We would like to thank the following people:

- Richard Kristof of Global Knowledge Network for championing the series and providing us access to some great people and information. And to Patrick Von Schlag, Robin Yunker, David Mantica, Stacey Cannon, and Kevin Murray for all their cooperation.

- To all the incredibly hard-working folks at Osborne/McGraw-Hill: Brandon Nordin, Scott Rogers, and Gareth Hancock for their help in launching a great series and being solid team players. In addition, Cynthia Douglas, Steve Emry, Jody McKenzie, Anne Ellingsen, and Bernadette Jurich for their help in fine-tuning the book.

- To Michelle Vahlkamp and Esther Kraft at CompTIA, for quickly answering our many questions.

# CONTENTS

We built this book for a specific reason. Every time we asked A+ certified technicians and A+ candidates what they wanted in their study materials, they answered "More questions!" Based on that resounding request, we built a book full of questions on the A+ exams so you can test yourself to your heart's content.

## In This Book

This book is organized in parts, or modules, by exam. We cover each of the exams in a separate section and we also have a separate "Test Yourself" module.

### The Q & A Modules

You will find one Q & A module for the Core exam and one for the Windows/DOS exam. Each module has 500 original questions, followed by an answer section that has full explanations of the correct choices.

Each module is divided into categories, so you will cover every topic tested by CompTIA. Each topic is a heading within the chapter, so you can study by topic if you like. Should you find you need further review on any particular topic, you will find that the topic headings correspond to the chapters of Osborne/McGraw-Hill's *A+ Certification Study Guide*. Want to simulate an actual exam? The section "The Test Yourself Module" explains how.

In addition, throughout the Q & A modules, we have sprinkled helpful notes in the form of Exam Watches and Q & A scenarios:

■ **Exam Watch** notes call attention to information about, and potential pitfalls in, the exam. These helpful hints are written by A+ certified technicians who have taken the exams and have received their certification—who better to tell you what to worry about? They know what you're about to go through!

■ **Q & A** sections lay out problems and solutions in a quick-read format.

## QUESTIONS AND ANSWERS

| | |
|---|---|
| "My computer is getting a keyboard error." | Either the keyboard needs cleaning, the connection has worked its way loose, or the keyboard must be replaced. |
| "The computer lost its BIOS settings." | This is commonly caused by a low CMOS battery. Replace the battery and reconfigure the CMOS. |

### The Test Yourself Module

If you have had your fill of exam questions, answers, and explanations, the time has come to test your knowledge. Or maybe, you want to start with a practice exam in the Test Yourself module to see where your strengths and weaknesses are, and then review only certain topics. Either way, turn to the final module of the book, Test Yourself Practice Exams. In this section we actually simulate the exams. We have given you one practice test per exam, with the number of questions corresponding to the actual exam. Lock yourself in your office or clear the kitchen table, set a timer, and jump in.

## The Global Knowledge Network Web Site

Global Knowledge Network invites you to become an active member of the Access Global web site. This site is an online mall and an information repository that you'll find invaluable. You can access many types of products to assist you in your preparation for the exams, and you'll be able to participate in forums, on-line discussions, and threaded discussions. No other book brings you unlimited access to such a resource. You'll find more information about this site in Appendix A.

# How to Take an A+ Certification Exam

This chapter covers the importance of your A+ certification as well as prepares you for taking the actual examinations. It gives you a few pointers on methods of preparing for the exams, including how to study, register, what to expect, and what to do on exam day.

## Importance of A+ Certification

The Computing Technology Industry Association (CompTIA) created the A+ certification to provide technicians with an industry-recognized and valued credential. Due to its acceptance as an industry-wide credential, it offers technicians an edge in a highly competitive computer job market. Additionally, it lets others know your achievement level and that you have the ability to do the job right. Prospective employers may use the A+ certification as a condition of employment or as a means to determine a bonus or job promotion.

Earning A+ certification means that you have the knowledge, the technical skills, and now, the customer relations skills necessary to be a successful computer service technician. Computer experts in the industry establish the standards of certification. Although the test covers a broad range of computer software and hardware, it is not vendor-specific. In fact, more than 45 organizations contributed and budgeted the resources to develop the A+ examination.

To become A+ certified you must pass two examinations: the Core exam and a Windows/DOS specialty exam. The Core exam measures essential competencies for a break/fix microcomputer hardware service technician with six months of experience. The exam covers basic knowledge of desktop and portable systems, basic networking concepts, and printers. Also included on the exam are safety and common preventive maintenance procedures.

With this new revision of the A+ certification, released in July of 1998, you now have only one choice for the specialty exam: Windows/DOS. The previous version of the A+ exam also offered Macintosh OS as a specialty, but because our world is becoming more and more PC-driven, the new exam also reflects this change. The Windows/DOS module covers basic knowledge of DOS, Windows 3.*x*, and Windows 95 operating systems for installing, upgrading, troubleshooting, and repairing microcomputer systems.

## Computerized Testing

As with Microsoft, Novell, Lotus, and various other companies, the most practical way to administer tests on a global level is through Sylvan Prometric testing centers. Sylvan Prometric provides proctored testing services for Microsoft, Oracle, Novell, Lotus, and the A+ computer technician certification. In addition to administering the tests, Sylvan Prometric also scores the exam and provides statistical feedback on each section of the exam to the companies and organizations that use their services.

Typically, several hundred questions are developed for a new exam. The questions are reviewed for technical accuracy by subject matter experts and are then presented in the form of a beta test. The beta test consists of many more questions than the actual test and provides for statistical feedback to CompTIA to check the performance of each question.

Based on the performance of the beta examination, questions are discarded based on how well or poorly the examinees performed on them. If a question is answered correctly by most of the test-takers, it is discarded as too easy. The same goes for questions that are too difficult. After analyzing the data from the beta test, CompTIA has a good idea of which questions to include in the question pool to be used on the actual exam.

## Test Structure

Currently the A+ exam consists of a *form* type test. This type of test draws from a question pool of some set value and randomly selects questions to generate the exam you will take. We will discuss the various question types in greater detail later.

Some certifications are using *adaptive* type tests. This interactive test weighs all of the questions based on their level of difficulty. For example, the questions in the form might be divided into levels one through five, with level one questions being the easiest and level five being the hardest. Every time you answer a question correctly, you are asked a question of a higher level of difficulty, and vice versa when you answer incorrectly. After answering about 15–20 questions in this manner, the scoring algorithm is able to determine whether or not you would pass or fail the exam if all the questions were answered. The scoring method is pass or fail. You won't find this type of exam for A+ certification as of yet. Currently Novell is employing the adaptive test format.

The exam questions for the A+ test are all equally weighted. This means that they all count the same when the test is scored. An interesting and useful characteristic of the form test is that questions may be marked and returned to later. This helps you manage your time while taking the test so that you don't spend too much time on any one question. Remember, unanswered questions are counted against you. Assuming you have time left when you finish the questions, you can return to the marked questions for further evaluation.

The form test also marks the questions that are incomplete with a letter "I" once you've finished all the questions. You'll see the whole list of questions after you finish the last question. The screen allows you to go back and finish incomplete items, finish unmarked items, and go to particular questions that you may want to look at again.

# Question Types

The computerized test questions you will see on the examination can be presented in a number of ways. You may see some of the possible formats on the A+ test, and some you may not.

### True/False

We are all familiar with True/False type questions, but due to the inherent 50 percent chance of guessing the right answer, you will probably not see any of these on the A+ exam. Sample questions on CompTIA's web site and on the beta exam did not include any True/False type questions.

## Multiple Choice

The majority of the A+ exam questions are of the multiple choice variety. Some questions require a single answer, whereas some require multiple answers. The easiest way to differentiate between the number of answers required is by the use of a radio button or a checkbox in front of possible answers. The radio button will only allow you to select one item from the given choices. The checkbox allows you to select any or all of the given answers in response to the question.

One interesting variation of multiple choice questions with multiple answers is whether or not the examinee is told how many answers are correct.

EXAMPLE:

Which files are processed immediately upon the completion of POST? (Choose two.)

OR

Which files are processed immediately upon the completion of POST? (Choose all that apply.)

You may see both variations of the multiple answer questions on the exam, but the trend seems to be toward the first type, where examinees are told explicitly how many answers are correct. Questions of the "choose all that apply" variety are more difficult and can be very confusing to the test taker. The majority of questions on the A+ exam are multiple choice with single answers.

## Graphical Questions

Some questions incorporate a graphical element to the question in the form of an exhibit either to aid the examinee in a visual representation of the problem or to present the question itself. These questions are easy to identify because they refer to the exhibit in the question and there is also an "Exhibit" button on the bottom of the question window. An example of a graphical question might be to identify a component on a drawing of a motherboard.

Test questions known as hotspots actually incorporate graphics as part of the answer. These types of questions ask the examinee to click on a location or graphical element to answer the question. As a variation of the above exhibit example, instead of selecting A, B, C, or D as your answer, you would simply click on the portion of the motherboard drawing where the component exists.

### Free Response Questions

Another type of question that can be presented on the form test requires a *free response,* or type-in answer. This is basically a fill-in-the-blank type question where a list of possible choices is not given. More than likely you will not see this type of question on the exam.

## Study Strategies

There are appropriate ways to study for the different types of questions you will see on an A+ certification exam. The amount of study time needed to pass the exam will vary with the candidate's level of experience as a computer technician. Someone with several years' experience might only need a quick review of materials and terms when preparing for the exam.

The rest of us may need several hours to identify weaknesses in knowledge and skill level and then to work on those areas to bring them up to par. If you know that you are weak in an area, work on it until you feel comfortable talking about it. You don't want to be surprised with a question, knowing it was your weak area.

### Knowledge-Based Questions

Knowledge-based questions require that you memorize facts. The questions may not cover material that you use on a daily basis, but they do cover material that CompTIA thinks a computer technician should be able to answer. Here are some keys to memorizing facts:

- **Repetition** The more times you expose your brain to a fact, the more it "sinks in" and increases your ability to remember it.

- **Association** Connecting facts within a logical framework makes them easier to remember.

- **Motor Association** It is easier to remember something if you write it down or perform another physical act, like clicking on the practice test answer.

### Performance-Based Questions

Although the majority of the questions on the A+ exam are knowledge-based, some questions are performance-based scenario questions. In other words, the performance-based questions on the exam actually measure the candidate's ability to apply one's knowledge in a given scenario.

The first step in preparing for these scenario type questions is to absorb as many facts relating to the exam content areas as you can. Of course, any actual hands-on experience will greatly help you in this area. For example, knowing how to discharge a CRT is greatly enhanced by having actually done the procedure at least once. Some of the questions will place you in a scenario and ask for the best solution to the problem at hand. It is in these scenarios that having a good knowledge level and some experience will help you.

The second step is to familiarize yourself with the format of the questions you are likely to see on the exam. The questions in this study guide are a good step in that direction. The more you're familiar with the types of questions that can be asked, the better prepared you will be on the day of the test.

# The Exam Makeup

To receive the A+ certification, you must pass both the Core and the Windows/DOS exams. You will see between 75 and 100 questions on each exam and you will have two and a half hours to complete each of them. As we are going to press with this book, CompTIA has not yet established the passing rate of the new exam. As it sits, a 72 percent is the passing rate for the Core portion and a 69 percent is the passing rate for the Windows/DOS portion. You would be well advised to check the CompTIA site at www.comptia.org for the most recent information.

# The Core Exam

The Core exam is broken down into eight categories. Note that the final category—customer satisfaction—will be tested, but will not count towards the passing or failing of the exam. The score on those particular questions will be posted on your score card, though, so your employer can see how you did on these types of questions. CompTIA lists the percentages as the following:

| Installation, configuration, upgrading | 30 percent |
|---|---|
| Diagnosing and troubleshooting | 20 percent |
| Safety and preventive maintenance | 10 percent |
| Motherboard, processors, memory | 10 percent |
| Printers | 10 percent |
| Portable systems | 5 percent |
| Basic networking | 5 percent |
| Customer satisfaction | 10 percent |

## The Windows/DOS Exam

The majority of the Windows/DOS exam will focus on Windows 95 (a whopping 75 percent), with the rest of the coverage divided between DOS and Windows 3.*x*. CompTIA's breakdown of this portion is as follows:

| Function, structure, operation, and file management | 30 percent |
|---|---|
| Memory management | 10 percent |
| Installation, configuration, and upgrading | 25 percent |
| Diagnosing and troubleshooting | 25 percent |
| Networks | 10 percent |

# Signing Up

After all the hard work preparing for the exam, signing up is a very easy process. Sylvan operators in each country can schedule tests at any authorized Sylvan Prometric Test center. To talk to a Sylvan registrar, call 1-800-77-MICRO. There are a few things to keep in mind when you call:

1. If you call Sylvan during a busy period, you might be in for a bit of a wait. Their busiest days tend to be Mondays, so avoid scheduling a test on Monday if at all possible.

2. Make sure that you have your social security number handy. Sylvan needs this number as a unique identifier for their records.

3. Payment can be made by credit card, which is usually the easiest payment method. If your employer is a member of CompTIA, you may be able to get a discount, or even obtain a voucher from your employer that will pay for the exam. Check with your employer before you dish out the money.

4. You may take one or both of the exams on the same day. However, if you only take one exam, you only have 90 days to complete the second exam. If more than 90 days elapse between tests, you must retake the first exam.

# Taking the Test

The best method of preparing for the exam is to create a study schedule and stick to it. Although teachers have told you time and time again not to cram for tests, there may be some information that just doesn't quite stick in your memory. It's this type of information that you want to look at right before you take the exam so that it remains fresh in your mind. Most testing centers provide you with a writing utensil and some scratch paper that you can use after the exam starts. You can brush up on good study techniques from any quality study book from the library, but some things to keep in mind when preparing and taking the test are:

1. Get a good night's sleep. Don't stay up all night cramming for this one. If you don't know the material by the time you go to sleep, your head won't be clear enough to remember it in the morning.

2. The test center needs two forms of identification, one of which must have your picture on it (e.g., driver's license). A social security card or credit card are also acceptable forms of identification.

3. Arrive at the test center a few minutes early. There's no reason to feel rushed right before taking an exam.

4. Don't spend too much time on one question. If you think you're spending too much time on it, just mark it and go back to it later if you have time. Unanswered questions are counted wrong whether you knew the answer to them or not.

5. If you don't know the answer to a question, think about it logically. Look at the answers and eliminate the ones that you know can't possibly be the answer. This may leave with you with only two possible answers. Give it your best guess if you have to, but most of the answers to the questions can be resolved by process of elimination.

6. Books, calculators, laptop computers, or any other reference materials are not allowed inside the testing center. The tests are computer based and do not require pens, pencils, or paper, although as mentioned above, some test centers provide scratch paper to aid you while taking the exam.

# After the Test

As soon as you complete the test, your results will show up in the form of a bar graph on the screen. As long as your score is greater than the required score, you pass! Also, a hard copy of the report is printed and embossed by the testing center to indicate that it's an official report. Don't lose this copy; it's the only hard copy of the report that is made. The results are sent electronically to CompTIA.

The printed report will also indicate how well you did in each section. You will be able to see the percentage of questions you got right in each section, but you will not be able to tell which questions you got wrong.

After you pass the Core exam and the Windows/DOS exam, an A+ certificate will be mailed to you within a few weeks. You'll also receive a lapel pin and a credit card–sized credential that shows your new status: A+ Certified Technician. You're also authorized to use the A+ logo on your business cards as long as you stay within the guidelines specified by CompTIA. If you don't pass the exam, don't fret. Take a look at the areas you didn't do so well in and work on those areas for the next time you register. Just remember that the Core and Windows/DOS exams must be taken within 90 days of each other to count toward certification.

Once you pass the exams and earn the title of A+ Certified Technician, your value and status in the IT industry increases. A+ certification carries with it an important proof of skills and knowledge that are valued by customers, employers, and professionals in the computer industry.

# Part 1

## Core

# Practice
# Questions

*Q & A*

The A+ question pool is very large and you never know what kind of questions you will get on the exam. The questions in this book are meant to help you determine what you still need to study. They cover all the subject areas that the test makers have said are relevant. By looking at these questions as a way to alert you to what you need to study further, you will end up being a much better technician than if you just memorized the questions and answers.

The types of questions on the A+ exam are very similar to what follows. You may find that there are more single-answer choices on the exam. The rationale behind having more multiple answers in these questions is to try to prepare you for the worst that the exam will throw at you. The exam makers claim that there are no trick questions. Be on your guard, though, for tricky questions or questions that, if you do not read them carefully, you might misread. Always think of what they are trying to test you on. Chances are they will be asking you about things that commonly occur, as opposed to some obscure exception to the rule that was not covered in the literature. Watch for acronyms and terms that you have never heard before.

# Installation, Configuration, and Upgrading

1. Which of the following graphics adapter's output was defined with the red, green, and blue colors plus an intensity bit?

   A. Color Graphics Adapter (CGA)
   B. Enhanced Graphics Adapter (EGA)
   C. Virtual Graphics Array (VGA)
   D. Super Virtual Graphics Array (SVGA)

2. Which of the following is not a type of mouse connector?

   A. DIN-8 connector
   B. PS/2 connector
   C. DB-9 connector
   D. DIN-6 connector

**3.** Which of the following are Standard Device Assignments for Interrupt
Request Lines (IRQs)? (Choose all that apply.)

   A. IRQ 4 = Serial port (COM1)

   B. IRQ 7 = Parallel port (LPT2)

   C. IRQ 6 = Keyboard

   D. IRQ 8 = Real-time clock

**4.** In the following table, what is the device that uses the Port Address (hex
range) of 2F8-2FF?

| 278-27F | Parallel port (LPT2) |
| --- | --- |
| 2F8-2FF | |
| 320-32F | Hard disk controller, 8-bit ISA |
| 378-37F | Parallel port (LPT1) |

   A. Serial port (COM1)

   B. Floppy controller

   C. Color graphics adapter

   D. Serial port (COM2)

**5.** Which type of port is used to connect the DB-25 connector?

   A. Parallel port

   B. SCSI port

   C. Serial port

   D. Both parallel and serial ports

**6.** Which type of connector is most commonly used to attach an unshielded
twisted-pair (UTP) cable with a network card?

   A. RJ-11

   B. RJ-14

   C. RJ-45

   D. RJ-55

**7.** You are upgrading a system that has two IDE hard disks, each totaling 528 megabytes. You are installing a new 1.2-gigabyte EIDE hard disk. You would like to keep the existing hard disks. How would you configure the hard disks?

A. Install the new hard disk as a master, and have both the IDE hard disks as slaves

B. Install the new hard disk as a slave, and configure one of the IDE hard disks as a slave

C. Install the new hard disk as a master on the secondary controller, with the two IDE drives on the primary controller

D. Install the new hard disk as a slave on the secondary controller, with the two IDE drives on the primary controller

**8.** Which of the following SCSI specifications yields a 16-bit bus with a total transfer rate of 20 Mbps?

A. SCSI-1

B. SCSI-2

C. Ultra SCSI-2

D. SCSI-3

**9.** An internal SCSI device uses which type of cabling?

A. 40-pin data ribbon cable

B. 50-pin data ribbon cable

C. DB-25 shielded cable

D. Keyed Centronics-50 cabling

**10.** When should an Electro-Static wristband be worn? (Choose all that apply.)

A. When working with CPUs

B. When working on laser printers

C. When working with monitors

D. Electro-Static wrist bands should *always* be worn

**11.** Which of the following are NOT required for an internal modem? (Choose all that apply.)

    A. An IRQ

    B. An I/O address

    C. A DMA channel

    D. A COM port

**12.** What is the most common measurement performed when using a multimeter?

    A. Current

    B. Voltage

    C. Resistance

    D. Tolerance

**13.** You are testing for resistance on a component with a multimeter. You place the probes on either end of the component and you get an infinite reading on the display. What is the reason for this?

    A. The multimeter is not set to read resistance

    B. This is normal for a working component

    C. This means the component is not working

    D. You cannot determine whether the component is not working until you measure the amount of voltage passing through the component

**14.** When installing a new power supply, you need to reattach the two power connectors to the motherboard in such a way that which two wires are facing each other?

    A. The black wires

    B. The red wires

    C. The yellow wires

    D. The black wire should face the red wire

**15.** Which of the following are types of keyboard connectors in use today? (Choose all that apply.)

A. Mini DIN-5

B. Mini DIN-6

C. DIN-5

D. DIN-6

**16.** You are installing a new SCSI host adapter in a system. You are also installing a SCSI hard disk and a SCSI CD-ROM drive. By default, what is the address of the SCSI host adapter?

A. 0

B. 1

C. 2

D. 7

**17.** The pins that attach the processor chip to the motherboard come in what two forms? (Choose all that apply.)

A. Single In-line Memory Module (SIMM)

B. Dual In-Line Package (DIP)

C. Pin Grid Array (PGA)

D. Zero Insertion Force (ZIF)

**18.** Which of the following devices uses a Dynamic Memory Access (DMA) Channel?

A. A modem

B. A sound card

C. A printer

D. A monitor

**19.** You are configuring a system that has many devices installed, such as a printer, sound card, modem, and network card. You need to find a free IRQ in order to install a card for the new scanner. Of the following IRQs, which are available for assignment according to the Standard Device Assignment settings?

A. IRQ 6

B. IRQ 7

C. IRQ 14

D. IRQ 15

**20.** Which of the following is the port address for the parallel port (LPT1)?

A. 278-27F

B. 378-37F

C. 2F8-2FF

D. 3F8-3FF

**21.** Which of the following devices are considered Field Replaceable Units (FRUs)? Choose all that apply.

A. System board

B. Floppy disk drive

C. Hard disk drive

D. Power supply

**22.** The power supply to the computer converts the wall current to what type of current?

A. Vac

B. AC

C. DC

D. 120 volts

**23.** A customer has opened up his computer and is looking at the system board. He tells you that the computer diagnostics says he has a 66 Mhz machine, but the CPU chip says 486 on it. Why is his machine not running that fast?

A. The 486 is the type of CPU
B. The manufacturer will not allow it to run at 486
C. FCC regulations say computers can run no faster than 300 Mhz
D. The diagnostic is wrong

**24.** Computers store information in the computer in which number system(s)?

A. Hexadecimal
B. Octal
C. Binary
D. Decimal

**25.** During bootup the computer reads what type memory to get the system configuration?

A. RAM
B. ROM
C. Cache
D. Decimal

**26.** A customer says his hard disk drive is broken. He can not slide the hard disk into the drive. His problem is which drive?

A. Hard disk drive
B. 3.5-inch floppy disk drive
C. 5.25-inch floppy disk drive
D. 8-inch floppy disk drive

**27.** CD-ROM drives use what to read the data on a CD?

A. Read-write head

B. Read Only head

C. Laser

D. Needle

**28.** The fan on the computer is not working. The customer complains that the system is slow and there is a burning odor. What should you do?

A. Replace system board

B. Replace power supply

C. Replace hard disk

D. Leave cover off

**29.** When replacing floppy drives the cables to be disconnected include:

A. Power

B. Floppy drive cable

C. Hard disk cable

D. Sound cable

**30.** EGA and CGA monitors have what type connector to attach to the computer?

A. D-15

B. D-9

C. RJ-45

D. Edge connector

**31.** The standard IRQ setting for floppy diskette controller is:

A. 1

B. 7

C. 3

D. 6

**32.** The standard IRQ settings for parallel port 1 and parallel port 2 are:

A. 5 and 7

B. 3 and 4

C. 4 and 3

D. 7 and 5

**33.** What device is assigned to IRQ 12?

A. Keyboard

B. Mouse

C. Hard disk controller

D. COM2

**34.** The standard I/O address setting for serial port 1 is :

A. 2F8-2FF

B. 3F8-3FF

C. 3F0-3F7

D. 1F0-1F8

**35.** The standard I/O address setting for parallel port 1 is:

A. 3F8-3FF

B. 2F8-2FF

C. 378-37F

D. 278-27F

**36.** Interrupts and I/O addresses can be set on hardware using:

A. Jumpers

B. ROM

C. DIP switches

D. Cache

**37.** Each DIP switch can be set to a value of :

A. 0 and 1
B. 0, 1, 2, 3, 4, 5, 6, 7, 8, 9
C. 0, 1, 2, 3, 4, 5, 6, 7
D. 0, 1, 2, 3, 4, 5, 6, 7, 8, 9, A. B. C. D. E. F

**38.** A customer wants cable run for a network. The area the cable will be run through includes fluorescent lights and other signal-generating appliances. What type cable should you use?

A. Shielded twisted pair
B. Unshielded twisted pair
C. Regular telephone wire
D. Electrical extension cord

**39.** You are preparing to plug a monitor into the computer. The connector has nine pins. What type of monitor and connector do you have?

A. VGA, DB-9
B. VGA, DB-15
C. EGA, DB-9
D. EGA, DB-15

**40** When plugging the phone into the modem, you notice the phone connector has eight pins. The modem fails to work. Why does the phone connector have eight pins?

A. Multi-line connector
B. Single line connector
C. Network connector
D. Bad connector

**41.** A network connection uses which connector?

A. RJ-45
B. RJ-11
C. RJ-14
D. DB-25

**42.** SCSI is an acronym for?

A. Small Computer Systems Interface
B. Special Computer Systems Interface
C. Small computer Serial Interface
D. Special Computer Systems Interface

**43.** A computer will typically have the following volts:

A. ±5 Vdc
B. ±12 Vdc
C. ±5 Vac
D. ±12 Vac
E. ±5 and ±12 amps

**44.** Read Only Memory typically stores the:

A. Basic Input Output System
B. Beginning Instructions for Operating System
C. Beginning Input Output System
D. Basic Integrated Output Settings
E. None of the above

---

**e x a m**
**ⓦ a t c h**    *Know your I/O addresses like the back of your hand. You will encounter several questions on the exam pertaining to I/O addresses.*

---

**45.** Which of the following types of monitors can display at least 64 different colors at the same time?

A. CGA

B. VGA

C. SVGA

D. EGA

E. Hercules

**46.** The best way to remove a network card from a computer is to use what technique?

A. Use a gentle pulling motion; slightly rock the card from end to end

B. Grab each side and pull firmly out

C. Use a small screwdriver to pry the card out

D. Hold by the center of the card and pull it out gently

E. Put one finger near the bus and the other on the opposite corner, and then pull on the other side until it comes out

**47.** The math co-processor is typically assigned this IRQ:

A. 14

B. 7

C. 6

D. 12

E. 13

**48.** The parallel port (LPT1) usually will take this IRQ:

A. 6

B. 7

C. 8

D. 13

E. 4

**49.** The following IRQs have been set up on a machine and it is locking up. What is a possible problem?

| Mouse | 12 |
| --- | --- |
| Hard disk controller | 14 |
| LPT2 | 7 |
| COM2 | 3 |

A. Bad setting of IRQs with the mouse at 12
B. Bad setting of IRQs with the hard disk controller at 14
C. Bad setting of IRQs with the LPT2 at 7
D. Bad setting of IRQs with the COM2 at 3
E. Non-IRQ problem

**50.** Which of the following are viable port addresses of an 8-bit ISA?

A. 320-32F
B. 1F0-1G8
C. 378-37H
D. 3F0-3I7
E. Not listed

**51.** COM2 will usually take this address:

A. 1F0-1F8
B. 378-37F
C. 278-27F
D. 3F8-3FF
E. 2F8-2FF

**52.** Signals normally follow the medium across the line, but sometimes a signal or stray electrons will stray into the atmosphere, producing noise, which is known as:

A.  Attenuation

B.  Crosstalk

C.  Interference

D.  Impedance

E.  Resistance

**53.** Which of the following is used to transmit data? This is input to the computer from the device.

A.  Serial Data Out (TxD)

B.  Data Terminal Ready (RxD)

C.  Serial Data Receive (TxD)

D.  Serial Data Out (RxD)

E.  Serial Data Receive (RxD)

**54.** In parallel communications, the receiving device to acknowledge a Slctin uses:

A.  Strobe-asserted

B.  Autofeed

C.  Busy

D.  Slct

E.  Init

**55.** What type of connector has five pins on the bottom row and four pins on the top row?

A.  DB-9

B.  DB-25

C.  RJ-11

D.  RJ-14

E.  P/2 Mini-Din

**56.** What type of connector is shown here?

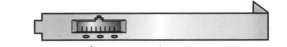

A. RJ-45

B. RJ-11

C. RJ-14

D. RJ-45b

E. RJ-11C

**57.** If you wanted to install four hard disks, and you were limited to using two ribbons, and you chose to number them 0 and 1 on each ribbon, which type of drive would you be installing?

A. ST-506

B. SCSI

C. EIDE

D. Integrated Drive Electronics

E. ESDI

**58.** To load MS-DOS into the HMA, you should do what?

A. Add the following line in the CONFIG.SYS: DOS = HIGH

B. Add the following line in the AUTOEXEC.BAT: LOADHIGH = DOS

C. Add the following line in the SYSTEM.INI: DOS = HIGH

D. Add the following line in the CONFIG.SYS: DEVICEHIGH = DOS

E. Add the following line in the AUTOEXEC.BAT: DOS = HIGHMEM.SYS

**59.** What command(s) would you use to look at the total XMS? (Choose all that apply.)

A. MEM /CLASSIFY /P
B. MEM /C /X
C. CHKDSK
D. CHKDSK /C
E. XMS /C

**60.** Which of the following are FRUs?

A. CPU
B. Power supply
C. ICs
D. Planar
E. CMOS chips

**61.** You are working at the help desk and you get a call from Joe down the hall that his monitor is blank, but the power light is on and the computer seems to still be running. What do you bring with you?

A. ESD wrist guard
B. A spare monitor
C. A video card
D. An extra power cord
E. Nothing extra

**62.** Which drive type(s) uses a 50-pin adapter?

A. SCSI
B. EDI
C. IDE
D. EIDE
E. SCSI2

**63.** What is the binary equivalent to the set for a device that is using the fifth binary ID in a SCSI chain?

A. 010
B. 011
C. 110
D. 100
E. 101

**64.** If you see the screw with the following shape in a machine, which of these statements will be true?

A. You are probably working on a Macintosh
B. You are probably working on a Compaq
C. You are probably working on an IBM
D. You should have a Torx wrench
E. You should have a Phillips head

**65.** You have correctly diagnosed a dead PC as having a bad power supply. After correctly installing the new power supply, which came with a new On/Off switch attached, the PC still appears dead after you attempt to power the system on. What would be the next most logical item to check?

A. Check the fuse in the new power supply
B. Check the 110/220 voltage selector switch on the power supply for the correct setting
C. Ohm out all of the power supply cables
D. Check the green chassis ground connector

**66.** Which type of socket (connector) would a 486DX-66 chip use?

A. DIP

B. ZIF

C. DIMM

D. SIMM

**67.** The standard address and interrupt setting for the second EIDE port is which of the following?

A. 1F0-1F8 IRQ 14

B. 3F0-3F7 IRQ 6

C. 3B0-3BF IRQ 12

D. 170-177 IRQ 15

**68.** In a PC that has a math co-processor, you are attempting to install a SCSI host adapter. Which interrupt setting will not work?

A. IRQ 10

B. IRQ 11

C. IRG 9

D. IRQ 13

**69.** A customer asks you to explain what his BIOS is. In simple terms how could you explain the terminology to him?

A. BIOS is the setting that controls the Bi-Polar settings for his CMOS battery life cycle

B. BIOS controls the Bi-Directional Input out system as in the newer parallel ports devices

C. BIOS is the low-level code that controls the PC input/output system

D. BIOS is the safety feature on the power supply crowbar circuit. It stands for Bar Iso Operation Safety.

---

e x a m
Ⓦatch    *Know your IRQs cold. There are several questions on interrupt*
*assignments on the exam.*

---

70. Which of the following is the standard Interrupt setting for a PS/2 type of
    mouse?

    A. IRQ 3
    B. IRQ 4
    C. IRQ 6
    D. IRQ 12

71. A serial mouse uses which type of connector?

    A. male (pins) DB-25
    B. female (sockets) DB-9
    C. female (sockets) DB-25
    D. male (pins) DB-9

72. Parallel Port LPT2 uses which standard IRQ and address?

    A. 378 IRQ 7
    B. 278 IRQ 5
    C. 3BC IRQ 9
    D. 3F8 IRQ 4

73. Which type of Video Display would you most likely find on a PC made in
    the early 1980s?

A. VGA

B. SVGA

C. RGB

D. CGA

**74.** You want to measure the current being drawn on a power supply in a PC with a suspect component. To do so you must do which of the following?

A. Use the +12 voltage scale and measure by shunting the + and - meter leads across the supply bus

B. Use the + 5 volt scale and measure by shunting the + and - meter leads across the supply bus

C. Open the circuit and, using the correct polarity, measure the current draw using the meter in series with the load

D. Measure the resistance and calculate the current based on ohm's law

**75.** You open a PC for service and find that the hard disk has a standard power cable and a wide and a narrow ribbon cable attached to it. What type of hard disk is it?

A. SCSI

B. IDE

C. EIDE

D. ESDI

**76.** You want to improve the performance of a PC. Which of the following upgrades will have the best effect on performance?

A. Add more ROM memory

B. Increase the size of the hard disk

C. Add more RAM memory

D. Install a more powerful power supply

**77.** You have a VGA card in a PC with 512 KB of memory. Which is the most likely setting that will work for this card?

A.  640 x 480 256 colors

B.  640 x 480 16 colors

C.  1024 x 800 32M colors

D.  600 x 800 256 colors

**78.** You are adding an ATAPI CD-ROM to a PC. What type of port should it be connected to?

A.  SCSI

B.  IDE

C.  USB

D.  None of the above. Proprietary hardware is required.

**79.** When soldering components you should always wear:

A.  An anti-static wristband

B.  An athletic supporter

C.  Protective eye wear

D.  Protective gloves

**80.** Which of these configuration files use the command syntax LOADHIGH?

A.  WIN.INI

B.  SYSTEM.INI

C.  CONFIG.SYS

D.  AUTOEXEC.BAT

**81.** The real time clock is located on the:

A.  Video Card

B.  Motherboard

C.  Desktop

D.  I/O card

**82.** A standard parallel printer cable has which two connectors on either end?

   A. DB-25 female (sockets) and DB-25 male (pins)

   B. DB-25 male (pins) and Centronics 50-pin (male)

   C. Centronics 36-pin male and Centronics 36-pin female (sockets)

   D. DB-25pin male and Centronics 36-pin male

**83.** In order for a serial communication device to work properly, the following parameters must be set properly: Baud Rate, Data-bits, Stop-bits, and _____.

   A. CTS

   B. DTR

   C. DSR

   D. PARITY

**84.** Identify the parallel port on a PC.

   A. DB-9 female (sockets) connector

   B. DB-25 male (pins) connector

   C. DB-15 female (sockets) connector

   D. DB-25 female (sockets) connector

# Diagnosing and Troubleshooting

**1.** You have just powered on a computer, and you hear a series of beeps, and see an error code that begins with the number 2. What is most likely the cause?

   A. Processor problem

   B. Memory problem

   C. Video problem

   D. System board problem

**2.** You have finished typing a report on a computer at school. You save the report to floppy disk to work on later. When you arrive at home on your computer, you put the floppy in the drive and receive an error trying to access the disk. Which of the following are potential reasons for this? Choose all that apply.

A. The two disk drives are not compatible

B. The disk has been write protected

C. The disk has been damaged

D. The disk drive has failed.

**3.** A dot matrix printer is printing characters that have missing spots. What is most likely the problem?

A. The ribbon is worn

B. The print head needs to be replaced

C. The roller is not rolling the paper correctly

D. The line feed is getting stuck

**4.** Users are complaining that the printer is printing garbage today. What would be the first thing you would check?

A. The rollers to make sure they are properly feeding the paper

B. The print heads to make sure they are properly cleaned

C. The printer software configuration

D. The cable is firmly connected

**5.** What is most likely the cause of the problem when a user can connect to his Internet Service Provider and browse the Internet, but only for a few minutes before the connection is dropped?

A. Bad phone line

B. Software configuration

C. Power supply problems

D. Loose cables

**6.** You make a connection to a remote system and you receive garbage characters on the screen. What is most likely the problem?

A.  Incompatible modems

B.  The connection is too fast for your modem

C.  The connection is too slow for you modem

D. Your software is configured incorrectly

# QUESTIONS AND ANSWERS

| | |
|---|---|
| "My computer is getting a keyboard error." | Either the keyboard needs cleaning, the connection has worked its way loose, or the keyboard must be replaced. |
| "The computer lost its BIOS settings." | This is commonly caused by a low CMOS battery. Replace the battery and reconfigure the CMOS. |
| "My monitor is dead." | Several issues revolve around this one. If it is a power-saver monitor, try hitting a few keys and see if it comes on. Check that the monitor is actually powered on and that the cable connection is secure. |
| "The mouse moves sporadically." | This is either a symptom of a dirty mouse or an incorrectly configured mouse. If it is a configuration problem, you probably have to raise the mouse-sensitivity property higher than it currently is. |
| "My printer won't print." | Run the printer's diagnostic routine, or *self-test*, and see if there is any problem. If it passes, the printer is not at fault and you need to check that the cable is correctly attached. Verify the device driver configuration, and if necessary, the software application's configuration. If the printer has a TCP/IP adapter card, the printer may have lost its TCP/IP configuration and you have to use the configuration utility and ensure that the settings are still intact. |
| "The output on the page from my printer is fuzzy." | If you are working with a dot-matrix printer, check the print head for stuck pins. However, a laser printer probably needs a good cleaning. |

**7.** In which circumstances will you not receive the Power On Self Test? Choose all that apply.

    A. When you restart the computer using CTRL-ALT-DEL

    B. When you cold boot the PC

    C. When you press the Reset button on the PC

    D. When you turn off the machine using the power switch

**8.** Which component has been removed from the following table, showing the error ranges on system startup?

| 300–399 | |
|---------|---|
| 400–499 | Video problems, monochrome |
| 500–599 | Video problems, color |

    A. Floppy disk errors

    B. Hard disk problems

    C. Keyboard problem

    D. Memory error

**9.** If you receive a "Memory Size Error" when you boot the system, how should you remedy the situation?

    A. Enter BIOS and change the size of memory

    B. Restart the computer and hold down the ESC key to reset the system memory

    C. Enter BIOS and reset the system defaults

    D. Hold down the ESC key on system startup

**10.** Where can you determine the amount of physical memory installed on a computer?

A. Enter BIOS, and look for the memory area

B. On system startup

C. On system startup, but you must subtract the amount of conventional memory from this number

D. By holding down the ESC key on system startup

11. What is the reason SIMM memory modules are now placed in sockets?

A. The capacity of RAM has grown in the past few years

B. The motherboards have become smaller

C. Chip creep

D. RAM cannot function on ATX form factor motherboards when soldered

12. What is the most common cause of mouse-related problems?

A. Incorrect drivers

B. Dirty mice

C. Improper connectors

D. Software configuration

13. Which of the following cause sporadic hardware errors that are difficult to pinpoint? (Choose all that apply.)

A. Operating near high-voltage devices

B. Incorrect drivers

C. Using an incorrect power supply

D. Operating in high temperatures

14. You have just installed a new hard disk in a system. When you restarted the computer, the screen was black and the computer did not boot. What should you check in this situation?

A. That the hard disk works
B. That the hard disk is configured correctly
C. That pin one on the data ribbon cable is correct
D. That the BIOS settings are correct

15. When you restart a computer after swapping out the floppy drive, you receive a beep from the system. What should you check in this situation?

A. That the floppy drive is working
B. That the data cable has been plugged in correctly
C. That the power cable has been plugged in
D. Nothing. This is the normal operation of the computer.

16. How will you know when you should replace the CMOS battery? (Choose all that apply.)

A. You will receive a warning message from a POST
B. You will begin losing CMOS settings
C. Your system will not boot
D. You never need to replace a CMOS battery

17. You received a hard disk controller error when restarting your system. You moved the hard disk from the primary to the secondary controller. However, you are still receiving the error. What is the cause of the problem?

A. The hard disk is not configured for the new controller
B. The settings in BIOS have been lost
C. The same cable used for both is bad
D. The secondary controller is bad

18. Which of the following should you check when you are diagnosing an external modem that cannot dial? (Choose all that apply.)

A. Improper parity setting
B. Loose cable
C. Bad phone line
D. Serial port failure

**19.** You are having problems installing a new sound card in a user's system. Which IRQ is the default sound card IRQ?

A. 3
B. 4
C. 5
D. 7

**20.** A user complains that he cannot get his CD-ROM to work with his DOS programs. He says the driver for the CD-ROM is being loaded, and he can play audio CDs by placing the headphone jack directly into the CD-ROM. What is most likely the problem?

A. The data cable is not plugged in
B. The CD-ROM is faulty
C. MSCDEX.EXE needs to be loaded in the AUTOEXEC.BAT
D. BIOS needs to be updated

**21.** Next to defective and worn media, what is the most common cause of tape drive failure?

A. Not cleaning the drive often enough
B. Using incorrect tapes
C. Not restoring data enough
D. Failing to realign the write heads after time

**22.** The customer states the mouse is jerky. When you use the mouse it bounces on the surface. What should you do?

A. Replace the mouse
B. Check the IRQ setting
C. Clean the mouse rollers
D. Clean the plug

23. A customer calls and says his mouse used to work fine, but now will not work when downloading pictures from the digital camera. What is the problem?

A. Digital camera and mouse use the same IRQ
B. Mouse is defective
C. Digital camera is not related to the problem
D. Digital camera and keyboard use the same IRQ

24. The customer has a flatbed scanner and reports it will not work. He has checked that it is plugged into the scanner and the computer. What is the first thing you check?

A. Scanner is plugged in the wall outlet
B. Correct IRQ is being used
C. Software installed correctly
D. Bad scanner cable

25. The customer calls and says that his floppy disk will not go in to the drive. It stops part way. What may be the problem?

A. A disk is already in the drive
B. Wrong IRQ setting
C. Trash is in the drive
D. Cable installed wrong

26. The customer reports that on January 1, 1999, the date in the computer shows December 31, 1998, and they have had to reset the date for a week. What is the problem?

A. Y2K problem

B. Bad CMOS battery

C. CPU is bad

D. Out-of-date computer

**27.** When starting up a computer that does not recognize the hard disk you also note that you can not hear the hard disk. What is the probable problem?

A. Bad hard disk

B. Power cable not attached

C. BIOS not set right

D. Bad CMOS battery

**28.** When attaching a ribbon cable to a connector, which side of the cable goes to pin 1?

A. Colored edge

B. Non-colored edge

C. Either edge

D. Ribbon cable has no coloring on the edge

**29.** The customer calls and says that the speakers that worked yesterday no longer work. What is the problem?

A. Conflict with hardware installed last month

B. Speakers are turned off

C. Conflict with software installed 10 days ago

D. CMOS battery dead

exam
Ⓦatch

*Keyboard errors usually generate a 3\*\* error code when POST runs at boot time.*

**30.** When using a laser printer, the printing becomes light in the middle of the page. What is the problem?

    A. Cheap paper

    B. Low on toner

    C. Bad cable

    D. Bad fuser

**31.** A dot matrix printer sounds like it is printing, but the paper is blank. What should you check first?

    A. Cable

    B. Print head

    C. Ribbon

    D. Printer driver

**32.** The customer calls and says the monitor is dead. What is the first thing to check?

    A. Cable to the computer

    B. If the switch is turned on

    C. IRQ conflict

    D. Check for virus

**33.** The modem does not work. You plug a phone in the wall outlet and do not get a dial tone. What is the problem?

    A. Bad modem

    B. Dead phone line

    C. IRQ conflict

    D. Call waiting

**34.** A POST error in the range of 100 – 199 indicates a _____ problem.

A.  System board
B.  Keyboard
C.  Floppy disk
D.  Memory

**35.** The computer has lost its BIOS settings. What is the problem?

A.  Bad RAM
B.  Bad AC power
C.  Bad hard disk
D.  Low or dead CMOS battery

**36.** When starting up the computer you get a 3** error code. This indicates what is bad?

A.  Keyboard
B.  Memory
C.  Floppy disk
D.  System board

**37.** The scanner produces smudgy scans. What is the probable problem?

A.  Dirty surface
B.  Bad cable
C.  Wrong IRQ
D.  Bad driver

**38.** A 3.5-inch diskette has one megabyte of data on it, on one machine. It has one hole in it. When put on a second machine the computer states it is not formatted. What is the problem?

A.  Disk formatted wrong
B.  Bad drive
C.  Wrong IRQ
D.  Diskette is blank

**39.** After installing a new diskette drive, the light stays on. What is the problem?

A. Bad drive
B. Wrong IRQ
C. Wrong type disk
D. Cable is backwards

**40.** The customer reports that the modem sporadically hangs up. They state there is no problem on the phone line. It works fine on a neighbor's computer. What may be the problem?

A. Call waiting not deactivated
B. Bad phone line
C. Bad modem
D. Wrong IRQ

**41.** CMOS is an acronym for:

A. Common Metal-Oxide Semiconductor
B. Complementary Metal-Oxide Semiconductor
C. Chips Memory Only System
D. Common Metal-Oxide System

**42.** If you see an error code of 2**, what is the probable source of the problem?

A. Mouse error
B. Keyboard error
C. RAM error
D. CPU error
E. Sound card error

**43.** You come across a computer that is sporadically rebooting itself. What are the possible causes?

A. Overheated power supply
B. Loose power cord
C. Dead battery
D. Bad IEPA regulator
E. Dead hard disk

**44.** You hear two beeps on your computer when you boot up. What are the possible hardware problems existing in your system?

A. Keyboard
B. Internal speaker
C. Mouse
D. Monitor
E. Sound card

**45.** You hear no beeps on your computer when you boot up. What are the hardware problems existing in your system?

A. Keyboard
B. Internal speaker
C. Mouse
D. Monitor
E. Sound card

**46.** What is the first number in the error code for a bad monochrome monitor?

A. 2
B. 3
C. 4
D. 5
E. 14

**47.** A user complains, "The output on the page from my printer is fuzzy." What is the likely problem on a dot matrix printer?

A. The transfer corona is broken
B. Paper jam
C. Poor paper feed
D. Fuser is broken
E. The print head has stuck pins

48. You have hooked up an external modem and you are ready to use it for outgoing calls. You tried it on one line and it worked, so you transfer it to another and it keeps hanging up. Your incoming fax line is working, and it is hooked up to the same line, so you know the problem is not the line. What is the problem?

    A. Device driver
    B. *70, not put in the dialing command of the modem
    C. Wiring
    D. Modem
    E. IRQ

49. You come across a blank screen on the computer. Which of the following could have caused this?

    A. Monitor settings on monitor
    B. Monitor settings on computer software
    C. Bad hard disk
    D. Bad video card
    E. Virus

50. Which of the following are bad for CD-ROM disks?

    A. ESD
    B. Magnetic fields
    C. High heat
    D. Scratches
    E. Attenuation

**51.** When you encounter a printer problem, the first thing you should do is:

    A. Restart the computer and see if it fixes itself

    B. Send another print job

    C. Examine the LED or LCD status

    D. Check for a paper jam

    E. Print a test page from the printer's controls

**52.** You turn on a computer and cannot hear the hard disk turning. What is the likely problem?

    A. Broken ribbon cable

    B. Disconnected ribbon cable

    C. Disconnected power supply

    D. Full hard disk

    E. Flipped ribbon cable

**53.** The POST program is located in the:

    A. CMOS

    B. ROM BIOS

    C. Operating system

    D. POST ROM

    E. Shadow ROM

**54.** The hard disk specifications are stored in the:

    A. CMOS

    B. BIOS

    C. Operating System

    D. POST ROM

    E. Control Panel

**55.** When cleaning a mouse, what is the best thing to use?

A. Water

B. Rubbing alcohol

C. Q-tip

D. Light soap and water

E. 10 grit sandpaper

**56.** When cleaning a monitor, what is the best thing to use?

A. Windex

B. Alcohol

C. Non-abrasive, lint-free cloth

D. Water

E. Light soap and water

**57.** Which of the following is an I/O device?

A. Mouse

B. Keyboard

C. Pen/Stylus

D. Network card

E. Sound Card (No Microphone)

**58.** Which of the following can act as input devices?

A. Mouse

B. Sound Card (No Microphone)

C. Keyboard

D. Pen/Stylus

E. Monitor

**59.** You come across a keyboard that is damaged. To get it working, you should:

A. Take out all the keys and fix the circuits inside, even if it requires soldering
B. Toss it and replace it with one that works
C. Take it in for repair
D. Find out your company policy on keyboards
E. With the power off, rinse it under warm water and let dry overnight while you replace the old one for the user

**60.** If you get an error number 423 after the POST, what does it mean?

A. Memory test failed
B. CMOS battery failed
C. Keyboard did not respond
D. Parallel port test failed
E. Memory size error

**61.** If you get an error number 201 after the POST, what does it mean?

A. Memory test failed
B. CMOS battery failed
C. Keyboard did not respond
D. Parallel port test failed
E. Memory size error

**62.** A customer calls and complains that his ink jet printer is printing pages with blank spots. Upon investigation you notice that he has already replaced the ink jet cartridge with a new one, but the print quality is sporadic. What would you do next?

A. Install a known good ink cartridge
B. Clean the paper path
C. Clean the printer head with denatured alcohol
D. Run the print head cleaning utility

**63.** A customer has a Windows 95 workstation. The Office97 CD is always in the CD-ROM drive so they can access the clip art folder. Every time the PC boots up, as soon as it starts to spin the CD, it shuts down and reboots. What is the most likely cause of this problem?

A. The CD-ROM is defective
B. The WIN.INI is corrupted
C. The Registry is corrupted
D. The power supply is bad

**64.** A customer calls and complains that his keyboard stops responding. After a reboot it works fine for a while, then stops responding again. What should you do to remedy this situation?

A. Clean the keyboard
B. Replace the motherboard
C. Replace the keyboard with a known good one
D. Check the Registry for a "Keyboard lock out" entry

**65.** A customer with a new, fast, Pentium-based PC claims that the keyboard responds slowly whenever he uses the left and right keyboard arrows. This is a Windows 95 system. Where could you adjust the response of the keyboard for the customer?

A. Edit the Registry
B. Edit the WIN.INI
C. Edit the SYSTEM.INI
D. Use the Control Panel keyboard setting applet to adjust the repeat rate

**66.** What is the correct order of events to begin troubleshooting a PC problem?

A. Re-boot the PC and see if the problem persists
B. Listen carefully to the customer's description of the problem
C. Isolate the problem to a hardware or software component
D. Replace the suspected item and thoroughly test the system

**67.** The most difficult type of PC problem to troubleshoot is:

A. A dead PC

B. A PC that is smoking or burned.

C. A PC that has been struck by lightening

D. An intermittent PC problem

**68.** You should test a suspected cable with a multimeter using the:

A. DC Volts mode

B. Ohm's mode

C. Current mode

D. AC Volts mode

**69.** A customer with a new Windows 95 PC is complaining that he can not use his modem to get online. You have gone through and confirmed that the dial-up networking settings are correct. The Faxing applet is working correctly to send and receive faxes. What is most likely causing the problem?

A. The IRQ settings of the modem are conflicting with another device

B. The handshaking settings should be changed from CTS/DTS to hardware

C. The Faxing applet has control of the modem to receive faxes

D. The RJ-11 jack is plugged into the wrong connector on the modem

**70.** You have just upgraded the floppy drive in a PC from a 5 ¼-inch 1.2MB to a 3 ½-inch 1.44MB drive. After successfully installing the new drive, it will not work properly. You notice that when you try to format a disk, the system attempts to format it as the wrong type. What must you do to correct this?

A. Check the CONFIG.SYS settings

B. Change the CMOS settings for the correct floppy drive type

C. Format the drive using the /F:144 switch

D. Format disks on another PC for the customer

**71.** The reason for the split in the cable on a floppy drive interface is:

 A. To enable two floppy drives on a port

 B. To enable two different format types of floppy drives on a port

 C. To correctly identify drive 1 and drive 2 for the operating system

 D. The cable is not supposed to be split. It is defective.

**72.** What is the physical size of 360K floppy disk?

 A. 3.5-inch

 B. 5.5-inch

 C. 3.25-inch

 D. 5.25-inch

**73.** You have a 286 PC with old BIOS and you need to install a 1.44 floppy disk in the system. The CMOS does not support this disk type. This PC has DOS version 5.0 installed on it. What can you to do enable the PC to correctly use the 1.44 disk drive?

 A. Edit the AUTOEXEC.BAT adding the line C:\DOS\SMARTDRV.EXE /F:144

 B. Edit the CONFIG.SYS by adding the line DRIVPARM=/D:1 /F:144

 C. Upload and install new flash BIOS

 D. It is not possible to use the 1.44 drive on this machine

**74.** A customer calls you and informs you that whenever he sits down at his PC and touches the keyboard, he notices a small static shock, and the PC locks up. How can you resolve this problem?

 A. Have the customer wear an anti-static wristband

 B. Arrange for the carpeting in the office to be sprayed with anti-static spray

 C. Ground the keyboard

 D. Install a grounding strap from the monitor to the keyboard

**75.** A customer is having a problem with his automatically scheduled tape backup program. The backup log is reporting a long list of errors stating that many files cannot be backed up because they are in use. You check the log and notice that these files in question are all Microsoft Word application files or document files. What should you advise the customer to do to resolve this issue?

A. Modify the backup list to not include these files

B. Re-format the backup tape

C. Verify that the expiration date on the tape cartridge has not expired

D. Advise the customer to be sure that all the applications are closed before the scheduled backup is run

**76.** A customer complains that his tape backup is reporting errors that it cannot read the tape. Trying different tape cartridges, you have the same problem on all cartridges. What would be a good thing to try first?

A. Check the cables connected to the tape drive

B. Re-install the backup software

C. Create a new backup set

D. Clean the tape heads and sensors with a Q-Tip and alcohol

**77.** The best protection against power surges and outages is:

A. Make sure that the power cable is using a grounded outlet

B. Use a surge-protected outlet strip

C. Make sure no heavy appliances are on the same power circuit

D. Use a battery backup UPS system

**78.** In order to use a CD-ROM on a Novell file server, you must first:

A. Create a supervisor account for all CD-ROM users

B. Create a group called CD-ROM users

C. Insert the CD media and use the MOUNT command

D. Log on to the network as Supervisor

**79.** A POST error in the 1*xx* range most likely indicates which problem?

 A. Video card problems

 B. Hard disk problems

 C. System board problems

 D. Floppy disk problems

**80.** Using a POST diagnostic test setup, you isolate the PC problem to error code 301. What should you do?

 A. Change the keyboard

 B. Change the Parallel Port

 C. Check the RAM memory

 D. Replace the ROM memory

**81.** You are on a field service call for a customer whose printer keeps having intermittent paper jams. You notice that the environment is very damp. What is the most likely cause of the problem?

 A. The paper is too thick for the printer

 B. The printer has something blocking the paper path

 C. The environment is too damp, causing the paper to stick together

 D. The printer needs to be removed for service

**82.** A residential customer complains that his modem periodically disconnects when he is online. He has only one telephone line, which he uses for the telephone as well as the PC. He also mentions that he has Call Waiting service on this line. What is the first thing to do to remedy this situation?

 A. Check the IRQ settings of the modem

 B. Check the telephone cable connections

 C. Install a newer, faster modem

 D. Disable Call Waiting by modifying the dialing string for the modem

# Safety and Preventive Maintenance

**1.** Under what circumstances should you not defragment a computer's hard disk?

A. When the hard disk is compressed

B. When the hard disk is smaller than 200MB

C. When the hard disk used clusters larger than 16KB

D. None of the above

**2.** Why is vacuuming the inside of a computer helpful for preventing problems? (Choose all that apply.)

A. The dust and debris can cause viruses

B. The dust and debris can build, causing the computer to overheat

C. The dust and debris can change data on a hard disk

D. The dust and debris can conduct a charge and damage components

**3.** Which of the following can prevent damage to your computer in the event of a power surge?

A. An extension cord

B. A switch box

C. A surge suppressor

D. A rubber mat

**4.** Which of the following are true for suppressors and noise filters?

A. A suppressor can absorb excess power

B. A noise filter can be used to reduce EMI

C. A suppressor can be used to reduce EMI

D. A noise filter can be used to eliminate harmful DC current

5. What must you do before you are going to store a UPS for long periods of time?

    A. Drain the battery, to keep the power from dissipating over time
    B. You should not discharge the battery
    C. You should discharge the battery
    D. You should recharge the UPS to full power before storing

6. When you work around laser equipment, what should you be most concerned with? (Choose all that apply.)

    A. Data loss from the intensely concentrated beam of light
    B. Burns on the skin from the concentrated beam of light
    C. Eye-related problems, such as blindness
    D. Shortage of devices nearby from the interference

7. In addition to not wearing an ESD wrist strap around high voltage equipment, what else should you be aware of to protect yourself? (Choose all that apply.)

    A. Never wear cotton around high voltage equipment
    B. Never touch the high voltage equipment with bare hands
    C. Never complete a circuit with your body
    D. Never touch the high voltage equipment without a multimeter

8. When should you open a power supply?

    A. Only after it has cooled down
    B. After the electricity has been discharged
    C. Only when using an ESD wrist strap
    D. Only if you are a qualified and trained technician

9. What does MSDS stand for?

A. Microsoft Developer Solutions

B. Material Source Data Sheet

C. Material Safety Disposal Sheet

D. Material Safety Data Sheet

10. When two objects come into contact with each other, _____ are transferred between them until they both have an equal charge.

A. Protons

B. Electrons

C. Neutrons

D. Atoms

11. A humidity level below what level will tend to lead to static electricity?

A. 30

B. 40

C. 50

D. 60

12. The lasers employed in CD-ROM drives are what level of laser beams?

A. Level 1

B. Level 2

C. Level 3

D. Level 4

13. Which of the following devices is used to check the AC voltage that is supplied to computer, and to detect surges and sags?

A. Line analyzer

B. Multimeter

C. Polarity tester

D. Line diffuser

**14.** What routine maintenance should you do on a hard disk drive? (Choose all that apply.)

    A. Clean the disk drive heads

    B. Run a defragment utility

    C. Run a utility such as SCANDISK

    D. Low-level format the drive often

**15.** If you have opened up a computer case to reveal a layer of dust, what should you use to remove the dust?

    A. A vacuum cleaner

    B. Damp cloth

    C. Compressed air

    D. Anti-static cloth with isopropyl alcohol

**16.** How do you know if you are working on high voltage equipment? (Choose all that apply.)

    A. A bright yellow and black sticker on the device that says "Danger—High Voltage"

    B. A "Warning" label of potential equipment damage and personal injury can occur

    C. A "Caution" label if personal injury can occur

    D. A label is not required for high voltage equipment

**17.** Why should you use compressed air rather than a vacuum for cleaning inside a dusty computer? (Choose all that apply.)

    A. Compressed air can be directed at the dust better

    B. Compressed air does not spread dust

    C. Compressed air is less likely to damage components than a vacuum

    D. Compressed air can provide more cleaning power in most cases

**18.** What is the best way to clean the outside of a computer case without damaging it?

   A.  Use a mild detergent and a damp cloth

   B.  Use acetone

   C.  Use isopropyl alcohol

   D.  Use an all-purpose spray cleaner

**19.** What can safely be used to remove hardened residue from metal components in a computer?

   A.  A screwdriver

   B.  Acetone

   C.  A rubber knife

   D.  Isopropyl alcohol

**20.** A(n) _____ lead looks like a small suction cup with a wire connected to it and is attached to the glass inside the monitor.

   A.  Diode

   B.  Matrix rod

   C.  Anode

   D.  Capacitor

**21.** Which of the following is the function of the battery located inside a personal computer?

   A.  To maintain a small amount of power to the devices during brownout

   B.  To maintain the time when a blackout has occurred

   C.  To maintain the system configuration when the machine is turned off

   D.  To maintain the system configuration when the machine is turned off and to back up temporary information during a temporary brownout

**22.** When cleaning dust from the computer case and keyboard you should use:

A. Compressed air
B. Isopropyl alcohol
C. Denatured alcohol
D. Vacuum cleaner

**23.** A customer calls and says the electrical contacts are heavily oxidized. What can be used to remove the oxidation?

A. Pencil eraser
B. Cleaner with wax
C. Isopropyl alcohol
D. Mild detergent

**24.** You are going to use Norton Utilities on a disk drive. The machine is using Windows 95. Which version of Norton Utilities should you use?

A. Windows 3.*x*
B. Windows 95
C. Windows NT
D. Any version

**25.** A power brownout is:

A. A low supply of power
B. A spike in power
C. A power outage
D. Noise in power

**26.** You have a monitor that demonstrates flickering of the image when placed near the refrigerator. What is causing this?

A. EMI
B. Brownout
C. ESD
D. Blackout

**27.** After removing a dead CMOS battery from a computer, you should do what with the battery?

    A. Place it in the trash

    B. Burn in the backyard

    C. Take to a recycling center

    D. Bury in yard

**28.** When shipping computer components you should:

    A. Put the in a Ziplock bag

    B. Put them in an ESD bag

    C. Place them uncovered in the box

    D. Wrap them in a static wrap

**29.** Dangers of working with live current include:

    A. Death

    B. Severe burns

    C. Computer damage

    D. All of the above

**30.** LaserJet III printers use what class laser beams?

    A. Class 1

    B. Class 2

    C. Class 4

    D. Class 3

**31.** The fan is not working on a power supply. After cleaning with compressed air, the fan still does not work. What do you do now?

    A. Open and service the power supply

    B. Replace the power supply

    C. Attach an external fan

    D. Tel the customer a fan is not required

**32.** When working on a computer you notice dust inside. What should you do?

    A. Leave it alone, as cleaning it may hurt something

    B. Vacuum it

    C. Wash the inside

    D. Only clean the part you are working on

**33.** The customer comments that the hard disk is getting slower and slower. This indicates what utility needs to be run?

    A. Virus software

    B. Back-up

    C. SCANDISK

    D. Defragmenter

**34.** A paper that describes how to handle environmentally dangerous and other hazardous material is called a:

    A. Material Safety Directions Sheet

    B. Material Safety Data Sheet

    C. Material Safety Directions System

    D. Material Safety Data System

**35.** A utility program supplied with Windows that is often used to mark corrupt sections on a disk is called:

    A. DEFRAG

    B. SCANDISK

    C. Norton Utilities

    D. COMMAND.COM

**36.** Used toner cartridges should be:

    A. Thrown away

    B. Refilled by user

    C. Sent back to the manufacturer or a recycler

    D. Put in an incinerator

**37.** The customer has gotten rid of a computer and has an extra UPS that will not be used for several months. After storing it for several months, they are now ready to use it. What should they first do to the UPS?

A. Fully discharge the battery

B. Leave it as it is

C. Fully charge the battery

D. A UPS cannot be stored.

**38.** A floppy disk drive is producing no errors. However, it has not been cleaned in two years. To clean the drive you should:

A. Use a mild detergent

B. Use alcohol

C. Use a special cleaning disk

D. You should not clean it

**39.** While doing work on a computer you notice an item wearing out. You should:

A. Ignore it

B. Tell the customer

C. Replace the item

D. Hope it breaks later

**40.** You are going to use a virus program on a disk drive. The machine is using Windows 95. Which version of the virus program should you use?

A. Windows 3.*x*

B. Windows 95

C. Windows NT

D. Any version

**41.** Common electrical charges that people generate in a dry environment that are not harmful to humans, but are harmful to computers are called:

A. EMI

B. ESD

C. A power spike

D. A power brownout

**42.** The customer has used the hard disk for two years and the only two utilities ever run on it are doing a regular backup and virus check. What utility probably needs running?

A. DEFRAG

B. SCANDISK

C. Norton Anti-Virus

D. CHKDSK

**43.** You should wear an ESD strap when working on which of the following?

A. Modems

B. Monitors

C. Power supply boxes

D. Sound cards

E. Planar boards

**44.** When you come across the sign shown here in a PC, you know that which of the following is true?

A. This is a hazard sign

B. This is a caution sign

C. By fixing what this is warning you about you may hurt yourself

D. By fixing what this is warning you about you may hurt the equipment

E. Not to worry, these are only for novices to obey

**45.** If you reach for your doorknob and you feel a shock from ESD, how many volts are beings discharged?

A. 2,000

B. 3,000

C. 20,000

D. 30,000

E. 200,000

**46.** A planar board goes into repair at the local shop and the repairman does not prevent static from affecting this board. Three more trips to the shop and the board is starting to get into trouble. What is this board suffering from at this point?

A. EMI

B. ESD

C. Spikes

D. UPS

E. Degradation

**47.** Dirty current is also known as:

A. EMI

B. ESD

C. UPS

D. Brownout

E. Semi-conductive resistance

---

exam
ⓌatcH

*Every A+ Certification Exam will have at least one question on battery disposal.*

---

**48.** A UPS contains a special filter that prevents magnetic fields caused by noise. What is this filter called?

  A. Noise suppressor
  B. Spike avoidance mechanism
  C. Conditioner
  D. Noise filter
  E. EMI protector

**49.** When discharging a monitor, which of the following should you use?

  A. Screwdriver
  B. Resistor
  C. Transformer
  D. ESD strap
  E. Jumper Wire

**50.** What is the attachment to the monitor that makes a small pop when it is pried open?

  A. Diode
  B. Anode
  C. Anode lead
  D. Anode cap
  E. None of the above

**51.** You find a monitor in your attic that hasn't been used in years, and you decide that you want to fix it. What should you do?

  A. Go ahead and work on it, since the charge is gone
  B. Discharge it and then work on it
  C. Have an experienced monitor repairperson discharge it while you watch
  D. Throw it in the garbage, since it is worthless
  E. Modify the cord so it can be tested on your new system

**52.** You find a monitor in your attic that hasn't been used in years, and you decide that you want to get rid of it. What should you do?

    A. Donate it and write off the donation, if possible

    B. Throw it in the trash

    C. Bury it in a fiberglass box to protect the environment

    D. Convert it to run on your new system by breaking a few pins

    E. Sell it to a computer resale shop

**53.** To dispose of batteries, what should you do?

    A. Throw them in the trash

    B. Bury them in a watertight container

    C. Put them in a fire

    D. Contact your state's EPA for disposal regulations

    E. Contact your state's EMI for disposal regulations

**54.** Which of the following may you do with used laser cartridges?

    A. Throw them away

    B. Sell them to laser print cartridge companies for them to reuse

    C. Refill them and use them if you are aware of the pros and cons

    D. All of the above

    E. None of the above

**55.** It is now unlawful to throw batteries away because:

    A. Congress passed the Battery Act

    B. The Senate passed the Battery Act

    C. The legislation passed the Clean Air, Water and Soil laws

    D. Congress passed the Pollution Control Act

**56.** Specialists who fix hard disks must work in a room termed a:

A. "Clean room"

B. "Sealed room"

C. "Dustless room"

D. "Dirtless room"

E. None of the above

**57.** Which of the following are preventive maintenance on a hard disk?

A. Oiling the hard disk

B. Opening it and spraying it with anti-static compressed air

C. Parking the heads, if it is an old hard disk

D. Low-level formatting it weekly

E. None of the above

**58.** Preventive maintenance of a PC includes the use of which of the following tools?

A. Anti-static compressed air

B. Soldering gun

C. Vacuum

D. Rubber knife

E. Eraser

**59.** If a power supply is not working you should:

A. Reverse the polarity of the power supply and try it

B. Switch the international settings to whatever it was not set on

C. Remove the power supply box and contact somebody to repair it

D. Remove the power supply box, open it up, and visually inspect it

E. Give it a good whack on the back side, since it is common for the contacts to be loose

**60.** If you don't follow safety recommendations for all PC repairs, what are the possible consequences?

A. Death

B. Shock

C. Burn

D. Blindness

E. Catastrophic equipment damage

**61.** How do you absolutely prevent catastrophic equipment damage from lightning during a storm?

A. Use a power surge protector

B. Use a UPS

C. Use a noise filter

D. Don't use the machine when there is lightning out

E. None of the above

**62.** What costs companies millions of dollars in lost productivity and should be avoided? (Choose one.)

A. ESD

B. EMI

C. Downtime

D. Hidden ESD

E. Degradation

**63.** What is true about a device that is affected by ESD?

A. When it occurred the person transferring the ESD may not have felt it

B. The affected component will always fail diagnostic tests

C. The person transferring the ESD had felt it

D. The affected component may pass a diagnostic test

E. The component can affect neighboring components

**64.** The type of damage that causes a component to function poorly is:

A. Catastrophic

B. Minimal

C. Intermittent

D. Degradation

65. You should never wear a _____ when working on any high-voltage equipment.

A. Protective eyewear

B. Lab Coat

C. Wrist Strap

D. Cowboy Hat

66. To dispose of chemical solvents, you could:

A. Dump them in a local sewer drain

B. Bury them in your back yard in a sealed metal box

C. Put them out on trash night for normal collections

D. Check with your local government for disposal procedures

67. Working on a CD-ROM with the cover off can be dangerous because:

A. There is high voltage in the motor circuit

B. There is high current in the control circuit

C. There are over 50,000 ohms on the controller card

D. The laser beam could blind you if you make eye contact with it

68. Whenever you encounter a new piece of equipment, you should always:

A. Read the operator's manual

B. Fill out the warranty card

C. Go to the manufacturer's web site to download the latest set of device drivers

D. Consult the manufacturer's suggested preventive maintenance guidelines

**69.** A Laser printer has a level _____ laser beam.

    A. 5

    B. 2

    C. 3

    D. 7

**70.** If you drop a screw into a PC when it is on, what should you do?

    A. Remove any floppy disks from the drive

    B. Shut the PC off and immediately retrieve the dropped screw

    C. Shunt the power supply with a load resistor to dissipate the ESD charge

    D. Don't tell anyone you did it

**71.** If you are attempting to install a RAM chip in a SIMM socket and it won't fit properly, you should:

    A. Order a different style of SIMM

    B. Try reversing it 180 degrees

    C. Use a flat-blade screwdriver to pry it into place

    D. Tell the customer the PC cannot be upgraded and sell him a new one

**72.** A good place to store a PC component card is:

    A. In your workbench drawer wrapped in a lint-free cloth

    B. In a cardboard box to prevent damage

    C. In an anti-static storage bag

    D. In an unused slot in the PC you are working on

**73.** A UPS will protect a PC from which possible causes of damage?

    A. ESD

    B. Power surges

    C. Brownouts

    D. Low Humidity

**74.** EMI is an acronym for:

    A. Electronic Metering Institute

    B. Electro-Magnetic Interference

    C. Environmental Management Institute

    D. Every Mother's Intuition

**75.** A UPS that has been stored offline for a long time may loose its:

    A. Battery charge

    B. Memory

    C. Warranty coverage

    D. EMI rating

**76.** An environment that has humidity over 80 percent can cause:

    A. ESD problems

    B. Condensation

    C. RFI

    D. Heat problems

**77.** When discharging a CRT tube, you should attach the discharge wire to:

    A. Your workbench

    B. A ground terminal on an electrical outlet

    C. An ESD mat

    D. Your supervisor's toolbox

**78.** A power supply that the fan has stopped working on can break down due to:

    A. Condensation accumulation

    B. Static buildup

    C. Heat buildup

    D. Current drain

**79.** A good thing to clean a monitor screen with would be:

    A. Rubber bladed knife

    B. Glass Cleaner

    C. Isotone solution

    D. Brown 25 Cleaner

**80.** Preventative maintenance on a hard disk includes which of the following?

    A. Formatting the drive

    B. FDISK the drive

    C. Running the DEFRAG utility

    D. Running the SCANDISK utility

**81.** Which types of storage media can be cleaned in the field?

    A. 1.44 disk drive

    B. 1.2MB disk drive

    C. 50MB hard disk

    D. A tape drive

**82.** When using a new chemical, always consult the.

    A. Advertised features

    B. Warning label

    C. Manufacturer's retail price schedule

    D. Almanac

**83.** Functioning computer equipment can best be disposed of by which method?

    A. Putting it in the trash

    B. Donating it to a charitable organization

    C. Giving it to someone you don't like

    D. Scrapping it for parts

**84.** Electrical contacts can be cleaned with which of the following items?

A. Soapy water
B. Contact cleaner
C. Isopropyl Alcohol
D. Pencil eraser

**85.** When using a chemical, what should be a major concern to you as a technician and a citizen? (Choose all that apply.)

A. The cost of the chemical
B. Its potential impact on the environment
C. The proper disposal procedures for the empty container
D. None of the above

# Motherboard/Processors/Memory

**1.** What does VLSI stand for?

A. Very Large Systematic Information
B. Very Large Scale Integration
C. Very Large System Integration
D. Very Large System Intelligence

**2.** Which CPU features a 32-bit register size, a 32-bit data bus, and a 32-bit address bus?

A. 286
B. 386SX
C. 386DX
D. 486

**3.** What is the data bus width of the 486SX processor?

A. 16-bit
B. 24-bit
C. 32-bit
D. 64-bit

**4.** What is the width of the address bus of a 286 processor?

A. 8-bit
B. 16-bit
C. 24-bit
D. 32-bit

**5.** If you have 16MB of physical memory installed on your computer, what would be the exact amount displayed when the system boots up?

A. 16,702,311
B. 16,811,536
C. 16,912,213
D. 16,777,216

**6.** Which of the following chips is large, expensive, and doesn't need a constant update, but does require a periodic update?

A. SRAM chips
B. SIMM chips
C. DIMM chips
D. DIP chips

**7.** What type of material is a motherboard made of?

A. Mylar
B. Fiberglass
C. Plastic
D. Kevlar

**8.** What is the size of the bus in an Extended Industry Standard Architecture (EISA) motherboard?

   A. 16-bit

   B. 24-bit

   C. 32-bit

   D. None of the above

**9.** Which mode of printing offers the same features as bi-directional, in addition to the use of a DMA channel for data transfer?

   A. ECC

   B. ECP

   C. EPP

   D. Bi-directional+

**10.** What is represented here?

   A. EPROM chip

   B. Processor

   C. BIOS chip

   D. Level 2 cache chip

**11.** What is the difference between SRAM and DRAM?

A. DRAM uses resistors

B. DRAM uses transistors

C. DRAM uses capacitors

D. DRAM is much slower than SRAM

**12.** Which of the following processors has a working math co-processor?

A. 386DX

B. 486SX

C. 486DX

D. 386SX

**13.** If the data bits of a memory chip equal 8 or 32, what is said about the memory chip?

A. The SIMM is 32MB

B. The SIMM does not use a parity bit

C. The SIMM is 8MB

D. The SIMM uses a parity bit

**14.** Which of the following are types of motherboards? (Choose all that apply.)

A. Full

B. ATX

C. AT

D. Baby

**15.** What was the purpose of VESA?

A. To increase the performance of the video subsystem

B. To create standards for the local bus

C. To regulate the use of nickel-cadmium batteries

D. To test motherboard speeds using electrolysis

**16.** The Intel 586 (Pentium) chip combined two 486DX chips into one. What was this technology called?

A. Double Intelligent Bus Mastering

B. Double Independent Parallel Architecture

C. Dual Independent Bus Architecture

D. Dual Independent Parallel Architecture

**17.** What did the 486SX introduce? (Choose all that apply.)

A. 66 Mhz processor speed

B. 8K on-board cache

C. Disabled math co-processor

D. Math co-processor

**18.** Fill in the missing data in the table shown here.

| Processor | Register | Data Bus | Address Bus |
|-----------|----------|----------|-------------|
| 80386DX | 32-bit | | |
| 80486SX | 32-bit | 32-bit | 32-bit |
| 80486DX | 32-bit | 32-bit | 32-bit |
| Pentium | 64-bit | 64-bit | 32-bit |

A. 24-bit data bus and 24-bit address bus

B. 24-bit data bus and 32-bit address bus

C. 32-bit data bus and 24-bit address bus

D. 32-bit data bus and 32-bit address bus

**19.** You have been called out to a customer's site to troubleshoot what has been described as a "system failure." When you arrive, you notice the error, "Cannot find operating system." Which of the following is not something you would check in this situation?

A. The hard disk cable is firmly plugged in

B. The correct line is present in the boot sector file

C. A floppy is in the drive

D. BIOS has the correct hard disk type specified

**20.** Which coprocessor would you use with a 386DX processor?

A. 386DX2

B. 386DX+

C. 387SX

D. 387DX

**21.** Specialized devices that work with the processor to speed up math operations are included with what chips?

A. 386SX

B. 386DX

C. 486DX

D. 486SX

**22.** A customer calls wanting to know about a problem. The computer he bought is supposed to have 16MB of memory, but it is showing 16,777,216 bytes. He wants to know where the extra memory came from.

A. The computer maker gave them extra memory

B. The 16,777,216 count is wrong

C. Both are correct. 16MB means 16 times 1048576

D. There is a problem in the computer

**23.** The 8088 processor can run at _____ speed.

A. 4.77 Mhz

B. 8 Mhz

C. 133 Mhz

D. 66 Mhz

**24.** The memory uses parity checking to check for bytes with errors. A machine using even parity adds a 1 to the parity bit if:

    A.  The number of bits that are 1 is an even number

    B.  The number of bits that are 1 is an odd number

    C.  The bits all add up to one

    D.  The bits all add up to zero

**25.** The memory uses parity checking to check for bytes with errors. A machine using odd parity adds a 1 to the parity bit if:

    A.  The number of bits that are 1 is an even number

    B.  The number of bits that are 1 is an odd number

    C.  The bits all add up to one

    D.  The bits all add up to zero.

**26.** If a byte does not have a parity error, this indicates:

    A.  The byte is correct

    B.  An even number of bits may be wrong

    C.  The byte is incorrect

    D.  An odd number of bits may be wrong

**27.** Serial ports transmit data over _____ conductors at a time.

    A.  Eight

    B.  One

    C.  Sixteen

    D.  Thirty-two

**28.** Parallel ports transmit data over _____ conductors at a time.

    A.  Eight

    B.  One

    C.  Sixteen

    D.  Thirty-two

**29.** The CMOS retains the settings of the BIOS by using a:

A. Hard disk

B. Little electricity from the wall outlet even when the computer is off

C. Battery

D. Static electricity

**30.** The _____ architecture was introduced by IBM to be used with the PS/2 computers.

A. ISA

B. MCA

C. EISA

D. VESA

**31.** Standard types and sizes of floppy diskette drives include:

A. 5.25-inch, 360KB

B. 5.25-inch, 1.44MB

C. 3.5-inch, 720KB

D. 3.5-inch, 2.88MB

**32.** Rings of concentric circles around a disk are called:

A. Sectors

B. Cylinders

C. Tracks

D. Slices

**33.** Combining the same track on each of the disks makes a:

A. Sector

B. Cylinder

C. Track

D. Slice

**34.** A kilobyte is _____ bytes in the memory of a computer.

A. 1,073,741,824
B. 1,000,000,000
C. 1,024
D. 1,048,576

**35.** A megabyte is _____ bytes in the memory of a computer.

A. 1,073,741,824
B. 1,000,000,000
C. 1,024
D. 1,048,576

**36.** The space to contain one character on a computer is called:

A. A byte, which contains 8 bits
B. A bit, which contains 8 bytes
C. A byte, which contains one hexadecimal number
D. A bit, which contains one bit

**37.** SIMMs are recognizable in that the memory chips are:

A. Installed separately in the motherboard
B. Embedded on one side of the module
C. Embedded on both sides of the module
D. Not used

**38.** DIMMs are recognizable in that the memory chips are:

A. Installed separately in the motherboard
B. Embedded on one side of the module
C. Embedded on both sides of the module
D. Not used

**39.** AT motherboards come in what sizes?

   A. AT
   B. Half-size
   C. AT Baby
   D. ATX Baby

**40.** SIMM stands for:

   A. Socket Integrated Modified Memory
   B. Scaled I/O Memory Management
   C. Serial Interactive Memory Mount
   D. Single In-line Memory Module
   E. Socket Induced Memory Management

**41.** The following CPUs have a 24-bit address:

   A. 8086
   B. 8088
   C. 80286
   D. 80386SX
   E. 80386DX

**42.** Which CPUs have a 16-bit data bus?

   A. 8086
   B. 8088
   C. 80386DX
   D. 80386SX
   E. 80286

exam
ⓦatch    *There are several questions on the exam that will test your knowledge*
*of different processors' bus sizes.*

**43.** Which CPUs have a 16-bit register?

A. 80486SX

B. 8088

C. 80386DX

D. 80386SX

E. 80286

**44.** A Pentium chip has what kind of address bus?

A. 8-bit

B. 16-bit

C. 24-bit

D. 32-bit

E. 64-bit

**45.** One kilobyte is equal to:

A. 1000 bytes

B. 1024 bytes

C. 1048 bytes

D. 102.4 bytes

E. 10244 bytes

**46.** One gigabyte is equal to:

A. 1,000,000,000 bytes

B. 1,024,000,000 bytes

C. 1,048,576,000 bytes

D. 1,073,741,824 bytes

E. 1,677,721,600 bytes

**47.** One megabyte is equal to how many kilobytes?

A. 1,000
B. 1,024
C. 1,048
D. 1,000,000
E. 1,048,000

**48.** The rate at which chips are refreshed is called:

A. Refresh
B. Purge rate
C. Recycle rate
D. Update rate
E. None of the above

**49.** EDO is an acronym for:

A. Extended Digital Optimizing
B. Extended Data Output
C. Enhanced Data Optimizing
D. Enhanced Digital Optimizing
E. Enhanced Digital Output

**50.** A memory bank is:

A. A single chip on a memory card
B. A series of four chips on a memory card
C. A series of eight chips on a memory card
D. The whole memory card
E. The slot/socket that the memory goes in

exam
ⓌatchRemember the interrupt and memory addresses for both COM1 and COM2 for the A+ Certification Exam.*

**51.** This stores the settings used by the BIOS:

    A. CMOS

    B. BIOS

    C. Hard disk

    D. RAM

    E. None of the above

**52.** Which architecture increased the bus size from 16-bit to 32-bit?

    A. MCA

    B. ISA

    C. EISA

    D. PCI

    E. PCMCIA

**53.** PCI stands for:

    A. Peripheral Component Interconnect

    B. Peripheral Card Interface

    C. Peripheral Card Interconnect

    D. PCMCIA Computer Interface

    E. Peripheral Component Interface

**54.** Previous to 1985, PCMCIA could handle up to how many bits?

    A. 8

    B. 16

    C. 20

    D. 32

    E. 64

**55.** VL-Bus stands for:

CORE
QUESTIONS

A. Version Logical Bus

B. Version Limitless Bus

C. Version Enhancement Standard Architecture Local Bus

D. Video Electronics Standards Association Local Bus

E. Version Enumerated Standard Architecture Local Bus

**56.** This parallel port offers an extended control code set:

A. Unidirectional

B. Bi-directional

C. ECP-Extended capability port

D. EPP-Enhanced parallel port

E. None of the above

**57.** What are the concentric circles on a disk, indicated by the arrows shown in the following illustration?

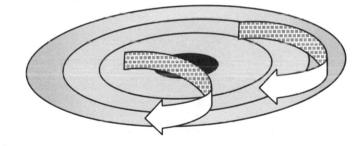

A. Tracks

B. Sector

C. Cylinder

D. Head

E. None of the above

**58.** What is the section on a platter that is shaped like a pie slice, as indicated by the arrows in the following illustration?

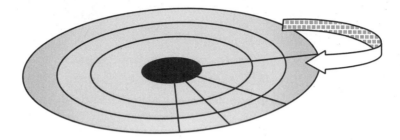

A. Tracks
B. Sector
C. Cylinder
D. Head
E. None of the above

**59.** The total of the tracks in each ring, indicated by the arrows in the following illustration, form what?

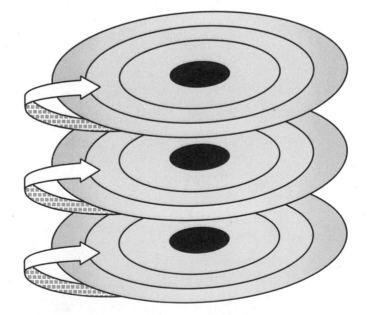

A. Tracks

B. Sectors

C. Cylinders

D. Head

E. None of the above

**60.** Which of the following includes a functional math co-processor?

A. 80386DX

B. 80486SX

C. 80486DX

D. Pentium

E. Pentium II

**61.** The ISA bus runs at what speed?

A. 33 Mhz

B. 16 Mhz

C. 8 Mhz

D. 12 Mhz

**62.** Which type of parallel port configuration will use DMA for better performance?

A. SPP

B. EPP

C. ECP

D. USB

**63.** PCI is an acronym for which of the following?

A. Proximity Component Interconnect

B. Peripheral Component Interconnect

C. Proxy Cache Interconnect

D. Peripheral Complimentary Interconnect

**64.** SIMM is an acronym for which of the following?

A. Simple In-line Memory Module
B. Single In-line Memory Module
C. Single Integer Memory Module
D. Solid Integrated Memory Module

**65.** DIMM is an acronym for which of the following?

A. Double Integer Memory Module
B. Dual Integer Memory Module
C. Dual In-line Memory Module
D. Density Intense Memory Module

**66.** The _____ type of memory requires a refresh rate.

A. ROM
B. SRAM
C. DRAM
D. WRAM

**67.** Which type of parallel port supports an extended command set?

A. SPP
B. ECP
C. EPP
D. NCP

**68.** The 386SX chip uses a _____ data bus.

A. 32-bit
B. 8-bit
C. 16-bit
D. 24-bit

**69.** The 386SX chip has a _____ address bus.

    A. 16-bit

    B. 8-bit

    C. 24-bit

    D. 32-bit

**70.** The 486DX chip has a _____ address bus.

    A. 16-bit

    B. 24-bit

    C. 32-bit

    D. 8-bit

**71.** The 8088 chip had a _____ address bus.

    A. 20-bit

    B. 16-bit

    C. 24-bit

    D. 32-bit

**72.** The Pentium Processor uses a _____ address bus.

    A. 32-bit

    B. 64-bit

    C. 24-bit

    D. 16-bit

**73.** The external clock speed of a 486DX4-chip is:

    A. 66 Mhz

    B. 33 Mhz

    C. 133 Mhz

    D. 72 Mhz

**74.** A customer calls you and wants to buy a modem for his laptop PC. Which type of modem should you recommend?

A. PCI bus
B. VESA bus
C. PCMCI bus
D. ISA

**75.** Which type of processors must have a heat sink to prevent damage to themselves?

A. 486DX4
B. 486DX2
C. Pentium II
D. Pentium

**76.** A customer calls and complains that his parallel port isn't working. What is the first thing you could check in the CMOS?

A. ECP settings
B. EPP settings
C. ENABLE/DISABLE setting
D. SPP setting

**77.** Which three items must be set correctly in CMOS for a hard disk to work properly?

A. HEADS
B. SIZE
C. CYLINDERS
D. SECTORS

**78.** The correct memory address and IRQ setting for COM2 is which of the following?

A. 3F8 IRQ 4

B. 2F8 IRQ 3

C. 3E8 IRQ 4

D. 2E8 IRQ 3

**79.** ISA is an acronym for:

A. Industrial Standard Archive

B. Industry Standard Architecture

C. International Standards Association

D. International Standard Architecture

**80.** Which type of memory offers increased bandwith by shortening the page mode cycle and is 10-15 percent faster than fast-page memory?

A. SRAM

B. DRAM

C. ROM

D. EDO RAM

**81.** A customer calls and reports to you that when he boots his PC he receives the following error, "Non system or disk error. Replace and press any key to continue." What is the most common cause of this problem?

A. A virus has destroyed the boot sector on the hard disk

B. The motherboard has gone bad

C. The CMOS is corrupted

D. The customer has inadvertently left a non-bootable floppy disk in the drive

exam
ⓦatch

*Know the different types of parallel ports for the exam, as many people get stuck on these types of questions.*

# Printers

**1.** What is the biggest disadvantage of daisy wheel printers?

    A. The replacement heads are extremely expensive

    B. The noise

    C. The electro-voice coil assembly is difficult to replace

    D. The roller unit is integrated into the head assembly

**2.** On a dot matrix printer, what controls a series of pins?

    A. Fuser

    B. Magno-resistive capacitor

    C. Solenoid

    D. Tension spring

**3.** Which of the following devices in a laser printer has the highest negative charge?

    A. The toner drum

    B. The fuser assembly

    C. The transfer corona

    D. The primary corona

**4.** How does the droplet of ink make its way to the page being printed in an Ink Jet printer?

    A. Gravity pulls the tiny droplet to the page

    B. Pressure forces the droplet of ink to the page

    C. A blast of air pushes the droplet to the page

    D. Magnets force the droplet out of the ink nozzle

**5.** How do laser printers receive their print job instructions one page at a time?

A. Photosynthesis

B. Page Description Query (PDQ)

C. Page Description Language (PDL)

D. Optical Character Resolution

**6.** The cleaning blade on a laser printer is made of what material?

A. Phosphor

B. Rubber

C. Plastic

D. Metal

**7.** What is the primary corona wire used for in a laser printer?

A. Fusing the image on the paper

B. Drawing the negative image on the photosensitive drum surface

C. Erasing the photosensitive drum

D. Pulling toner from the drum to the positively charged paper surface

**8.** What is the purpose of the transfer corona in a laser printer?

A. Pulls the toner off of the photosensitive drum

B. Charges the photosensitive drum

C. Erases the photosensitive drum

D. Fuses the image on the paper

**9.** What component is responsible in the last phase of the laser printing process?

A. Primary corona wire

B. Fusing rollers

C. Transfer corona

D. Roller wire assembly

10. What is the first phase of the laser printing process?

    A. Charging
    B. Writing
    C. Developing
    D. Cleaning

11. What happens after the developing phase in the laser printing process?

    A. Cleaning
    B. Writing
    C. Transferring
    D. Charging

12. What phase in the laser printing process ensures that the drum has been electrostatically erased so that it can receive a new image?

    A. Charging
    B. Transferring
    C. Cleaning
    D. Writing

13. Which component of a laser printer is responsible for transferring the image to the drum?

    A. Primary corona
    B. Fusing roller
    C. Corona wire
    D. Laser diodes

14. Which of the following parts is not a portion of the fuser assembly?

    A. A rubberized pressure roller
    B. A electrostatic sensor clip
    C. A Teflon-coated aluminum fusing roller
    D. A halogen heating lamp

**15.** Which type of printer roller does not advance the paper until the EP cartridge is ready to process the next line of the image?

  A. Fuser roller

  B. Exit roller

  C. Registration roller

  D. Feed rollers

**16.** A parallel cable consists of what connectors?

  A. Male DB-15 connector for the computer and a 36-pin Centronics connector for the printer

  B. Male DB-25 connector for the computer and a 24-pin Centronics connector for the printer

  C. Male DB-25 connector for the computer and a 36-pin Centronics connector for the printer

  D. Male DB-15 connector for the computer and a 24-pin Centronics connector for the printer

**17.** A coworker has just made a parallel cable to connect the laser printer in the office. While he is printing, strange things are occurring. You think the parallel cable may be too long. What is the maximum cable length for the parallel printer cable?

  A. 5 feet

  B. 8 feet

  C. 10 feet

  D. 12 feet

**18.** What are the only types of field-replaceable units that an end user should replace? (Choose all that apply.)

  A. Toner cartridges

  B. Roller assemblies

  C. Print heads

  D. Power supplies

19. Which of the following is not a reason for a laser printer to print a blank page?

    A. Fuser assembly failure
    B. No toner
    C. Transfer corona failure
    D. HVPS failure

20. What will happen if an element of the fusing process fails?

    A. Ghosted images will appear
    B. Blank pages will be printed
    C. Speckled pages will appear
    D. Smudged images will appear

21. Which of the following should you consider when storing printing paper? (Choose all that apply.)

    A. Humidity
    B. Temperature
    C. Ream size
    D. Location

22. Printers are classified in two major groups. These two groups are:

    A. Impact and laser
    B. Impact and non-impact
    C. Laser and non-impact
    D. Ink Jet and laser

23. The process a laser printer uses to print is:

    A. Charging, cleaning, writing, developing, transferring, fusing
    B. Charging, fusing, writing, developing, transferring, cleaning
    C. Cleaning, charging, writing, developing, transferring, fusing
    D. Cleaning, charging, fusing, developing, transferring, writing

**24.** During the fusing step of the electro-photographic print process:

    A. The toner is permanently bonded to the paper

    B. The photosensitive drum is cleaned and electrically erased

    C. A high voltage negative charge is applied to the drum

    D. The image is transferred to the paper

**25.** During the writing step of the electro-photographic print process:

    A. The toner is permanently bonded to the paper

    B. The photosensitive drum is cleaned and electrically erased

    C. A high voltage negative charge is applied to the drum

    D. The image is transferred to the paper

**26.** The customer reports that his HP LaserJet 5 printer is showing a paper jam. He says that he removed the paper jam from the toner cartridge area, but the error will not disappear. What is the problem?

    A. Did not clear paper jam

    B. Must press Reset

    C. Failed to close cover

    D. Open and close the back side

**27.** Parallel printer cables normally come in what two lengths?

    A. 6 feet and 10 feet

    B. 10 feet and 25 feet

    C. 6 feet and 25 feet

    D. 6 inches and 10 feet

**28.** Serial printer cables normally come in what two lengths?

    A. 6 feet and 10 feet

    B. 10 feet and 25 feet

    C. 6 feet and 25 feet

    D. 6 inches and 10 feet

29. A LaserJet printer shows the toner is low, but is still printing fine. What action should the user take?

   A. Replace the toner cartridge
   B. Have the printer serviced
   C. Refill the toner cartridge
   D. Watch the output, and when it starts getting light, replace the cartridge

30. When using a Dot Matrix printer, the complaint is that there is a white line through the print. What needs replacing?

   A. Ribbon
   B. Print head
   C. Roller
   D. Printer cable

31. When using a Dot Matrix printer, the complaint is that there are strange characters through the print. What needs replacing?

   A. Ribbon
   B. Print head
   C. Roller
   D. Printer cable

32. The parallel port sends data to the printer _____ at a time.

   A. Eight bits
   B. One bit
   C. 25 bits
   D. 10 bytes

exam
**W**atch   *Understanding the theory of the Electrophotographic Print process is a key to passing the Printers section of the exam.*

**33.** The COM port sends data to the printer _____ at a time.

A. One byte

B. One bit

C. 25 bits

D. 10 bytes

**34.** Printers may be connected to a computer via:

A. Network connection

B. Infrared

C. Parallel cables

D. Serial cables

**35.** When a job is sent to the printer, garbage is printed with page breaks. The print preview looks fine. The customer uses two different printers on the PC. What is the problem?

A. Wrong printer driver used

B. Bad cable

C. Wrong IRQ

D. Out of toner

**36.** When a job is sent to the printer, it prints blank pages. The print preview looks fine. The customer uses two different printers on the PC. What is the problem?

A. Wrong printer driver used

B. Bad cable

C. Wrong IRQ

D. Out of toner

**37.** The customer reports that the Ink Jet cartridges she gets from you keep clogging up. She says that at her office, they always turn off the system every night via the power strip. What is the problem?

A. Bad ink cartridges

B. Ink Jet printers should never be turned off

C. They are using the power strip to turn off the printer

D. Bad printer

38. When installing a new cartridge on an inkjet printer, what is installed?

A. Only new ink

B. New nozzles and ink

C. New ink (and the nozzles are cleaned)

D. New photosensitive drum and new ink

39. Printers that have print considered to be letter quality include:

A. Laser

B. Dot Matrix

C. Ink Jet

D. Daisy wheel

40. A printer prints strange characters. You move only the printer to a second computer and hook the second printer to the first computer. The first printer now prints fine, but the second printer now prints strange characters. What should you do?

A. Replace the first printer's toner cartridge

B. Replace the second printer's toner cartridge

C. Replace the first computer's printer cable

D. Repair the second computer

41. A parallel printer cable with a bar connector is a:

A. Male DB-25

B. Female DB-25

C. Female 36-pin Centronics

D. Male 36-pin Centronics

**42.** Replacing an empty toner cartridge is a:

   A. User task

   B. Manufacturer task

   C. Trained service technician task

   D. Not permitted

**43.** Which of these are components of a laser printer?

   A. Cleaning blade

   B. Photosensitive drum

   C. Primary corona wire

   D. Transfer corona

   E. Fusing rollers

**44.** This highly negatively charged wire electronically erases the photosensitive drum:

   A. Cleaning blade

   B. Photosensitive drum

   C. Primary corona wire

   D. Transfer corona

   E. Fusing rollers

**45.** Photosensitivity is affected by which of the following print processes?

   A. Charging

   B. Developing

   C. Cleaning

   D. Transferring

   E. Writing

exam
Ⓦatch  *Minimize your cable lengths for reliable communications. Parallel cables should be limited to 10 feet; serial cables to less than 25 feet.*

**46.** In the print process, what occurs after developing?

   A. Fusing
   B. Writing
   C. Charging
   D. Transferring
   E. Cleaning

**47.** What is the second step of the print process?

   A. Cleaning
   B. Charging
   C. Corona transfer
   D. Corona sweep
   E. Copying

**48.** In the third step of printing, what is the point at which the laser hits the drum?

   A. -5000 Vdc
   B. -100 Vdc
   C. 0 Vdc
   D. +100 Vdc
   E. +5000 Vdc

**49.** If you are getting black specks on your printouts, what step in the process is probably failing?

   A. Fusing
   B. Writing
   C. Charging
   D. Transferring
   E. Cleaning

**50.** You have checked that the paper path is clear, and the power light is on, and the cables are all connected, but your network print job is not printing. What are the possible reasons?

 A. Someone printed a poorly formatted document and it has stopped the print jobs
 B. Paper jam
 C. Low toner
 D. Printer is not online
 E. None of the above

**51.** A user wants to print three copies of an invoice at the same time. What kind of printer can he use?

 A. Daisy Wheel
 B. Ink Jet
 C. Thermal
 D. Dot Matrix
 E. Laser

**52.** Which of the following can cause the printer to send out blank pages?

 A. No toner
 B. Transfer corona failure
 C. HPVS failure
 D. All of the above

**53.** You have a dry ink cartridge and it is out of ink. Which of the following are acceptable procedures?

 A. Refill cartridge
 B. Refill cartridge and clean with isopropyl alcohol
 C. Replace with new one
 D. Refill and run cartridge cleaning software
 E. Refill and run several blank sheets

**54.** Which of the following are ways to connect a printer?

A. DB-9
B. DB-24
C. Parallel
D. Serial
E. Infrared

**55.** The location of a serial printer can be within: (Choose all that apply.)

A. 10 feet
B. 20 feet
C. 25 feet
D. 75 feet
E. 50 feet

**56.** On a daisy wheel printer, a _____ is energized, causing it to strike the back of a _____ containing the character.

A. Electromechanical hammer, petal
B. Solenoid, petal
C. Resistive coil, petal
D. Solenoid, drum
E. Resistive coil, drum

**57.** On a dot matrix printer, the earliest print heads had _____ pins, while today's have _____ .

A. 8, 24
B. 7, 24
C. 8, 25
D. 16, 24
E. 12, 32

**58.** Which of the following are true about using dot addressable mode in printers, instead of font addressable?

A. It is faster

B. It is slower

C. Each printed dot requires an input

D. Each of the pins is pre-configured for each font

E. None of the above

**59.** Laser printers use what to produce high quality prints?

A. Light

B. Electricity

C. Chemistry

D. Pressure

E. Heat

**60.** What are the main types of rollers?

A. Spiked

B. Feed

C. Register

D. Fuser

E. Exit

**61.** What are the three main motors in a printer?

A. Transfer corona

B. Main drive

C. Paper feed

D. Roller motor

E. Transport

**62.** If you see a following printout happening periodically on a dot matrix printer, what is the probable cause?

**Test print job**

A. Ribbon advancement
B. Paper advance
C. Paper slippage
D. Ink cartridge low
E. Bad print head

**63.** On a Macintosh computer you have put the drivers in the system folder connected to the AppleTalk network, and you have cleaned the printhead. Why is it still not printing on the network dot matrix printer?

A. The drivers do not go here
B. Macintoshes don't use AppleTalk networks
C. You should not have lubricated the printhead
D. None of the above

**64.** You are consulting with a new client who wishes to generate high-quality, black-and-white documents for their law office. Which is the best type of printer for this part of the system?

A. Bubble Jet
B. LaserJet
C. Dot Matrix
D. Daisy Wheel

**65.** Identify the printer that uses a pump and ink well to spray the ink onto the page.

   A.  LaserJet
   B.  Bubble Jet
   C.  Dot Matrix
   D.  Ink Jet

**66.** Identify all of the printers that could be considered line mode printers.

   A.  LaserJet
   B.  Dot Matrix
   C.  Ink Jet
   D.  Bubble Jet

**67.** Which of the following can cause LaserJet printed pages to smear when touched?

   A.  Charging
   B.  Fusing
   C.  Cleaning
   D.  Developing

**68.** Before servicing a printer, you should first:

   A.  Remove the plug from the AC wall outlet
   B.  Check the toner cartridge
   C.  Consult the manufacturer's guidelines
   D.  Try to print a test page

exam
ⓦatch    *A corrective measure for a dry ink cartridge should never be refilling the ink cartridge! Replacing the cartridge not only replenishes the ink, but replaces the old worn-out nozzles with new ones.*

**69.** The easiest way to test a printer on a Windows 95 PC is to:

A. Start Word, create a document, and try to print it

B. Open a simple text file and try to print it

C. Use the Print Test Page applet included in the Printers folder of My Computer

D. Run the Self Test utility that comes with the printer

**70.** What low-level DOS command is helpful to test the hardware port, printer cable, and printer itself, bypassing any possibly corrupted printer drivers?

A. PRINT <filename> LPTx

B. COPY CON

C. CAPTURE SH

D. DIR > LPTx

**71.** A PC using Windows is printing intermittently. Small documents print, but large print jobs never complete. Either they print partially or not at all. What is the most likely cause of the problem?

A. The printer drivers are corrupted

B. The printer cable is bad

C. The printer is low on ink

D. The hard disk is very low on space

**72.** When servicing a LaserJet printer, which items below are potentially dangerous and can cause bodily harm if caution is not used?

A. Heated fusion rollers

B. Drum cleaning blade

C. High voltage corona

D. Class 3 Laser beam

**73.** Which is the third step of the six-step LaserJet EP printing process?

A. Charging

B. Developing

C. Writing

D. Transferring

**74.** Which is the fifth step of the LaserJet EP printing process?

A. Developing

B. Writing

C. Transferring

D. Fusing

**75.** Prior to the LaserJet EP printing process of writing, the drum is charged to approximately what voltage potential?

A. +3000 volts

B. -5000 volts

C. 3000 volts

D. +5000 volts

**76.** Identify the printers that are normally capable of printing graphic images.

A. Dot Matrix

B. Daisy Wheel

C. LaserJet

D. Bubble Jet

**77.** Identify the parts that all types of printers have in common.

A. Power Supply

B. Paper Feeding Mechanism

C. Ink Well

D. Fusing Assembly

**78.** Identify the two common types of ports used for printer interfaces.

    A. SCSI

    B. Parallel

    C. USB

    D. Serial

**79.** The serial printer cable has a _____ connector on the PC end and a _____ connector on the printer end.

    A. DB-25 female (sockets)

    B. DB-25 male (pins)

    C. Centronics 36-pin (male)

    D. Centronics 50-pin (female)

**80.** You are on a service call to repair a printer. The printer online light keeps flashing, indicating that it is out of paper. You have verified that there is paper in the printer and that the proper paper path is selected. What should you check first?

    A. The printer cable

    B. The ink ribbon

    C. The fusion roller

    D. The paper path and sensor

**81.** Printer cables that are longer than 10 feet may experience what kind of problems? (Choose all that apply.)

    A. Noise and interference

    B. Data skew

    C. Paper jams

    D. All of the above

**82.** What type of switch is usually found on a printer to control its option settings?

A. DIP switch

B. Power switch

C. Sensor switch

D. Voltage Selector switch

83. A LaserJet printer is printing blank pages. Select all of the possible causes.

A. Toner cartridge is empty

B. Fusion roller is malfunctioning

C. Transfer corona has failed

D. HVPS failure

# Portable Systems

1. Which of the following laptop components is more likely be replaced or upgraded without sending the laptop to the original manufacturer?

A. Hard disk

B. Keyboard

C. Display

D. Power supply

2. Active matrix displays are based on what type of technology?

A. Transistor Type Technology (TTT)

B. True Refresh Technology (TRT)

C. True Crystal Transistor (TCT)

D. Thin Film Transistor (TFT)

3. How can you use PCI components with a portable computer, without the use of a docking station?

A. Use a PCI adapter

B. Use a serial PCI interface

C. Use a PCMCIA adapter

D. You can't

**4.** What is the least expensive way to add external VGA and keyboard connectors to a laptop?

    A. Use a serial port converter

    B. Use a port replicator

    C. Use a parallel replicator

    D. Use a PCMCIA converter

**5.** Most portable computers today are shipping with what type of hard disks?

    A. IDE and EIDE

    B. IDE and SCSI

    C. EIDE and UDMA

    D. EIDE and SCSI

**6.** What does the acronym PCMCIA stand for?

    A. People Can't Memorize Computer Industry Acronyms

    B. Personal Computer Messaging Center Installation Architecture

    C. Personal Computer Memory Card Installation Architecture

    D. Personal Computer Memory Card International Association

**7.** PCMCIA version 1.0 defined an interface with how many pins?

    A. 40 pins

    B. 50 pins

    C. 62 pins

    D. 68 pins

**8.** Which type of PCMCIA card is the thinnest?

    A. Type I

    B. Type II

    C. Type III

    D. Type IV

**e x a m**
**ⓦatch**  *All PC Cards are 85.6 mm by 54.0 mm. Type I cards are 3.3 mm thick,*
*Type II are 5.0 mm thick, and Type III 10.5 mm thick.*

**9.** What is Socket Services?

A. A hardware abstraction layer responsible for ejecting PC cards

B. A layer of BIOS-level software that detects insertion of PC cards

C. A software interface that isolates PC card internal errors

D. A software interface that enables PC cards to run in ISA emulation mode

**10.** What does Card Services manage?

A. The ISA emulation mode

B. The allocation of system resources automatically, such as memory and interrupts

C. The layer of BIOS-level software that detects insertion of PC cards

D. The software interface that isolates PC card internal errors

**11.** What type of PC card is generally used only for memory?

A. Type 1

B. Type 2

C. Type 3

D. Type 4

**12.** Which type of PC card is generally reserved for rotating mass storage devices?

A. Type I

B. Type II

C. Type III

D. Type IV

**13.** Fill in the missing data in the following table.

| Type | Size |
|------|------|
| Type I | 3.3 mm |
| Type II | |
| Type IV | 10.5 mm |

A. 4.0 mm

B. 5.0 mm

C. 6.0 mm

D. 7.0 mm

**14.** Which of the following is not a disadvantage with a laptop computer?

A. Harder to repair

B. Not as upgradable

C. Less resale value

D. Hardware and drivers can be difficult to find

**15.** You are working on a user's laptop, which frequently loses its battery life after only a couple hours, even when it has recharged for over 12 hours. What is most likely the problem?

A. Nickel/metal hydride batteries are being used, not nickel cadmium

B. The user is running demanding spreadsheet software

C. The battery needs to be fully discharged

D. The battery is bad

**16.** How do enhanced port replicators extend the capabilities of port replicators?

A. By adding infrared adapters and PCI adapters

B. By minimizing space and including RAM and video enhancements

C. By adding sound capabilities and more PC Card slots

D. By adding ISA-compatible slots and dual monitor connectors

**17.** Identify the statement that is true from the following statements.

    A. Type 3 PC cards are the most flexible, as they can fit into Type 3 and Type 2 slots

    B. Type 1 PC cards are the most flexible, as they can fit into Type 1 and Type 2 slots

    C. Type 2 PC cards are thicker than Type 3 cards, and only work in Type 2 slots

    D. Type 3 PC cards are thicker than Type 2 cards, and can only fit into a Type 2 slot

**18.** Which laptop battery is slightly heavier and produces less power?

    A. NiCad

    B. NiMH

    C. LiIon

    D. HiLon

**19.** Which of the following are the most common areas for a RAM upgrade on a laptop computer? (Choose all that apply.)

    A. Port replicator

    B. PCMCIA slots

    C. Proprietary expansion slots

    D. Parallel port

**20.** How can you configure a user's laptop so that he does not need to load drivers for the docking station when he is not using it?

    A. Install the operating system twice; one with docking station drivers, the other without. Instruct the user to boot into the operating system of his choice

    B. Create two hardware profiles, and select the appropriate profile on startup

    C. Create desktop shortcuts that turn off devices and drivers when not in use

    D. Create a batch file on startup that disables the devices and drivers a user does not wish to load

**21.** A user would like to remove the modem PC card and insert the Ethernet network PC card. What is the simplest way to do this? (Choose all that apply.)

A. If you are using Windows NT, remove the card and insert the new card while the operating system is running

B. If you are using Windows 95 or Windows 98, remove the card and insert the new card while the operating system is running

C. If you are using Windows NT, you may have to shut down or suspend the computer while you insert the new card

D. If you are using Windows 95 or Windows 98, you may have to shut down or suspend the computer while you insert the new card

**22.** Replacing a portable computer battery is a:

A. User task

B. Manufacturer task

C. Trained service technician task

D. Not permitted

**23.** Type I PC Cards (PCMCIA) are _____ thick.

A. 3.3 mm

B. 5.0 mm

C. 10.5 mm

D. 54.0 mm

**24.** Type II PC Cards (PCMCIA) are _____ wide.

A. 3.3 mm

B. 5.0 mm

C. 10.5 mm

D. 54.0 mm

**25.** Type III PC Cards (PCMCIA) are _____ long.

A. 3.3 mm

B. 5.0 mm

C. 10.5 mm

D. 85.6 mm

**26.** Memory is usually upgraded on portable computers by adding a:

A. SIMM

B. DIMM

C. Proprietary expansion card

D. Memory chips

**27.** A pointing device on a portable computer that looks like a rubber stick in the center of the keyboard is called:

A. Mouse

B. Trackball

C. Pointing stick

D. Touch pad

**28.** A pointing device on a portable computer that is a small plastic square, over which you rub your finger, is called:

A. Mouse

B. Trackball

C. Pointing stick

D. Touch pad

**29.** Common keyboard styles used in a portable computer are:

A. Dvorak

B. 84-key

C. 101-key

D. Numeric

**30.** The battery does not charge well or not at all on a portable computer. The battery checks out fine. What should you do?

    A. Replace battery

    B. Clean contacts in computer

    C. Replace AC converter

    D. Tell customer it can't be fixed

**31.** An AC adapter converts power to what type for a portable computer?

    A. 110 Vac

    B. DC

    C. 110 Vdc

    D. 220 Vac

**32.** Passive matrix LCDs are chosen for use because they:

    A. Are cheaper to buy and use less energy

    B. Are easier to see from an angle

    C. Have superior quality image

    D. Have superior capability to handle a changing image

**33.** Active matrix LCDs are chosen for use because they:

    A. Are cheaper to buy and use less energy

    B. Are easier to see from an angle

    C. Have superior quality image

    D. Have superior capability to handle a changing image

**34.** When cleaning an LCD display you should use:

    A. Alcohol

    B. AJAX

    C. A damp cloth

    D. Steel wool

exam
**ⓦatch** *Portable computer batteries must be disposed of properly. Check the label of the battery and with local agencies for disposal directions. Do no just throw batteries in the trash!*

**35.** The display on a portable computer is bad. What parts may you replace?

   A. Display as a whole
   B. Wires in the LCD
   C. LCD cover
   D. Transistors in the LCD

**36.** The user states that, when turning on the portable computer, he can not get it to start. The power LED does not light. What is the probable problem?

   A. Bad hard disk
   B. Dead battery
   C. Bad motherboard
   D. Brightness turned down

**37.** The user states that, when turning on the portable computer, he can not get it to start. The power LED does light. What is the probable problem?

   A. Bad hard disk
   B. Dead battery
   C. Bad motherboard
   D. Brightness turned down

**38.** Type I, II, and III cards were developed by the:

   A. Video Electronics Standards Association
   B. Joint Photographic Experts Group
   C. Moving Picture Experts Group
   D. Personal Computer Memory Card International Association

**39.** The customer reports that ever since he recharged the NiCad battery to the computer, which was not fully discharged, it does not fully recharge. This is caused by:

A. Memory effect

B. A dead battery

C. Defective portable computer

D. Recharge effect

**40.** A customer complains that whenever he moves his mouse quickly in Windows, the pointer is not there. How do you fix this?

A. Tell him to move the mouse slowly

B. Adjust the brightness control

C. Get an active matrix LCD panel

D. Set mouse trails in Windows

**41.** Which of the following laptop batteries can be thrown out and swapped with another of the same type when they finally wear out?

A. LiIon

B. NiCad

C. NiMH

D. CMOS

E. None of the above

**42.** You have bought a used laptop and you notice the battery, which is a LiIon, is not lasting very long. You order a new battery and you are having the same problem after three days. What could be the cause?

A. The POWER.DRV in the CONFIG.SYS has the wrong switch

B. The plug in the wall is backwards

C. The battery is collecting too much memory

D. The contacts need cleaning

E. The battery isn't being drained fully

**43.** What kind of monitor is sent a signal to x and y transistors, which then send voltage down the wire, which turns on the LCD at the intersection of the two wires?

   A.  CRT
   B.  Active Matrix
   C.  LED
   D.  Passive Matrix
   E.  None of the above

**44.** Which of the following is the cheapest version of a docking station and just extends the existing ports into the station?

   A.  Socket Extender
   B.  Carry Through
   C.  Jack Extender
   D.  Interface Extension
   E.  Port Replicator

**45.** You have put a laptop into a docking station and are having problems with the modem. Which of the following should you check?

   A.  That the laptop is properly seated into the docking station
   B.  That the computer has rebooted since you installed the modem
   C.  That the docking station and the laptop are hardware compatible
   D.  All of the above
   E.  None of the above

**46.** You need to replace an EIDE IBM 2.0GB internal hard disk on a laptop. Which types can you replace it with to ensure compatibility?

   A.  OEM EIDE hard disk
   B.  OEM UDMA hard disk
   C.  Generic EIDE hard disk
   D.  Generic UDMA hard disk
   E.  Generic IDE hard disk

**47.** What does PCMCIA stand for?

   A. Personal Computer Memory Card International Association

   B. Peripheral Components Manufacturing Computer Interfaces Association

   C. Portable Computer Manufacturing Card Integrated Architecture

   D. Port Cartridge Manufactured Component Intelligent Adapter

   E. None of the above

**48.** Type III cards are usually used for:

   A. 56K modems

   B. Ethernet cards

   C. External mice

   D. Mass storage devices

   E. SCSI adapters

**49.** You can't figure out what kind of card you have, so you get out a ruler. It measures 5mm thick. What kind of card do you have?

   A. Type I

   B. Type II

   C. Type III

   D. Can't tell, because they are all the same thickness

   E. A bad ruler, since none of these are this thick

**50.** Which of the following are uses of a PC card?

   A. Cellular Phone Interface

   B. Global Positioning System Card

   C. Smart Card Readers

   D. Braille Monitors

   E. None of the above

**51.** In 1985 the PCMCIA added to their specification support on PC Cards for:

A. ZV

B. VR

C. Bus Mastering

D. DMA

E. 32-Bit Card Bus operation

**52.** How many pins does the Type II PCMCIA card interface have?

A. 24

B. 56

C. 64

D. 68

E. 128

**53.** The following are commonly used as mice on laptops:

A. Touch pad

B. Pointing stick

C. Trackball

D. External mouse

E. Rubber arm

**54.** Where in the Windows 95 desktop can you enable the battery meter on the task bar?

A. Start | Settings | Control Panel | Power

B. Start | Settings | Control Panel | Power | Advanced

C. Start | Settings | Control Panel | Power | Meters

D. Start | Settings | Control Panel | Power | Options

E. Start | Settings | Control Panel | Power | Battery

**55.** Which of the following is a layer of the BIOS-level software that detects the insertion and removal of PC Cards?

A. PCMCIA Sensor
B. PC Card Sensor
C. Plug & Play ROM
D. Active Matrix Sensor
E. Socket Services

**56.** Generally, NiCad is limited to about _____ recharges.

A. 100
B. 1,000
C. 10,000
D. 100,000
E. Unlimited

**57.** What kind of software manages the allocation of system resources automatically on today's operating systems?

A. Socket Services
B. Card Services
C. Dynamic Resource Allocator
D. Hardware Manager
E. None of the above

**58.** When working with a laptop, you see the plastic part shown in the following illustration on the laptop. What is it for?

A. Ejecting the floppy
B. Ejecting the PC card
C. Front space key
D. Right move key
E. Standing the laptop up at a slight angle

**59.** You see the lever shown here on the side of a docking station. What could it possibly be?

    A.  Power On/Off lever

    B.  Laptop Eject lever

    C.  Monitor Control lever

    D. PCMCIA toggle

    E.  Lever used to choose internal or docking stations components

**60.** Which of the following operating systems will detect that you are on a docking station, and configure itself accordingly?

    A.  Windows NT 3.51

    B.  Windows NT 4.0

    C.  Windows 95

    D. Windows 3.1

    E.  DOS

**61.** A full-feature docking station can provide you with _____ support.

    A.  EIDE

    B.  SCSI

    C.  ISA

    D. PCI

    E.  Full size hard disk

**62.** Because of the _____ of laptop computers, it is often difficult to upgrade them.

A. Size
B. Proprietary nature
C. Power requirements
D. Weight

**63.** The most popular laptop battery today is:

A. NiMH
B. Nickel Cadmium
C. Eveready Energizer
D. Lithium Ion

**64.** You are recommending a laptop for a customer. The most important requirement is the length of battery life between charging. Which two components will maximize this feature for your customer and should be considered for this proposed purchase?

A. An active matrix screen
B. A lithium ion battery
C. A nickel cadmium battery
D. A passive matrix screen

**65.** An older customer comes to you to purchase a laptop. You notice that he is wearing glasses, and he expresses a concern to you about being able to read the smaller screen. What type of displays and options should you recommend to this customer?

A. Passive matrix screen
B. LCD monochrome screen
C. Active matrix screen
D. External VGA monitor

**66.** If a customer wishes to use his or her laptop on the road, as well as have extra features in the office, what would you recommend?

A. Purchase a laptop with the biggest active screen possible

B. Purchase a docking station and monitor for use in the office

C. Purchase a laptop and a desktop for office use

D. Purchase a desktop model for the office, and don't purchase a laptop at all

**67.** Most laptops manufactured today come with which type of pointing device?

A. Mouse

B. Pointing Stick

C. Trackball

D. Touch Pad

**68.** Choose from the items below the advantages of owning a laptop PC, compared with a desktop system.

A. Small size and portability

B. Faster processing speed

C. Better screen display

D. Better resale value

**69.** A laptop battery that only will run the laptop for a short period of time has suffered from which symptom?

A. Battery fatigue

B. Overcharge heat

C. Poor contacts

D. Memory effect

**70.** What is the thickness of a Type III PC card?

A. 3.3.mm

B. 5.0 mm

C. 10.5mm

D. 10.2 mm

**71.** Joe has been eating fried chicken while working on his school project with his laptop. His laptop uses a trackball. He calls you and asks for help. His mouse (trackball) is working sporadically. What would you suggest that he do?

A. Purchase an external mouse for his laptop

B. Replace the trackball with a new one

C. Clean the track ball with a damp cloth

D. Use the Mouse Control applet in Windows to adjust the ballistics of the mouse movements

**72.** A Type I PC card is manufactured to which dimensions?

A. 85.6mm x 54.0mm x 5.0mm

B. 85.6mm x 54.2mm x 3.3mm

C. 85.6mm x 54.0mm x 3.3mm

D. 85.6mm x 54.5 mm x 3.3mm

**73.** To change a PC card in a Windows 95 laptop, you must do which of the following?

A. Shut down the PC, change the PC card, and re-boot

B. Remove the card and replace it

C. Use the Remove Card applet by clicking the icon in the lower-right task bar

D. Edit the WIN.INI to allow this feature

**74.** To run a laptop on land power you need:

A. A DC to DC converter

B. An AC power adapter

C. A DC to AC adapter

D. A power inverter

**75.** To add a device to a laptop, the most common interface type is:

A. PCI

B. ISA

C. VESA

D. PCMCIA

**76.** The three most common pointing devices for a laptop include which of the following?

A. Trackball

B. Standard Mouse

C. Touch Pad

D. Digitizing Pad

**77.** The mouse may be hard to see as it is moved on a laptop with a _____ type of display.

A. Active matrix

B. CRT

C. Passive matrix

D. Monochrome LCD

**78.** Using a docking station with a laptop usually allows the use of which optional devices?

A. PCI-based cards

B. External monitors

C. DC converters

D. ISA-based network interface cards

79. Some disadvantages to owning a laptop when compared to a desktop PC include which of following? (Choose all that apply.)

   A. Lower resale value
   B. Higher cost of ownership
   C. Compatibility with peripheral devices
   D. Easily dropped

80. A PCMCIA card has how many sockets on the interface?

   A. 70
   B. 68
   C. 72
   D. 50

81. Release 2.*x* of the PCMCIA standards included which new features?

   A. Specification for the Type II card
   B. Specifications for the Type III card
   C. Increase in bus speed of the Type II card
   D. Bus mastering

82. The 1995 standards for the PCMCIA card included which of the following features?

   A. The Type III specification
   B. Zoomed Video
   C. 32-bit bus support
   D. 33 Mhz transfer speed

# Basic Networking

1. Which is the most common network cable in use today?

   A. Coaxial

   B. UTP

   C. STP

   D. Fiber optic

**2.** Which of the following is not identified with thin coaxial cable?

   A. BNC

   B. 10BaseT

   C. ThinNet

   D. 10Base2

**3.** What type of cable is shown here?

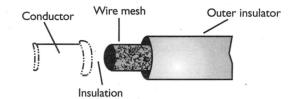

   A. UTP

   B. STP

   C. ThinNet

   D. BNC

**4.** Which cable is most resistant to EMI?

   A. ThinNet

   B. STP

   C. Fiber optic

   D. ThickNet

**5.** What is the maximum cable distance for twisted-pair cabling?

    A. 100 meters
    B. 185 meters
    C. 320 meters
    D. 400 meters

**6.** What does CSMA/CD stand for?

    A. Communication Sensing Multiple Access / Communication Detection
    B. Carrier Sense Multiple Access / Collision Detection
    C. Carrier Sensing Multiple Accessible / Contention Device
    D. Complete Sense Multiple Accessing / Collision Detection

**7.** Which network access method is faster on a small network and why?

    A. Token Ring, because the token travels much faster
    B. CSMA/CD, because the device does not need a token to communicate
    C. Token Ring, because CSMA/CD requires every computer to broadcast their intent to transmit
    D. CSMA/CD, because every device can communicate at the same time

**8.** What does TCP/IP stand for?

    A. Transport Control Protocol/Internet Proxy
    B. Transmission Controlled Packet/Internet Packet
    C. Transfer Control Packet/Internet Protocol
    D. Transmission Control Protocol/Internet Protocol

**9.** Which protocol is not routable?

    A. TCP/IP
    B. IPX/SPX
    C. NetBEUI
    D. AppleTalk

**10.** Which protocol requires the least configuration?

A. TCP/IP

B. IPX/SPX

C. NetBEUI

D. AppleTalk

11. Which type of networking device is most often used to connect a computer to the network?

A. CSU

B. NIC

C. DCS

D. DSU

12. Which device will need to be terminated when using 10BaseT?

A. Both ends of the cable in a bus topology

B. The hub

C. Every workstation

D. Nothing will need to be terminated

13. What is being represented in the following illustration?

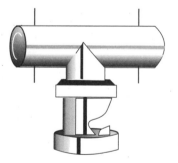

A. An AUI T-connector

B. A fiber optic T-connector

C. A BNC T-connector

D. A DSU T-connector

**14.** Identify the maximum cable distance of fiber optic cable.

    A. 1000 meters

    B. 1500 meters

    C. 2500 meters

    D. None of the above

**15.** Which type of cable does RJ-45 specify?

    A. Standard phone line

    B. Coaxial

    C. UTP

    D. Thick coaxial

**16.** The 2 in 10Base2 refers to what?

    A. 200 meter cable distance

    B. 200 feet cable distance

    C. 2 Mbps

    D. 2 forms of transmission (Full duplex and Half duplex)

**17.** Which type of cabling is used in a physical bus topology? (Choose all that apply.)

    A. UTP

    B. Coaxial

    C. STP

    D. ThinNet

**18.** Garth is having problems configuring his network card. After installation, he configured the network card with a unique IRQ, but it still will not work. What else could he check before he buys a new network card?

    A. The unique host ID on the network card

    B. The hardware address on the network card

    C. The I/O memory address

    D. The port replicator IRQ

**19.** Which of the following are common network problems? (Choose all that apply.)

    A. Network congestion

    B. Damaged cable

    C. Incorrectly configured NIC

    D. Missing terminator

**20.** Which topology does 10Base5 use?

    A. Star

    B. Bus

    C. Ring

    D. Clustered Ring

**21.** What happens when two devices transmit at the same time on a CSMA/CD network?

    A. All communication stops

    B. They can both transmit at once

    C. They will retransmit after waiting a random amount of time

    D. The station with the highest priority will continue to transmit

**22.** Types of cable used for network cabling include:

A. Twisted pair
B. Telephone
C. Coaxial
D. Fiber optic

23. Cable that is used on a network and that is referred to as UTP is:

A. Uniform Twisted Pair
B. Unrated Twisted Pair
C. Unshielded Twisted Pair
D. Uniform Telephone Pair

24. Cable that is used on a network and that is referred to as STP is:

A. Super Twisted Pair
B. Super Telephone Pair
C. Shielded Twisted Pair
D. Shielded Telephone Pair

25. The ends of a cable on a 10base2 coaxial network:

A. Have a 50-ohm terminator
B. Have an open end
C. Must circle back to the other end
D. Have a T-connector

26. Devices are connected to a coaxial network via what type connector?

A. 50ohm connector
B. T-connector
C. Splice
D. RJ-45

27. The maximum length of a 10base2 coaxial cable is:

A. 100 meters

B. 180 meters

C. no limit

D. 6 feet

**28.** The maximum length of a fiber optic cable is:

A. 100 meters

B. 180 meters

C. no limit

D. 6 feet

**29.** Connecting a personal computer to a network requires what type of hardware?

A. NIC

B. Hardware

C. Docking station

D. T connector

**30.** When using token ring cards on a network, the customer reports that the cards are set to 16 Mbps, but are running at 4 Mbps. What is the problem?

A. Server wrong

B. Software wrong

C. One NIC running at 4 Mbps

D. One NIC running at 16 Mbps

**31.** There are a variety of common network access methods available. Some of these methods include:

A. CSMA/CD

B. CSA/USA

C. Token passing

D. Baton passing

**32.** During routine groundskeeping, the backhoe operator cuts the fiber optic cable for the company's token ring network. What effect will this have on the network?

A. All network activity stops
B. Only those users below the break are disabled
C. Only those users above the break are disabled
D. No effect

**33.** What type of network architecture is shown here?

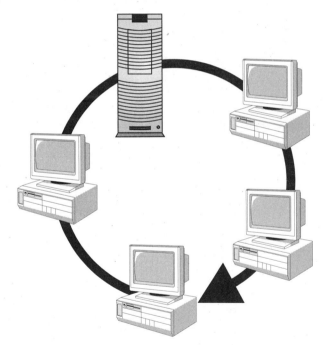

A. Star
B. Bus
C. Ring
D. Ethernet

**34.** What type of network architecture is shown here?

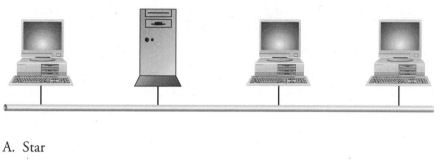

A. Star
B. Bus
C. Ring
D. Ethernet

**35.** What type of network architecture is shown here?

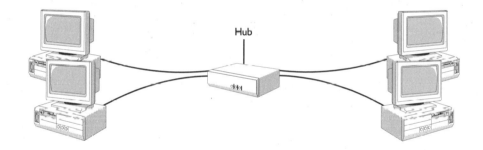

A. Star
B. Bus
C. Ring
D. Ethernet

**36.** In a star network, if the server goes down, then:

A. The network is down
B. The host is not accessible
C. Only devices with higher addresses are disabled
D. There is no effect

**37.** In a Token ring network running peer to peer services in addition to client/server services and the server goes down, then:

A. The network is down

B. The server is not accessible

C. Only devices with higher addresses are disabled

D. There is no effect

**38.** In a bus network running peer to peer services in addition to client/server services and the server goes down, then:

A. The network is down

B. The server is not accessible

C. Only devices with higher addresses are disabled

D. There is no effect

**39.** Your client states that he can no longer access the network. What should you check first for the source of the problem?

A. Power cord

B. IRQ on NIC

C. Connection from NIC to network

D. Network

**40.** The client states that Netscape works, but WordPerfect no longer works. In your company, all PCs run WordPerfect from a network server. The problem is:

A. Bad NIC

B. Server down

C. Network down

D. WordPerfect not on client machine

**41.** Rate the types of cable in the order of least to greatest susceptibility to interference.

A.  Fiber optic, coaxial, STP, UTP
B.  Fiber optic, coaxial, UTP, STP
C.  UTP, STP, coaxial, fiber optic
D.  Fiber optic, STP, UTP, coaxial

**42.** When using fiber optic cable, what must be done with the ends of the cable?

A.  Leave open
B.  Install 50 ohm terminators
C.  Install special transceivers
D.  Connect the shield to the cable

**43.** Why is the network shown here having problems?

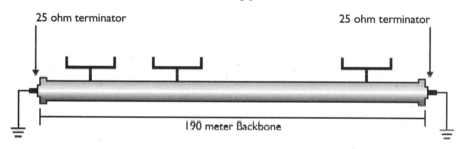

A.  Bad ground
B.  Bad terminators
C.  Backbone is too long
D.  All of the above
E.  None of the above

**44.** The following can connect a computer to a network

A.  NIC card
B.  PC card
C.  Modem
D.  Network adapter card
E.  Jet Direct card

**45.** What does the cable used with cable TV closely resemble?

A. UTP

B. STP

C. Thinnet

D. 10baseT

E. Fiber Optic

**46.** What does BNC stand for?

A. Broadband Network Connector

B. Baseband Network Connector

C. Broadband Network Cable

D. Bold New Connector

E. British Naval Connector

**47.** Which of the following lengths of wire will be suitable for a Cat V twisted pair cable?

A. 99 meters

B. 101 meters

C. 340 feet

D. 320 feet

E. 100 yards

**48.** Coaxial has a limitation of:

A. 180 meters

B. 590 feet

C. 200 yards

D. 623 feet

E. 100 meters

**49.** What is the most common speed at which fiber optic data transfers?

A. 100 megabits per second

B. 100 megabytes per second

C. 10 megabits per second

D. 10 megabytes per second

E. Over 100 megabytes per second

**50.** You have four star networks connected together by routers. One hub goes down with four workstations connected to it. What happens to the network?

A. The whole network goes down

B. The four workstations connected directly to the hub lose network connectivity

C. Nothing

D. Data is lost on all computers

E. None of the above

**51.** Which of the following is a LAN?

A. Dialing up the Internet on your home computer

B. Dialing up your neighbor's computer through dial-up networking

C. Connecting a computer by T1 line in San Francisco to a computer in New York

D. Hooking up a local printer by serial port

E. All of the above

**52.** Setting up a DHCP client workstation using TCP/IP always involves manually entering:

A. Subnet Mask

B. Default Gateway

C. IP address

D. DNS Server IP address

E. None of the above

**53.** 10baseT uses the following connector:

    A. AUI

    B. BNC

    C. RJ-11

    D. RJ-45

    E. DIX

**54.** A guy at a computer show says he has a network card that can handle two types of wires. What could these be?

    A. UTP

    B. Thinnet

    C. 10Base2

    D. 10BaseT

    E. Each network card can only support one kind of wiring scheme

**55.** Token passing is used mostly on _____ networks.

    A. Fiber

    B. Bus

    C. Ethernet

    D. Token Ring

    E. None of the above

**56.** Which of these are protocols?

    A. TCP/IP

    B. IPX/SPX

    C. NetBEUI

    D. DLC

    E. NetBIOS

**57.** If you are setting up a giant WAN and you have many different types of computers, such as IBM and Macintosh, what protocol would you bind first?

A. TCP/IP

B. IPX/SPX

C. NetBEUI

D. DLC

E. NetBIOS

**58.** What size unit is transferred on a network?

A. Packet

B. Bit

C. Byte

D. Megabyte

E. None of the above

**59.** A method by which devices can communicate across the network is:

A. Token passing

B. Terminator

C. Network access

D. 10Base8

E. CSMA/CD

**60.** Most network cards require a:

A. DMA channel

B. Driver

C. IRQ address

D. IO memory address

E. All of the above

**61.** Which of the following is possible?

A. A network card with a BNC connector joining directly by cable to a fiber optic backbone

B. A network card with a RJ-45 connector joining directly by cable to a fiber optic backbone

C. A network card with a BNC connector joining directly by cable to a Token Ring

D. A network card with a RJ-45 connector joining directly by cable to a Token Ring

E. A network card with a BNC connector joining directly by cable to a 10Base5 backbone

**62.** What is the cheapest type of cable?

A. UTP

B. STP

C. 10Base2

D. 10Base5

E. Fiber

**63.** What type of network is shown here?

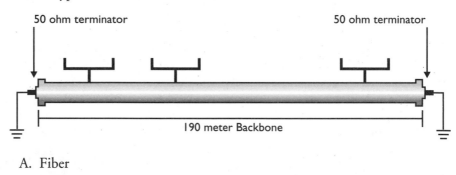

A. Fiber

B. StarBus

C. Bus

D. Arcnet

E. Token Ring

**64.** The reason that twisted-pair cable is constructed with each pair tightly twisted together is to reduce:

   A. Bandwidth

   B. Interference

   C. Crosstalk

   D. Cable Length Requirements.

**65.** Identify the least expensive type of network cabling.

   A. Coaxial ThinNet

   B. ThickNet

   C. Twisted pair

   D. Fiber optic

**66.** Which of the following acronyms correctly identifies twisted-pair cable?

   A. TWP

   B. FDDI

   C. UTP

   D. STP

**67.** What is the correct impedance of a ThinNet coaxial network?

   A. 75 ohm

   B. 200 ohm

   C. 50 ohm

   D. 100 ohm

exam
ⓦatch    *Coaxial cable requires that each device be connected to a T-connector, which is then connected to the coaxial cable. In addition, each end of the cable must have a 50Ω terminator installed.*

**68.** In a coaxial ThinNet network, each workstation will use a _____ connector to connect to the network.

   A. T
   B. RJ-45
   C. RJ-11
   D. DB-9

**69.** An ethernet network uses which type of access control?

   A. CSMA/CD
   B. Token Ring
   C. ARC technology
   D. FDDI

**70.** Which type of network protocol requires a unique IP address for each workstation?

   A. IPX/SPX
   B. NetBIOS
   C. NetBEUI
   D. TCP/IP

**71.** Which type of network protocol is considered native for a Novell network?

   A. NetBEUI
   B. TCP/IP
   C. IPX/SPX
   D. Token Ring

**72.** The de facto protocol for the Internet is:

   A. IPX
   B. IP
   C. NetBEUI
   D. Token Ring

**73.** IPX/SPX is an acronym for which of the following?

A. Internet Packet Exchange/Serial Packet Exchange

B. Internetwork Packet Exchange/Sequenced Packet Exchange

C. International Protocol Exchange/Sequential Packet Exchange

D. Internal Packet Exchange/Serial Protocol Exchange

**74.** Which of the following network protocols is NOT considered to be routable?

A. TCP/IP

B. IPX/SPX

C. NetBEUI

D. Token Ring

**75.** Which type of network connection would be considered to be a WAN connection?

A. 10Base2

B. 10BaseT

C. Dial-up networking

D. ThinNet

**76.** A customer requires a network link between two points that should be approximately 1000 meters in length. Which type of network cabling do you recommend?

A. ThickNet

B. ThinNet

C. UTP

D. Fiber

**77.** To properly configure an ethernet network card in a workstation, you must do which of the following? (Choose all that apply.)

A. Assign a Frame type
B. Assign a DMA channel
C. Assign an IRQ channel
D. All of the above

78. The two possible speeds for a Token Ring network are:

A. 10 Mhz
B. 4 Mhz
C. 100 Mhz
D. 16 Mhz

79. If you need to work on a LAN for a business, it is always best to first consult with:

A. The Novell Manual set
B. The Microsoft Networking Essentials Guide
C. The Network Administrator
D. The Banyon Vines Administrators Guide

80. A small network with several workstations and no dedicated server is considered to be a _____ network.

A. Client / Server
B. Peer to Peer
C. Peer to Client
D. Hybrid

81. Some common network problems include:

A. Damaged cable
B. Fragmented hard disk
C. Excessive traffic
D. Missing terminator

**82.** Which type of network checks for activity before sending a packet?

    A. Token Ring

    B. FDDI

    C. Ethernet

    D. None of the Above

**83.** NetBEUI is an acronym for which of the following?

    A. Network Broadcast User Interface

    B. NetBIOS Extended User Interface

    C. Network Basic User Interface

    D. NetBIOS Broad User Interface

**84.** Which two items below identify a NetWare native frame type?

    A. Ethernet 802.2

    B. Ethernet SNAP

    C. Token Ring

    D. Ethernet 802.3

# Customer Satisfaction

**1.** What should be the first thing you do when repairing a user's computer?

    A. Have the correct tools with you

    B. Document the current configuration

    C. Find out what the problem is with the computer

    D. Write down the hardware information of the computer

**2.** Why should you be aware of non-verbal cues when you are working on a user's computer?

A. He may look worried that you are moving things around. This would indicate you should probably not continue, or ask for permission.

B. He may be asleep

C. You may solve the problem by his facial expression

D. The user may not be interested in what you are doing, and you should take the opportunity to train him

**3.** What should you do if you found out a user broke a printer?

A. Tell his boss, and make them pay for it

B. Inform your boss that the user broke the printer

C. Tell the user you have seen this happen before

D. Remove the printing software from the user's computer

**4.** After you have asked the customer what problems she is having with her computer, what should you ask next?

A. What did you do to the computer?

B. Who else has worked on this computer?

C. What has changed on the machine since it worked?

D. What applications were you using before the computer stopped working?

**5.** When you are through asking the user questions, what should you do before continuing?

A. Tell him to show you exactly what he was doing when the problem occurred

B. Paraphrase what the user has said, just in case you misinterpreted him

C. Give him your pager, and have him call you when the problem happens again

D. Document the problem, and the solution you came up with

**6.** Why should you try to be calm during a situation with the user?

A. Because sudden moves may frighten the user

B. Because it will calm the user

C. Because you should always appear like you know what you are doing

D. Because the user may not know what has happened to the computer

**7.** Why should you be conscious of the way you are reacting when working on a user's computer?

A. Because the user doesn't care about what the problem is

B. Because you know what you are doing, and do not need any help from the user

C. Because the user mostly sees how you react to the problem

D. Because you can get fired

**8.** Why should you always put yourself in the customer's shoes?

A. To remember what it was like when you were inexperienced

B. To understand what it's like to not be very intelligent

C. To determine the solution to the problem

D. To determine the nature of the problem

**9.** Why should you take the time to train the users?

A. So they can help you diagnose and troubleshoot problems in the future

B. So they will give you a good recommendation

C. It will help you and the company in the future

D. Because you are paid to help the user

**10.** Why should you try and have a good rapport with users?

A. They will call you less often, therefore you don't have to see them much

B. They will trust you, and call you with many more small problems

C. They will trust you, and therefore will be less likely to withhold information from you

D. Because you won't have to do a good job if they like you

11. Other than being unprofessional, why should you not swear while fixing a user's computer?

    A. It can personally offend a user
    B. It can appear as if you are incompetent
    C. It will take you longer to fix the problem
    D. The user may feel afraid of you

12. Which of the following are examples of intruding on a user? (Choose all that apply.)

    A. Interrupting a meeting
    B. Spending too much time fixing their PC
    C. Eavesdropping on their phone calls
    D. Asking what is wrong with the computer

13. What should you do if you go to a user's cubicle for a repair, and the user is not there?

    A. Start working on the problem
    B. Do not proceed
    C. Ask the person in the next cubicle if it's safe to work on this user's computer
    D. Go find the user

14. What quality means that you are not going to compromise yourself or ask others to do so in order to achieve something?

    A. Honesty
    B. Professionalism
    C. Integrity
    D. Loyalty

15. What should you do if you find a few games on the store room PC, when you know games aren't allowed in the organization?

A. Delete the games

B. Confront the user

C. Notify management, but don't name names

D. Notify management, and name names

**16.** What is the best way to deal with angry users?

A. Ignore them

B. Quickly resolve their problems

C. Notify management of this difficult user

D. Fix their computer when they are not around

**17.** A user calls you into his office and tells you he cannot access a file like he could before you started working on his system. He is becoming irate because he is expected to give a lecture, and needs his notes to be printed. What should you do in this situation?

A. Insist it wasn't working before you started on the computer

B. Refer the problem to a higher source, such as your boss, because this customer is upset

C. Pretend that you did make a mistake configuring the computer

D. Apologize for any inconvenience, and begin troubleshooting the problem

**18.** You are doing phone support for your company when a user calls and is upset that she has been transferred many times. How should you handle this situation?

A. Place the user on hold until you find the original technician who answered the call

B. Forward the call to your supervisor so the caller will feel she is getting results

C. Apologize and ask what you can do for the customer

D. Apologize and forward the call to your supervisor

**19.** You are called out to work on a computer that has been badly configured by another technician in your department. When you arrive, the customer is upset with the service from the first technician. How should you handle this situation?

    A. Apologize for the inconvenience, and begin troubleshooting the problem

    B. Find out the name of the first technician

    C. Notify your manager of the first technician's performance

    D. Apologize for the inconvenience and agree with the customer about the performance of the first technician

**20.** You are working on a problem that you remember a technician having just the other day. The user is currently in the office, waiting for you to finish. What should you do in this situation?

    A. Call the employee while you are in the user's office, and ask how to fix the problem

    B. Do not look incompetent in front of the user. Continue with your diagnosis.

    C. Leave the office, and find the other employee

    D. Continue with the troubleshooting, and hope the resolution comes to you

**21.** You arrive to work on a computer with a trouble ticket. After introducing yourself you should:

    A. Immediately begin repair

    B. Ask user to explain problem

    C. Tell user what you are going to do and do it

    D. Leave to take a coffee break

**22.** When arriving at the user's desk, and after the user has explained the problem, what should you do next if there is not an obvious solution?

A. Start taking the machine apart

B. Say it is impossible and leave

C. Ask the user what may have changed on the machine prior to the problem

D. Tell the user the problem is imagined

**23.** After the user explains the problem with his computer, you should:

A. Start work on the machine

B. Summarize what the user has said and then give a possible solution

C. Tell the user a solution to a different problem

D. Comment on last night's ball game

**24.** You have received a call from a user. She reports that she cannot turn on the power to her computer. What should you then ask?

A. Did you plug the computer in?

B. Does the LED light on the computer come on?

C. Did you unplug the computer?

D. Did you turn off the power strip?

**25.** You are repairing PCs for a software company. What can you assume about the users' hardware knowledge?

A. They are experts

B. They are idiots

C. Don't assume anything. Find out from them what their level of knowledge is.

D. They are dumber than you

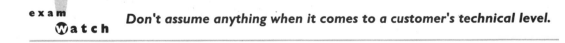

**exam**
**ⓌatcH**    *Don't assume anything when it comes to a customer's technical level.*

**26.** You have come across users who talk a lot about computers. You therefore know that:

A. They are experts
B. They know very little about computers
C. You need to talk with them to establish a knowledge level
D. They can fix anything themselves

**27.** When you are finished fixing a computer, what should you always say to the user?

A. Don't call me again with such a dumb problem.
B. Are there other problems?
C. Nothing. Pack up and go.
D. Are you satisfied that the problem is fixed?

**28.** A client calls back and says that the correction you made created another problem. You should:

A. State that you never make mistakes
B. Apologize and state that you did not realize your fix would cause this
C. Blame the customer for the problem
D. Go back and correct the problem

**29.** You are going to an office to fix a computer. Your appearance should be:

A. Neat and clean
B. Casual and comfortable
C. Nerdy, to inspire confidence
D. Whatever; they only want your technical knowledge

**30.** When working on computers, what type of attitude does the customer want you to have?

A. As long as you fix it, the customer does not care
B. A non-caring attitude
C. A friendly attitude
D. Concerned about their business

**31.** If you arrive at a cubicle or office and you see the customer is on the phone:

A. You should barge on in
B. Wait quietly until he is off the phone
C. Listen intently to his conversation
D. Shout for his attention

**32.** You are attempting to correct a problem on a machine. No matter what you try, the problem still exists. You should:

A. Talk with other technicians
B. Refuse to leave the machine until you get it
C. Go and research the problem
D. Blame the problem on a previous technician

**33.** When you first come up to a user to work on a machine you should:

A. Let her know what you will do
B. Let her know what she needs to do
C. Tell her to leave
D. Just start working

**34.** While you are working, your user and the person in the next cubicle get in an argument over Word versus WordPerfect. They ask you to say which is better. You should:

A. Ignore them
B. Give the pros and cons of both programs
C. Tell them one is great and one is horrible
D. Tell them your preference

**35.** You have received a call to fix a PC monitor for a user. It turns out that he just failed to turn it on. You discover that he is a new user. You should:

A. Tell him to go to school before calling again

B. Show him how to start the computer

C. Speak with lots of acronyms to show him you are an expert

D. Keep language simple

**36.** A customer has just gotten a new monitor. He says the monitor is bad and needs replacing. You know it is set wrong from the old monitor. You should:

A. Tell him you need to change the settings. Then change them.

B. Get him a new monitor

C. Allow him to tell why the monitor is bad and then explain the settings you will change

D. Just fix it and ignore the customer

**37.** You are attempting to fix a PC and the user keeps saying that you don't know what you're doing. You should:

A. Finish the job

B. Tell him where to go

C. Send another technician to do the job

D. Just leave and tell no one

**38.** A user calls and says that there is nothing on his hard disk. After checking the drive, you discover it was formatted. You should:

A. Tell the customer it is their fault and that they can fix it

B. Tell the customer what happened and fix it

C. Report the incident to his boss

D. Remove the FORMAT command

**39.** A user says his Internet connection stopped working and wants you to fix it. The company does not let an employee of this user's level have access to the Internet. You should:

   A. Tell his supervisor

   B. Fix the problem

   C. Tell him it is against company policy to have Internet access

   D. Delete all his Internet files

**40.** A user has Microsoft Office licensed and installed on her machine. She wants you to add Access. She says that it is part of Office. What should you do?

   A. Check to see if she is licensed to Access

   B. Install Access

   C. Tell her that without a license, company policy does not allow the installation

   D. Uninstall Office

**41.** While fixing a PC, you discover that the user has an unlicensed copy of Office on the machine. You should:

   A. Refuse to fix the PC

   B. Immediately erase the Office folder

   C. Report the user to his supervisor

   D. Tell the user that the copy needs a license

**42.** A customer complains that a file is missing, and you were the last one to use the machine. What do you do?

   A. Tell him you are certain that it was not you who deleted it

   B. Run UNDELETE in hopes of retrieving the file

   C. Tell him he should be more careful next time

   D. Do a file search and try to use a text string that is in the document

   E. None of the above

**43.** A customer is stating his problem and you get a page. You should:

   A. Politely excuse yourself and ask to use the phone

   B. Tell the customer that you understand his problem, and if you have any questions you will ask him (in hopes he will let you go at that point)

   C. Say, "not another one of these darn things today"

   D. Keep listening and turn off the sound on your pager and look at the number

   E. Keep listening and turn off the sound on your pager without looking at the number

**44.** *Customer:* I've had this problem trying to save items in Microsoft Word as templates.
*Tech:* Oh yes, the auto-open virus. Let me sit down and get rid of it.
*Customer:* I don't have a virus. I scanned this morning.
*Tech:* Well, you must not have the update patch for it. Let me download it.
*Customer:* This has nothing to do with a virus. I am just trying to save a template to make a form letter with.
*Tech:* Oh.
What should the tech have done? (Choose the best answer.)

   A. Listened fully to the customer, before jumping to conclusions

   B. After the customer said his first sentence, asked him if he was having a problem with a virus trying to save the program or if it was just the user trying to save as a template

   C. Updated the customer with a batch file over the network, so he would not have viruses in the first place

   D. Apologized for being ignorant

   E. Wrote the template for the customer to build rapport

---

exam
ⓦatch     ***Don't go for the misleading answer, which might solve the problem right away, but the one that maintains the customer satisfaction requirements.***

---

**exam**
 **Ⓦatch** *When repairing a computer, let the user explain the problem fully before starting to work on it. Many times the exam takes into account exceptions that technicians would run into if they did not listen fully to the customer and ask pertinent questions.*

**45.** The best way to carry a new monitor to a user's desk is:

 A. Very rapidly so that the user can get his monitor quickly

 B. Very slowly so that you don't appear to be reckless

 C. With two people so that you don't hurt you back

 D. Over your head like Hercules

 E. At a pace that is as fast as you can safely carry it without walking faster than you normally would

**46.** A customer would like to put a copy of MS Office on his machine, but it appears to be a pirated copy. The customer has insisted that it is not one. What should you do? (Choose the best answer.)

 A. Install it since the customer is always right

 B. Call the anonymous anti-piracy hot line

 C. Ask his boss

 D. Ask your boss

 E. Tell the customer that it is company policy to record and register all software and you would like to see his EULA so you can record the number and send it in

**47.** When listening to a customer a tech should:

 A. Nod his head to show he is listening

 B. Take notes on all that the customer says

 C. Lead the conversation so that it does not go astray

 D. Ask appropriate questions

 E. Be at the computer in order to reenact what the user did that got him into trouble

**48.** If a user asks you to show her how to make a shortcut on the desktop you should:

A. Make the shortcut as fast as you can to show the user how quick you are
B. Use only shortcut keys and tell the user each shortcut
C. Go extremely slowly and talk slowly in order for the user to understand
D. Assume the user knows nothing and explain every single thing you are doing
E. Go at a pace that you would be able to follow if you did not know how to create a shortcut

**49.** You find a laptop computer with coffee spilled on the keyboard. You should:

A. Tell the user not to drink coffee while using the laptop
B. Tell the user the story of when you spilled pop in your laptop
C. Consult with a couple of other techs to appraise the situation
D. Take the laptop and walk away quietly
E. Inform the user that this laptop may take some time to dry and that he might try to use another computer in the office for a while

**50.** When you approach a user about what you plan to do with her printer, how should you act?

A. Confidently
B. Animated
C. Serious
D. Light-hearted
E. Demure

**51.** What is the best action to take when you can't solve a problem and it's nearing 5:00, when everyone goes home?

A. Ask the user if you can stay over and you'll lock up
B. Ask the user when would be a good time to come back
C. Ask the user to call you back when he is ready
D. Tell the user you'll drop by later
E. Act like you fixed the problem and shut down the computer

**52.** Two users are arguing about who formatted the hard disk by accident. You should:

    A. Run some utilities to see who was logged on the system when this happened

    B. Refer the problem to your boss

    C. Fix the problem and let the users figure out who caused it

    D. Say that you did it, just to get them to shut up

    E. None of the above

**53.** You have an upset customer on the phone. What is the first thing you do?

    A. Calm him down

    B. Listen to what he has to say

    C. Transfer the call to a crisis specialist

    D. Tell him why he should not be upset

    E. None of the above

**54.** A user on the phone just can't seem to understand what you are trying to walk him through after 25 minutes. He is ten miles away. What should you do?

    A. Keep talking; maybe he will catch on

    B. Put another technician on the line to see if the user will understand this person better

    C. Drive the ten miles and fix the problem

    D. Tell the user to put someone with more experience on their phone

    E. Tell the user to use the online help

**55.** A user is asking your honest opinion about a computer he wants to buy for home. It is very similar to the one he has at work. You happen to hate the system he has at work. You should tell the user:

    A. "That's a great choice, no better PC on the market."

    B. "This PC is EISA only, the planar is obsolete."

    C. "I'll bring you in a magazine that rates all the new computers."

    D. "This PC is junk, buy a another brand."

    E. "I can't answer computer questions that are not work related."

**56.** You told the customer you would meet him at 2:00. It is now 2:15 and you missed him. What should you do?

A. Apologize when you next talk to him

B. Page him

C. Leave a note on his desk

D. Ask a co-worker when he is expected back

E. None of the above

**57.** A user is complaining about an extraordinarily loud hub next to her desk. What should you do? (Choose two.)

A. Tell the user you will see about moving it

B. Tell the user that is the way it is

C. Tell the user that you would not want to listen to this all day

D. Tell the user you will talk to some people about it

E. Tell the user you'll get it fixed

**58.** A customer keeps looking at his watch; you should say:

A. "Is that a Rolex?"

B. "This may take a while. Do you have the time to wait?"

C. "Do you need to be somewhere?"

D. "What time is it?"

E. "I notice you've been looking at your watch. Do you need to be somewhere?"

**59.** A user keeps changing the video settings on a computer and causing the screen to turn into a mess that you can't read. You are getting tired of going out to fix the problem. What do you do?

A. Tell the user you are not going to fix this problem again

B. Just keep on fixing it; it's good job security

C. Tell the user he should not mess with things he doesn't understand

D. Show him exactly how to fix the problem himself in an understandable manner

E. Delete every driver but the ones that work

**60.** A customer says that his PC is slow. You think his PC is fast. Your boss thinks his PC is fast enough. Your company's accountant thinks the PC is fast. The purchasing manager in your company thinks it's fast. Who is right?

A. Customer

B. Your boss

C. The purchasing manager

D. The corporate CPA

E. Yourself

**61.** What is the best way to leave a customer? (Choose one.)

A. Better educated

B. Delighted

C. On good terms

D. With a fixed PC

E. None of the above

**62.** Professional conduct includes: (Choose all that apply.)

A. Appearance

B. Attitude

C. Integrity

D. Competence

E. Time management

**63.** Most PC users in the workplace fit into which category of user? (Choose all that apply.)

A. They may be intimately familiar with their own workstation, but most likely do not fully understand the operating system intricacies

B. They are power users. They fully understand the workings of their office PC system.

C. They understand their particular business software package, but know little about their LAN

D. They can easily become frustrated when their daily work routine is interrupted or hindered by PC problems

**64.** Why is setting up an on-site trouble log for a customer's LAN a good idea? (Choose all that apply.)

A. It can help you to get paid in a timely manner

B. If the log book is heavy enough, you can use it to whack an intermittent PC

C. It shows the customer that you are genuinely concerned with their system and can also aid in working out more difficult or intermittent problems

D. It can save you time and the customer money, especially if more than one technician is involved in a particular incident

**65.** You encounter a strange or unique problem that you cannot seem to work out in a timely manner. Which would be the best procedure for customer satisfaction?

A. Tell the customer that the PC has to be taken back to the shop for repair

B. Explain the difficult nature of this problem to the customer and suggest that you perform some research into this issue with the proper manufacturer and return at a later date to finish the repair

C. Stay on the problem until it is fixed, no matter how long or how much it will cost the customer

D. Tell them a plausible excuse for not making the repair, but explain that you need to get paid for the time you worked on it anyway

**66.** After you have listened to a customer's explanation of a particular PC problem, what are some good questions that you can ask to aid in the troubleshooting process?

A. How long has the problem been occurring?

B. Has anything been changed on the PC recently?

C. Who broke the PC?

D. Can you duplicate the problem now and show it to me?

**67.** You are on site, working on a customer's PC, and your pager goes off. What should you do? (Choose all that apply.)

A. Immediately pick up their desk-phone and respond to the page
B. Try to finish up the part of the procedure you are working on and ask if they would mind if you used the telephone
C. Check the number on the pager and try to determine if it can wait a few minutes or requires an immediate response
D. Stop what you are working on with this customer and explain to them what the problem is for the customer who has just paged you. It will make them feel better to know that other people are having problems, too.

**68.** If you work on a PC for a customer and the normal user is not there at the time, what would be some good procedures to follow?

A. Take advantage of the fact that the workstation user is not there and perform any upgrades or optimizations you feel are necessary
B. Ask to speak with his or her supervisor and try to determine what the reason for the service call is from someone in authority
C. Leave a note for the person who is absent, explaining what you did, along with a telephone number or pager number for them to contact if they have any questions or problems
D. Clean up their desk area for them, just for a nice extra touch

**69.** If you need to work on a workstation that someone is currently using, what would be the preferred procedure to follow? (Choose all that apply.)

A. Tell the person who is working on the PC how busy you are and that you have to work on that PC now
B. Politely ask him if he could save his work and let you sit down and work on that PC for awhile
C. Ask him if he is planning to take a break soon and offer to come back at that time to make the repair
D. Reach over his shoulder and click the Save button to save his work as is

**70.** When working on a multi-user LAN for a company, it is always best to follow which of the procedures listed below?

A. Maintain a friendly working relationship with the LAN Administrator

B. Keep your own secret list of all of the security passwords

C. Request an Administrator- or Supervisor-level password for your own use and maintain that security

D. Change all the passwords to a clear setting so you can log on as anyone you need to

71. You are working on a system in an office where there is obviously a lot of politics and gossip. How could you best handle a situation like this? (Choose all that apply.)

A. Find out who the most popular person is and take that person to lunch

B. Find out who the least popular person is and befriend that person

C. Always try to avoid getting involved in such matters

D. Spread a few rumors yourself to gain some popularity

72. You are sent to an office to work on a particular problem. When you arrive you are hit with a barrage of requests to take care of several other issues "… as long as you are here…." How could you best handle this situation? (Choose all that apply.)

A. Fix as many things as you can to make everyone like you

B. Stay focused on your main task and refuse to work on anything else

C. Work on what you came to do first. Then get permission from the office manager before addressing the other issues mentioned

D. Listen carefully first to the other issues to see if any of them may relate to the task at hand

73. Non-verbal communication is said to convey what percentage of the message?

A. 50 percent

B. 75 percent

C. 90 percent

D. 80 percent

**74.** You are called to take care of a LAN printing problem. The LAN has several similar printers but one is not printing. You know you cannot immediately fix the problem, but the customer is stressed out and needs to get a report printed immediately. What should you do? (Choose all that apply.)

A. Tell the customer that you can't fix the printer and he is out of luck

B. Temporarily capture another printer of the same type for the customer's immediate use, and help him to get his report printed out

C. Have the customer copy the report to a floppy and bring it back to your shop to print it for him

D. Suggest that the customer e-mail the report to someone else so they can print it out for him

**75.** To qualify PC users, you should determine which level of expertise they are at. List the four levels below in ascending order of competence.

A. Casual user

B. Novice

C. Power user

D. Administrator

**76.** A user at a site has obviously misconfigured a PC. What would be the best course of action to take? (Choose all that apply.)

A. Immediately report that user to the supervisor or LAN Administrator

B. Never say anything to make the user feel stupid

C. Correct the errors, and while doing so, try to explain to that user how he can avoid these problems in the future

D. Share some of your own experience in this same area with the customer, explaining how confusing these things were for you at one time

**77.** Good rapport with a customer will usually result in which of the following? (Choose all that apply.)

A. The customer is more likely to be honest with you when he knows that he did something wrong
B. The customer is more likely to trust your abilities as a technician
C. The customer will deny mistakes he made so you won't make fun of him
D. The customer will call you and pester you with his petty personal problems

78. Why is it a good idea to talk with customers about other subjects besides PCs? (Choose all that apply.)

A. You could get lucky and meet someone who is cute
B. It helps break the ice and builds rapport
C. Most people like to talk about things other than just PCs
D. You can get more billable hours for your time by wasting it on idle chit-chat

79. The workplace is a good place to _____ . (Choose all that apply.)

A. Meet someone special
B. Build professional business relationships
C. Gain referrals for other potential customers
D. Get someone to buy you a free lunch

80. To maintain a professional appearance you should avoid which of the following? (Choose all that apply.)

A. Wearing heavy cologne
B. Keeping your hair neat and trimmed
C. Wearing neat and pressed clothing
D. Showering regularly

81. If a particular PC is giving you a tough time effecting a repair, you should avoid which of the following? (Choose all that apply.)

A. Taking time out to re-assess the situation

B. Cursing or swearing at the PC

C. Banging on the PC or desktop

D. Blaming other people for the problem

**82.** You are upgrading a PC for a customer. This process involves replacing several parts with better ones than are currently in the PC. The old parts are still good. What should you offer to do with the old parts? (Choose all that apply.)

A. Slip them into your tool case and take them home for your personal use

B. Offer to upgrade the home PC of one of the office workers

C. Offer the customer or business for which you are working a trade-in credit for these parts against the bill

D. Suggest to the customer that they might use the parts on another PC at their business

**83.** Before leaving a job site, it is always a good idea to do what? (Choose all that apply.)

A. Demonstrate to the customer that the problem you were called to fix is repaired

B. Clean up any mess you might have made

C. Use the phone to call home

D. Ask if there is anything else that needs to be taken care of

**84.** You are running late, and as you are trying to leave, a customer asks you to take care of a Microsoft Word problem. What should be the best course of action? (Choose all that apply.)

A. Listen to the customer's explanation

B. Politely explain that you have another appointment waiting, and schedule another appointment

C. Call your next appointment to see if you can delay it

D. Say, "Sorry, I've gotta run. I'll call you later."

# Answers

*Q & A*

The answers to the questions are in boldface, followed by a brief explanation. Some of the explanations detail the logic you should use to choose the correct answer, while others give factual reasons why the answer is correct. If you miss several questions on a similar topic, you should review the corresponding section in the *A+ Certification Study Guide* (Osborne/McGraw-Hill) before taking the A+ Certification test.

# Installation, Configuration, and Upgrading

1. **A.** Color Graphics Adapters (CGA) provide for four types of digital output. This means that by combining all three colors, and changing the intensity of those colors, you could get a total of 16 different colors on the display (remember, digital output).

2. **A.** Connectors for mice include DB-9, which uses a serial connector and requires a free COM port, PS/2 mouse, which is similar to a bus mouse but does not require an expansion slot, and a bus mouse, which will use a DIN-6 connector and require a free IRQ.

3. **A, D.** The Standard Device Assignment for IRQ 7 is Parallel port (LPT1), and IRQ 6 is the Floppy controller. The computer industry has come up with these standard IRQ settings. They should be used whenever you are installing a device.

4. **D.** The Standard I/O Address Settings for Port Address of 2F8-2FF is the Serial port (COM2). Serial ports I/O address settings and IRQ device assignments are very important for the exam.

5. **D.** The DB-25 connector, similar to DB-9s in that it is trapezoidal in shape, is the type of connector for parallel and serial ports. When used with parallel ports, the DB-25 connector will have *sockets*, and when used with the serial port, the DB-25 connector will have *pins*.

**6. C.** The RJ-45 connector has 8 pins, and is similar to the RJ-11 connector, although the RJ-11 (standard telephone connector) has only four pins. The RJ-45 connector is the most common connector used on an Ethernet network.

**7. C.** If you are adding a third hard disk to an IDE system, you must install the new hard disk as a master on the secondary controller, with the two IDE drives on the primary controller. Each IDE controller can only contain two devices, which will be configured as master and slave.

**8. B.** SCSI-2 includes a 16-bit bus and a total transfer rate of 20 Mbps. Because SCSI-3 is fairly new, it's highly unlikely that your A+ exam will contain questions about the characteristics of SCSI-3.

**9. B.** SCSI cabling and connectors vary according to whether the SCSI device is internal or external. Internal devices use a single, unshielded 50-pin cable that is similar to the 40-pin IDE hard disk cable. External devices use shielded cables that can have a female DB-25, Centronics-50, Mini 50, or Mini 68 connector attached to it.

**10. A, B.** Electro-Static wrist bands should be worn in all situations when you are repairing electronic devices, with the exception of when you are working with monitors. Monitors can build large amounts of static electricity that, when discharged, could kill you.

**11. C.** With an internal modem you must make sure that you already have a free IRQ, I/O address, and COM port prior to installation. A DMA channel is not required when configuring any type of modem, either internal or external.

**12. A.** The most common measurement performed with the multimeter is current. Current is measured in *Amperes*, or amps, and is measured by placing the negative probe against the negative contact point, and placing the positive probe against the positive contact point.

**13.** **C.** When using a multimeter to measure resistance, if you receive a reading of infinite, this means the component is not allowing electricity to pass from one probe to the other and must be replaced.

**14.** **A.** When replacing a power supply, you must remember that when you reattach the two power connectors to the motherboard, the black wires that are located on each connector must be facing each other.

**15.** **B, C.** There are two types of keyboard connectors in use, the DIN-5 connector and the Mini DIN-6 connector. DIN-5s are generally found on AT style keyboards and have a round port with 5 pins. The Mini DIN-6 also has a round port but differs in that it has 6 pins with one square pin.

**16.** **D.** The SCSI host adapter usually defaults to the address of 7, which is the last address available on the SCSI bus. Since the SCSI host adapter uses an address, you will have seven available addresses left for adding SCSI devices.

**17.** **B, C.** DIP pins are identified as two rows, located on opposing sides of the chip, of 20 pins. PGA chips are identified as four rows of pins that surround the bottom of the chip.

**18.** **B.** A sound card uses a Dynamic Memory Access (DMA) Channel to write information directly into main memory. This method improves the module's performance, as you are basically removing the overhead of having the processor move the information from the device to main memory.

**19.** **D.** The IRQ number of 15 is available by default, unless you have configured another device to use this IRQ. Notice that the other IRQs listed are either reserved for system use, or used for the printer (IRQ 7).

**20. B.** The default port address for the parallel port (LPT1) is 378-37F. Be aware that it is possible to override the default settings from BIOS.

**21. A, B, C, D.** All of the devices listed are devices that can be replaced in the field. A device that is not field replaceable must have special equipment, or requires soldering to be repaired. In the computer industry, these types of devices are becoming rare. Many components are much easier to replace than to repair.

**22. C.** The current is converted to DC (direct current). The power supplied to the computer is AC or Vac (alternating current). AC power is 120 volts.

**23. A.** A 486 CPU will often have a speed of 66 Mhz. 486 is the type of CPU, not the speed. The FCC does not regulate the speed of computers. The manufacturer will not set the chip to run less than the rated speed. Sometimes they do run them higher than the rated speed.

**24. C.** The computer works in binary. Humans work in the decimal system. Hexadecimal and octal are often used to display the memory in the computer, as they are easier to read.

**25. B.** The computer reads the BIOS at bootup for the system configuration. The BIOS is stored in ROM. RAM and cache memory are erased when the machine is turned off. The computer uses the binary numbering system, not the decimal numbering system, to store information.

**26. B.** Many people call the 3.5-inch floppy disk a hard disk because of the hard cover. Answers C and D are incorrect as they have soft covers and are considered floppy. Since the customer was inserting the disk, you can eliminate answer A.

**27. C.** CD-ROM drives use a laser to read CDs. Read-Write heads are used to read disks (floppy and hard). Needles and Read Only heads are not used to read data for computers.

**28.** **B.** Leaving the cover off may be a temporary fix, but it is not a good one. The fan is on the power supply, so replace the power supply. The burning is probably in the power supply. Unless they have been heat-damaged, the system board and the hard disks should be fine.

**29.** **A, B.** The only cables on a floppy disk drive are the power and floppy disk drive cables. The hard disk drive cable is attached to the hard disk drive, and the sound cable attaches the CD drive to the sound card.

**30.** **B.** CGA and EGA use the D-9 connector. The RJ-45 connector is used to connect to networks. Edge connectors are used by boards to connect to the system board. VGA and SVGA monitors use the D-15.

**31.** **D.** IRQ 6 is used by floppy diskette controller. (IRQ 1 is used by the keyboard, IRQ 7 is used by LPT1, IRQ 3 is used by COM2.)

**32.** **D.** IRQ 7 is used by parallel port 1, and IRQ 5 is used by parallel port 2.

**33.** **B.** The mouse uses IRQ 12. (The keyboard uses IRQ 1, the hard disk controller uses IRQ 14, COM2 uses IRQ 3.)

**34.** **B.** Serial port 1 uses 3F8-3FF. (Serial port 2 uses 2F8-2FF, the floppy controller uses 3F0-3F7, the 16 bit ISA hard disk controller uses 1F0-1F8.)

**35.** **C.** Parallel port 1 uses 378-37F. (COM1 uses 3F8-3FF, COM2 uses 2F8-2FF, parallel port 2 uses 278-27F.)

**36.** **A, C.** ROM and cache cannot be used to set values on the hardware. DIP switches and jumpers are used to provide hardware settings.

**37.** **A.** A DIP switch can only have a value of one or zero. A group of switches may be displayed as decimal (B), octal (C), or hexadecimal (D) number.

**38.** **A.** Shielded twisted pair cable is the best answer, as it will reduce the interference. Unshielded twisted pair cable would work fine if there were no interference. Telephone wire and electrical cord are not designed to carry electronic data.

**39.** **C.** The EGA monitor and DB-9 connector. VGA uses a DB-15 connector (15-pin) and EGA uses a DB-9 connector (9-pin).

**40.** **A.** You have a multi-line plug (8 pins) and it will not work with the modem. A single line plug has four pins, and is used for modems. A network plug (RJ-45) would have eight pins, but would not be connected to the phone.

**41.** **A.** RJ-45 is used for network connections. (RJ-11 is used for single line telephones, RJ-14 is used for multi-line telephones, DB-25 is used for the parallel port.)

**42.** **A.** SCSI is an acronym for Small Computer Systems Interface.

**43.** **A, B.** The power supply of the computer will convert volts of alternating current (Vac) into DC, also known as volts direct current (Vdc). ±5 Vdc as well as ±12 Vdc are found in computers.

**44.** **A.** The Basic Input Output System, otherwise known as BIOS, is stored in Read Only Memory.

**45. B, C.** Remember that CGA monitors can only display four colors at a time, and Hercules can only display monochrome. EGA can only display 16 colors at a time. VGA can display 256. SVGA can have 16 million.

**46. A.** Beware of this question on the exam. Try and imagine what they are saying and think of what will be the best solution. All the answers will sound good and they might indeed even work. The key here is that you want to rock it from end to end gently.

**47. E.** Know the IRQs like the back of your hand. You will be given questions such as this, as well as possible lengthy scenarios involving the wrong IRQ as the culprit of the problem.

**48. B.** Not only is it good to learn IRQs for the exam, but in the real world this knowledge is indispensable. I can't tell you how many times I've impressed my fellow techs by rattling off the correct IRQs when they ask for them.

**49. C.** If LPT1 is already assigned to this IRQ, you may have a conflict. Beware of the examination trying to slip LPT1 and 2, and COM1 and 2 questions at you. They may try and reverse these, so keep an eye out for that.

**50. A.** Know these addresses as well as you know your IRQs. While they are not typically as heavily emphasized as the IRQs, don't be surprised if you see some on the exam. Also, some books list these differently from how they may be in another book or on the exam. If this is the case, think in terms of hexadecimal and decide if the answer is right. Hexadecimal is 0–15, assigning letters to the numbers 10 through 15 (a, b, c, d, e, f).

**51. E.** Don't be fooled by things that look similar. Not only do COM1 and COM2 sound alike, their hexadecimal numbers are very similar. Once again, if you have these memorized and you take your time when answering these questions, you will not have a problem with them.

**52. B.** Crosstalk can happen on wires that are next to each other. Using shielded cables prevents this. Crosstalk can interfere with computers trying to communicate. Therefore, it is always important not to have crosstalk.

**53. E.** Only by careful study will you be able to recognize the details required to answer many of the test questions. These are primary control signals sent by serial communications. Know the chart well and expect to be tested on the finer points of it. Notice that this question tried to reverse the RxD and the TxD in the answers.

**54. E.** Only by rote memorization of the parallel communications will you be able to answer the questions that they throw at you regarding this topic.

**55. A.** The DB-9 is a trapezoid connector and is usually used for monitors and serial ports. DB-25 connectors are used for serial and parallel ports. The RJ-11 and 14 are used for phones. The P/2 Mini-Din is typically used for mice and keyboards.

**56. A.** These types of connections have eight pins and they are usually associated with network cards. Modem connectors like the RJ-11 or RJ-14 typically have only four connection points.

**57. C.** Enhanced Integrated Drive Electronic (EIDE) advanced the limit of hard disks from the IDE standard of two, to four. Each ribbon is limited to two drives, and you are limited to two ribbons. SCSI is a chain and the devices are all strung together. The IDs start at zero and start going up by increments of 1.

**58. A.** This line should be in the CONFIG.SYS. HMA is an acronym for High Memory Area. Don't get confused by the HIGHMEM.SYS that also resides in the CONFIG.SYS. Make sure before you take the exam that you fully understand the different types of memory and the related commands, purposes, and properties of all of them.

**59. A.** MEM/CLASSIFY/P will show you the XMS. (CHKDSK is for hard disks, therefore answers C and D are wrong. XMS is a fictitious DOS command.) Answer A has a switch of /CLASSIFY, which is usually just written as /C. This is a good command to view TSRs and other memory-related items.

**60. A, B, C, D.** An FRU is a Field Replaceable Unit. Expect to be asked this on the exam. An IC is an integrated circuit. You would not replace this. You would instead replace whatever it was attached to. The planar is an example of something that IC is attached to. The planar is the motherboard.

**61. E.** You would not bring a power cord with you since it already shows that it has power. Secondly, while the problem may indeed be the monitor, do not bring a spare one with you unless you enjoy carrying around heavy equipment with you all day. An ESD wrist guard will not help you in this situation. Finally, you cannot carry all the possible hardware around that you may need for a given repair. You may not know what their existing setup is, so you would not know which card to bring. Plus, most computer problems can be caused by a variety of reasons. It is better to troubleshoot first, then get the hardware.

**62. A, E.** Remember that the SCSI uses a female DB-25 or Centronics-50 connector. Answers B, C, and D all use the standard 40-pin connector. It may be a good idea for you to memorize all the types of connectors inside and outside of the computer before taking the exam. Take a good look at the number of pins, and whether they are male or female. Also, note any markings on the ribbons and power cords, and note their orientation.

**63. D.** First of all, in order to understand binary, study the following chart:
000=0
001=1
010=2
011=3

100=4
101=5
110=6
111=7

Note that the numbering starts at zero, therefore you must take the 100 number. On all binary questions, carefully look at what the question is asking for. The test makers have been known to try and trick you on these.

**64.** **A, B, D.** These screws are found on Macintosh and Compaq machines, although their popularity is increasing. They have various sizes. These are denoted by a T instead of the # sign. You need to obtain a torx wrench to work on these screws.

**65.** **B.** The most logical item to check is the 110/220 voltage selector switch. I have seen cases where this switch could be dirty or in the "limbo" position: not on 110 or 220, but somewhere in the middle. This can be a result of vibration during shipping. Never overlook the obvious, simple solution!

**66.** **B.** A ZIF (zero insertion force) connector is the type of socket that is used to mount a 486 style of chip to a motherboard. There are a few exceptions to this on some older or less expensive motherboards, but this is what you will find holding the processor chip on 90 percent of motherboards. The DIMM and SIMM sockets are for memory. The DIP (dual in-line package) is common for other misc 14- and 16-pin support chips.

**67.** **D.** The standard address and interrupt setting for the second EIDE port is 170-177 with an Interrupt of IRQ 15. There are always exceptions, and many newer PCI based motherboards may give more choices than this, but the other choices are used by other hardware. 1F0-1F8/IRQ 14 is reserved for the primary IDE port. 3F0-3F7/IRQ6 is reserved for the floppy controller. 3B0-3BF is reserved for a monochrome display, and IRQ 12 is normally used for a PS/2 mouse. Many times you can move these items around, but it is always best to stick to the standard addresses and interrupts. It will make life a lot easier for the next technician to work on the PC!

**68.** D. In a PC that has a math co-processor, IRQ 13 is used for that device. Since most modern PCs have a math co-processor, avoid using IRQ 13. On some newer Pentium-based PCs with the co-processor built into the processor, you may on occasion get away with this, but it is always safer to leave this interrupt alone.

**69.** C. You could explain to the customer that BIOS stands for Basic Input Output System. It is the low-level code that controls the PC hardware. It is designed into the motherboard in ROM.

**70.** D. IRQ 12 is the standard Interrupt setting for a PS/2 type of mouse. If the PC only has a serial mouse, then you could use this IRQ. However, there has been resurgence in the use of PS/2 mice in IBM clones. Maybe the IBM patent ran out, so now everyone is taking advantage of that. This frees up the standard COM ports for other neat stuff like modems and other devices.

**71.** D. A serial mouse uses a male (pins) DB-9 connector. You can use the male DB-25-pin serial connector with an adapter if necessary. All the little mice come with a female DB-9 connector. Remember the PS/2 mouse comes with the mini DIN type of connector. Some generic mice come with a mini DIN and an adapter for DB-9 so you can use them on either connection.

**72.** B. Parallel Port LPT2 normally uses 278 and IRQ 5. The choices for parallel port addresses are 378, 278, and 3BC. The operating system will map whichever address you assign to the logical LPT ports. We could argue this question all night but the de-facto standard is 278 IRQ 5 for the second parallel port. It is also possible to have a second parallel port work without an assigned IRQ in many cases. I have seen Windows 95 work with a second parallel port without an IRQ assigned.

**73. D.** The most likely display type for that vintage PC would be CGA or Color Graphics Adapter. The VGA and SVGA had not been invented. RGB is a generic type of display terminology that goes back to the world of video. Most VGA monitors are actually analog RGB monitors with an additional sync channel to allow multiple scan rates. Most generic RGB monitors, made for television, use a standard scan rate that is different than what PCs use. So don't use them on a PC!

**74. C.** To measure the current being drawn on a power supply you must place the meter in series with the load. Remember that volts are measured in parallel (shunted across the load) and resistance measurements should always be performed with the power off!

**75. D.** The ESDI or MFM type of hard disk uses two ribbon cables. This is because the controller for the drive is not integrated into the drive electronics as are the newer style IDE and EIDE drives. Chances are that if you are working on something this old, you are a curator in a PC museum. If you ever have the pleasure of working on a system with this much legacy, remember that you must low-level format the drive with the hard disk controller card it will be used with. This is done using the debug utility. Low-level formatting an IDE or EIDE drive is something to be avoided unless you have the specific utilities provided by the manufacturer.

**76. C.** Considering the available choices, adding more RAM memory will have the best effect on performance improvement in a PC. This is especially true in Windows 95, and memory is dirt cheap these days. Most new PCs are being shipped with 32MB. Windows 95 just eats this up and loves it! Low memory is the main cause of disk thrashing.

**77. A.** The correct answer is 640 x 480 256 colors. A VGA card in a PC with only 512 KB of memory will not support any color depth greater than 256 colors. To be able to support any color depths greater than 256, additional memory would have to be installed on the VGA card. Most modern VGA cards have a minimum of 2MB to 4MB of RAM and can display up to 32 million colors.

**78. B.** The ATAPI CD-ROM standard is designed to work on an IDE or EIDE port. Be sure to correctly set the settings for master/slave before installing the device. Also, double-check the CONFIG.SYS file for command-line switches that may be necessary to specify the IDE port, especially if you are using a non-standard IDE port address.

**79. C.** When soldering components you should always use protective eye wear. Molten solder hurts if it gets in your eyes. Our eyes are a great troubleshooting tool. Always protect them.

**80. D.** LOADHIGH can be used in AUTOEXEC.BAT or any other batch file to load a mouse driver such as MOUSE.COM or another type of program such as SMARTDRV.EXE high into upper memory. It can also be abbreviated LH in some versions of DOS.

**81. B.** The real time clock is located on the motherboard. This device keeps time when you shut off the PC. They do go bad. Sometimes they are replaceable. Sometimes they are soldered in and are not replaceable, or not worth the time to do so. Often, a bad RTC is mis-diagnosed as a low CMOS battery problem. That is an incorrect assumption. The CMOS battery holds the BIOS settings for the hard disk type and various other settings.

**82. D.** A standard parallel printer cable has a male (pins) DB-25 connector on the end that is supposed to be connected to the PC and a Centronics 36-pin male on the printer end of the cable.

**83. D.** Parity. Failure to set all of these parameters properly will result in a communications failure for the associated device or worse yet, data transfer corruption.

**84. D.** The parallel port on a PC uses a DB-25 female (sockets) connector. The second serial port often uses a DB-25 male (pins) connector. Look twice, connect once.

# Diagnosing and Troubleshooting

**1. B.** Memory-related errors are usually preceded by a 2**, where the ** can be any set of numbers. In most cases, you may receive a message along with the number code, such as "Memory parity error."

**2. A, C, D.** There are a number of problems that can go wrong when using floppy disks and floppy drives. Of the possibilities listed, only answer B would not result in an error. If you were trying to write to a disk that was write protected you would not receive an error.

**3. B.** When you are seeing characters with missing spots on a dot matrix printer, you may need to clean or replace the print head. The reason is that some of the print heads are dirty and they are sticking.

**4. C.** When the printer is suddenly printing garbage, you should check that the software for the printer is properly configured. Specifying a wrong printer driver or print processor usually is responsible for this.

**5. A.** The most common cause of modems mysteriously losing connection is a bad or noisy phone line. The fact that the user is connecting, and able to use the modem for a period of time before the failure indicates this.

**6. D.** The most common symptom for an incorrect configuration is receiving garbage characters after making a connection. For example, if the software is configured to use an Even Parity and the connecting modem expects the parity to be set to None, you will see a steady stream of garbage coming across the screen right after connection.

**7. A.** You only receive the Power On Self Test (POST) when you are cold booting your PC. An example of a cold boot is when you start your computer in the morning using the power switch, or turn off your computer with the power switch, and turn it back on again.

**8. C.** Keyboard problems are displayed in the error range of 300-399. The most common keyboard-related errors are stuck key and keyboard not found.

**9. D.** Enter BIOS the Setup program then exit.

**10. B.** Most computers display the amount of physical memory installed in the system on the main startup screen. Usually the system quickly counts up the memory. The number is determined by the actual size of a megabyte: 1,024 kilobytes.

**11. C.** The condition of chip creep refers to the thermal expansion of integrated circuits, which causes them to lose connection with the socket. SIMM sockets are elevated from the motherboard and eliminate the chip creep condition.

**12. B.** Dirty mice can cause jerky motion, unresponsiveness, and sporadic movement problems. Remove the ball and clean it, as well as the roll bars. If the mouse is too dirty, just replace it.

**13. A, D.** Operating your computer near high-voltage devices and in high temperatures may cause sporadic problems. Although an incorrect device driver may cause sporadic problems, this can be fixed with software. Using an incorrect power supply is never recommended; you can damage the entire computer as a result.

**14. C.** Whenever you see problems with the screen turning black and the computer not booting up after working with a hard disk or floppy drive, you should check that pin one is correct. Pin one corresponds with the red stripe on the flat data ribbon cable for this reason.

**15. D.** Whenever a computer has a successful POST, it will respond with one audible beep. This is the normal operation of the computer, and assures you the system is functioning normally.

**16. A, B.** Most BIOS will inform you with a warning message when the CMOS battery has become low. Failure to replace the CMOS battery in a timely manner will result in losing all of your BIOS settings.

**17. C.** When you are working with the disk subsystem, you must isolate the problem to one of the three disk subsystem components: disk drive, cable, and controller. In this case, you only replaced the controller, and did not isolate the problem. Using a new cable in addition to changing the controller would isolate the problem.

**18. B, C, D.** All are important to check when determining why a modem will not dial, except the parity setting. Improperly configuring start and stop bits, as well as parity will not cause the modem to not dial.

**19. C.** The default sound card IRQ is 5, the default I/O address is 220, and the default DMA channel is 1. These settings are important to remember when configuring sound cards.

**20. C.** A common problem when dealing with CD-ROM drives is failure to load the CD-ROM driver and the MSCDEX.EXE, which makes the CD-ROM drive accessible to DOS. The CD-ROM driver does load into memory, even when MSCDEX.EXE is not loaded correctly.

**21.** **A.** Not cleaning a tape drive often enough is very destructive to the unit. I have personally witnessed two tape drives fail within a few months due to lack of cleaning. The drives should be cleaned at least once a week, or after every 10 hours of use.

**22.** **C.** Since the mouse operates on the screen, the IRQ setting and plug are fine. As it is bouncing, the rollers probably are dirty. Clean the rollers. Then the mouse will act normally and not need replacing.

**23.** **A.** Since the digital camera is in use when the mouse fails, they are probably both using the same IRQ.

**24.** **A.** If the customer reports the scanner will not work, first make sure it is plugged in the wall outlet and is turned on. The customer may not realize the scanner needs separate power. Then check the IRQ, the software, and the cable in that order.

**25.** **A, C.** If it was the wrong IRQ or the cable was wrong, the disk would still go in the drive. Something is in the drive, either another disk or trash.

**26.** **B.** Since the date has been going wrong for a week, you know the battery is dying. The problem is not Y2K, as it is not year 2000.

**27.** **B.** Even if the BIOS is not set right or the CMOS battery is bad, the hard disk will still turn when powered up. The first thing to check is if the power cord is fully connected.

**28.** **A.** The ribbon cable has a colored edge that always goes to pin 1.

**29.** **B.** The CMOS battery does not affect the speakers. A conflict with the hardware or software would turn up when they were installed. The customer forgot to turn on the speakers, or someone turned them off.

**30.** **B.** If the printing is light in one area, you are low on toner. Cheap paper would not cause this. A bad fuser would put streaks on the paper and a bad cable will either not print or throw out garbage characters.

**31.** **C.** If the printer driver, cable, or print head is bad you will probably get garbage characters. Since it sounds like it is printing, but no print appears, the ribbon is not installed or is worn out.

**32.** **B.** As the customer reports that the monitor is dead, first check if it is turned on. Then check the cable to the computer, then check for a virus. The IRQ will not affect the monitor.

**33.** **B.** If the phone plugged in the jack does not get a dial tone, then the phone line is dead and needs fixing. A bad modem, IRQ conflict, or call waiting problem will not affect the dial tone.

**34.** **A.** System board errors are those from 100 to 199. (Keyboard errors are 300–399, floppy disk errors are 600–699, memory errors are 200–299.)

**35.** **D.** The RAM, AC power and the hard disk do not affect the BIOS. The CMOS battery is low or dead.

**36.** **A.** Keyboard errors are in the range 300–399. Therefore it is a keyboard error.

**37.** **A.** A dirty surface will cause a smudgy scan. A wrong IRQ or bad driver will normally result in no scan. A bad cable would produce no scan or bad characters.

**38.** **A.** You know the diskette is not blank, as it read on another machine. The IRQ would cause the machine to not recognize the drive. The disk was formatted as a 1.4MB disk when it actually is a 720KB diskette (one hole). The drive is trying to read it as a 720KB diskette.

39. **D.** If the light stays on, this indicates the cable was installed backwards. With a wrong IRQ, the light will not come on. With a wrong type disk the light will go out. The drive may be bad, but check the cable first.

40. **A.** Since it works at the neighbors, it is not a bad modem or wrong IRQ. If the customer has call waiting and does not deactivate it (*70), then when the call comes in, the modem may hang up.

41. **B.** CMOS is an acronym for Complementary Metal Oxide Semiconductor.

42. **C.** RAM error. Know these error codes and what they represent. You may be tested on many different numbered error codes, as well as beeps and graphical errors.

43. **A, B.** A dead battery may reset the date and cause the computer not to boot, but it won't try to reboot. A dead hard disk will have the same non-booting effect.

44. **A, C, D.** These will trigger two beeps, as well as an associated error code number. The problem would not be an internal speaker, since this is what would sound these beeps in the first place.

45. **B.** How could you hear the beep if it was coming out of the broken speaker? It would probably sound like one hand clapping. Look for obvious answers on the exam like this one. Sometimes you have to think about what they are asking instead of just reciting what you have memorized.

46. **C.** There are many error codes, and you're not expected to learn thousands of them. Just memorize the common ones and you will be fine. You can always look up the rare ones in a book when you are out in the field.

**47.** E. The transfer corona and the fuser are found on laser printers, not dot matrix. Paper jams and poor paper feed won't cause fuzziness. Poor paper feed results in streaking.

**48.** B. By putting in *70, you are disabling the call waiting feature found on many phones. This is the culprit when you lose the connection sporadically and you are sharing two lines. If the modem worked on another line, this should tell you right away that it is not any of the other choices.

**49.** A, B, D, E. Monitors can have the contrast set to an extreme and cause a black monitor. Bad settings on the software can also cause this. The hard disk will not affect the monitor. The video card actually will affect monitors. And finally, remember that viruses can cause all sorts of hardware problems.

**50.** C, D. Electrostatic Discharge (ESD) will not hurt a CD, nor will magnetic fields. Attenuation is an example of an unrelated term that the test makers like to throw in.

**51.** C. The proper first step is to examine the printer. Many times these displays will alert you to problems that are sporadic. For instance, many of the new laser printers will turn off their printing functions when the toner gets low. If you simply turn the machine on and off, this problem may go away, but only temporarily. The goal of being a good tech is to minimize the number of visits to a machine.

**52.** C. is the right answer here. The power supply is responsible for making the drive turn. If it is missing, then there is not anything else that can make the drive turn. Usually ribbon problems will cause the drive to turn continuously.

**53.** B. The answer to this one is in the ROM BIOS. Be sure that you understand the difference between the BIOS and the CMOS when you take the exam.

**54.** **A.** CMOS is not the BIOS, but over time people have referred to it as the BIOS. The CMOS actually stores the BIOS. Think of the BIOS as the information (settings) and the CMOS as the hardware (storage).

**55.** **A, B, C.** Try a dry Q-Tip first and if it doesn't work, then put a small amount of water on the Q-Tip. Lastly, try a small amount of rubbing alcohol. Soap would only gunk up the mouse, and the sandpaper would simply wreck it.

**56.** **C, E.** Windex is not recommended. Alcohol may be good for mice, but not for monitors. Light soap and water seem to work the best. A tip when cleaning: never get any liquid inside of the monitor case.

**57.** **D.** An I/O device is an input/output device. A network card will receive data as well as send it. The other ones are unidirectional (meaning one direction of communication).

**58.** **A, C, D, E.** While the first three choices seem obvious, since they do indeed input information into a computer, the last may not be. Some monitors can have touch screens that enable the user to input data into them. This just goes to show that you must read each question carefully.

**59.** **D.** While the other solutions may work, the exam is always asking you for the best answer. With keyboards so cheap nowadays, it may be best to pitch them. Fixing them just may take too much time. However, management can view things in peculiar ways and they may have a policy of repairing keyboards.

**60.** **D.** The 423 is a code for a bad parallel port test outcome. Memorize all of these. They will most likely be on the test.

**61.** **A.** The 201 is a code for a memory test that has failed. Memorize all the codes. They will most likely be on the test.

**62.** **D.** Run the print head cleaning utility. Most bubblejet and inkjet printers come with a print head cleaning utility. Pressing a sequence of buttons located on the printer enables this utility, or it may be part of the Printing Utilities applet that came with the printer.

**63.** **D.** The power supply is bad. This was a real-world experience of mine. Coincidentally, the problem appeared right after I had added more RAM to the PC. Removing the CD-ROM from the drive allowed the PC to boot Windows 95 correctly, but the PC would intermittently restart when the customer tried to access the CD-ROM. What we discovered was that the power supply would crowbar when the additional current was drawn to spin-up the CD-ROM.

**64.** **C.** Replace the keyboard with a known good one. I believe the UART in the keyboard stops working after warming up in such cases, and there is no longer any communication with the keyboard port. Keyboards are cheap and I personally don't even waste time cleaning them anymore.

**65.** **D.** Use the Control Panel keyboard setting applet to adjust the repeat rate. There are other keyboard-related settings located in this handy applet included with Windows 95. It is definitely worth a visit to note what else you can tune up in this area of performance.

**66.** **B, A, C, D.** Listen carefully to the customer's description of the problem. Try not to interrupt. Often his description of the problem is accurate, even if his diagnosis is incorrect. Never be afraid to admit that you don't know. These situations can be a good opportunity to "earn as you learn." Reboot the PC to see if the problem goes away. It may go away and return after a short period. Careful observation is one of your greatest troubleshooting tools. Isolate the problem to a hardware or software component. You may have to try more than one thing. Be patient. Finally, replace the suspected item and thoroughly test the system.

**67. D.** An intermittent PC problem is the most difficult type to troubleshoot. I would rather find a charred and smoking PC than one with an intermittent problem. One struck by lightening is easy. Change the power supply first, then the motherboard, and so on, until it comes back to life. The intermittent PC problem will separate the novices from the pros. Use all of your available resources for this type of service call. The Internet is a great source of information for product support, driver updates, and service bulletins.

**68. B.** Ohm's mode is the correct multimeter setting to check continuity on a cable. Many multimeters come with a helpful beeping continuity setting. Use a paperclip if necessary to get to the pins, and always check it twice!

**69. C.** The Faxing applet has control of the modem to receive faxes. This is common in many brand-name PCs that come loaded with all types of faxing and communications software. Make sure that the fax-modem application is set to Send Faxes Only. If the customer needs to have this feature enabled, then you could install a second modem to be used for their online activities.

**70. B.** Change the CMOS settings for the correct floppy drive type. If the PC thinks it has a type of drive different from the one installed, it will not work properly.

**71. A.** To enable two floppy drives on a port, you must have each one set as a different logical drive number. This could be done by jumper settings on the drive itself, but the most popular method is the "split" cable. The first drive should be connected to the connector that is located after the split. The split changes the pin-out relationship of that connector to set that drive as the first one.

**72.** **D.** 5.25-inch is the physical size of a good old-fashioned 360K disk. Unfortunately, it looks exactly like the newer 1.2MB 5.25-inch floppy disks. To tell which is which you would have to place it in a drive and query the disk with a DIR command.

**73.** **B.** Edit the CONFIG.SYS by adding the line DRIVPARM= /D:1 /F:144. This command as shown assumes that it is the second drive. The drives are identified as 0 and 1, with 0 being the first and 1 being the second. Consult the DOS manual for more information on this handy command to support newer drives in legacy machines.

**74.** **B.** Arrange for the carpeting to be sprayed with anti-static spray. Having the customer wear a wristband is silly and could be potentially dangerous if they were to come in contact with the static charge on the Monitor screen. Running ground straps is also not a viable solution, as it will only provide more paths to distribute the ESD charge. Eliminating the problem at the source is the best solution.

**75.** **D.** Advise the customer to be sure that all applications are closed before scheduled backup is run. A tape backup will try to lock each file before it is archived to the tape. If a file is open this cannot be achieved. All applications should be closed prior to running a backup. This is true whether it is run manually or on a schedule.

**76.** **D.** Clean the tape heads and sensors with a Q-Tip and alcohol. This is a common problem. Always remember to clean the end of tape sensors whenever you clean the tape head. Failure to do so may cause a tape to get ripped off at the end of the supply or take-up spool.

**77.** **D.** Use a battery backup UPS system to ensure the maximum protection. Many failures, including hard disk crashes, can be caused by power surges and outages. Files left open during the power outage can also become corrupted. You can use SCANDISK to attempt to repair problems such as these, but the horse had already been let out of the stable at that point.

**78.** **C.** Insert the CD media and use the MOUNT command. It is often best to ask your network administrator to do this. Disgruntled network administrators have shot many technicians on site for lurking about the Novell server. Always respect their turf when you are called in to work in a network environment. They can be your best ally or your worst enemy!

**79.** **C.** System board problems. Consult the chart in the companion study guide and memorize this for the test.

**80.** **C.** Change the keyboard. It is possible that the problem could be with the onboard UART located on the motherboard, but changing the keyboard is faster and easier, so try that first.

**81.** **C.** The environment is too damp, causing the paper to stick together. Always look at the surrounding area for clues to problems. A dry, high-static environment can also cause paper jams, and other problems.

**82.** **D.** Disable Call Waiting by modifying the dialing string for the modem. Windows 95 makes this easy by modifying the dialing properties to add *70 to the string, so all of your numbers will dial with that appended to the head of the string. Some areas use a different set of characters to disable Call Waiting, so you may have to check with your local telephone company for the correct Call Waiting disable character sequence.

# Safety and Preventive Maintenance

1. **D.** You should always defragment a computer's hard disk to increase performance. Over time, data gets fragmented all over the disk and the hard disk has to spend a considerable amount of time attempting to read the data.

2. **B, D.** Vacuuming your computer removes dust and debris that can cause a computer to overheat, and eliminates the potential for conducting an electrical charge, which can short a system or destroy components.

3. **C.** Of the devices listed, only the surge suppressor can be used to prevent damage to your computer in the event of a power surge. However, surge suppressors are not without fault; the surge of electricity can jump across the wire and complete the circuit, causing damage to your computer.

4. **A, B.** Suppressors are used to absorb or block harmful spikes of energy, while a noise filter is designed to reduce the amount of noise present in electrical current and eliminate magnetic fields caused by noise.

5. **B.** A discharged UPS that is stored for a long period of time may lose some of its capacity to store power, or may become unable to accept a charge at all. To ensure that your UPS is stored in the proper manner, review the manufacturer's documentation for any other recommended procedures.

6. **B, C.** Whenever you work around lasers or high-voltage equipment, you must be extremely careful not to injure yourself. These forms of equipment can cause damage in the form of burns, eye-related problems, including blindness, or even death.

7. **B, C.** You never want to complete a high voltage circuit with your body. This means that you should never use both hands on the equipment itself. If you do, you are forming a "live" circuit between you and the equipment, resulting in an electrical pathway that leads from one hand and passes through your body to the other hand. You should always be careful with high voltage equipment, which means handling high voltage properly, and not with your bare hands.

8. **D.** You should only open the power supply if you are trained and skilled with these devices. This is the same for monitors; never open them unless you are trained and have the proper equipment. Even if you are trained, you probably won't need to open a power supply.

9. **D.** Material Safety Data Sheets are white pages that contain information on any substance that is deemed hazardous, most notably cleaning solvents. MSDS is required by the United States Department of Occupational Safety and Health Administration, and must be posted in obvious locations.

10. **B.** This electron transfer is an electrostatic discharge that may not hurt you, but it can still harm a computer component. Unless precautions are taken, you can actually destroy a device without even realizing it.

11. **C.** A humidity level below 50 percent tends to lead to static electricity. You will notice this especially in the winter months, when humidity levels are low naturally. Ensure that you check any air-handling equipment in the room for a properly set humidity level.

12. **C.** Level 3 laser beams are of a significantly lower intensity than those employed in construction or scientific applications. As a result, you will not get a severe burn from them, but should nevertheless be cautious when working with them.

**13. A.** A line analyzer should be used to detect surges, spikes, and sags in the AC voltage for your computer. Use this as preventive maintenance for detecting bad AC sources, and developing a strategy for safeguarding the computer and peripherals.

**14. B, C.** With modern hard disk drives, there is not much preventive maintenance that is required to keep a disk drive running. However, to increase performance and reduce errors, there are a few utilities you can run to defragment the drive and check for inconsistencies.

**15. C.** The most effective way to remove dust from the inside of a computer is to use compressed air. This stream of high compressed air can remove dust in the deepest places of the system, and will not damage any delicate system components.

**16. A, B, C.** High voltage equipment must carry labels to warn the user of potential danger to themselves or equipment. These labels usually consist of "Caution", "Warning", and "Danger—High Voltage," with an explanation of the possible danger.

**17. A, C, D.** Compressed air is something that should be in every technician's toolkit. The stream of air can be directed easily, without damaging components, and provides more cleaning power than a vacuum.

**18. A.** A damp cloth with a small amount of mild detergent should be used to clean the outside of a computer's case. Be careful to not use too much detergent, as it may stain the exterior of the case. Also, make sure the cloth is not too damp, as there is potential for the moisture to seep through cracks and into the case.

**19. C.** A rubber knife can be used to remove the hardened residue from the metal components in the computer that the vacuum or compressed air could not remove. This knife is sturdy enough to scrape residue off, and does not conduct electricity.

20. **C.** You will need to locate the anode lead in the event you are discharging a monitor. Gently prying the lead away from the monitor until you hear a pop discharges any buildup that has accumulated on the glass.

21. **C.** The battery in your personal computer is used to maintain the CMOS system settings, date, and time when the system is powered down. This battery does not provide any power supply in the event of blackout.

22. **A, D.** Compressed air or a vacuum cleaner may be used to clean dust. Alcohol will affect the appearance of the plastic. AJAX powder will scratch the surface.

23. **A, C.** You can use either isopropyl alcohol or a pencil eraser to clean oxidation on metal contacts. Using a cleaner with wax or a mild detergent will leave a layer on the contact, causing it to not make a good connection.

24. **B.** When using utilities you must use the version for that operating system or you will damage your disk structure. The correct answer is Windows 95.

25. **A.** A low supply of power is called a brownout. A blackout is a power outage. Noise on a power line is EMI and a power spike is a sudden increase in power for a short period.

26. **A.** Electro-magnetic Interference (EMI) is being produced by the refrigerator motor and causing the interference.

27. **C.** Batteries contain environmentally harmful substances. Therefore, burning them, burying them, or putting them in the trash will harm the environment. Take them to a recycling center.

**28. B.** Place computer components in an ESD bag to reduce static damage. Ziploc bags and static wrap will increase the likelihood of static damage.

**29. D.** Live current that is misdirected can cause death, severe burns, and damage to the computer.

**30. D.** LaserJet III printers use class 1 lasers.

**31. B.** Power supplies hold high voltages, so they are not serviceable. The fan is necessary to draw off the heat generated. Replace the power supply.

**32. B.** Dust build-up will cause parts to fail, so vacuum the computer. Water may cause a short and damage to you or the computer.

**33. D.** Although a backup may need to be run, viruses checked for, and SCANDISK run, a drive that is progressively slowing down definitely needs defragmenting.

**34. B.** The paper is a Material Safety Directions Sheet (MSDS). It tells how to handle, store, and dispose of material.

**35. B.** SCANDISK is a Microsoft program to mark corrupt sectors. COMMAND.COM is not a disk utility program. Norton Utilities can do this, but it is not part of Windows. DEFRAG does not mark corrupt sectors.

**36. C.** Used toner cartridges should be returned to the manufacturer or a recycler to protect the environment.

**37. C.** They should first fully charge the UPS battery, as it will have lost power in storage.

**38. D.** Diskette drives should only be cleaned when they are producing errors, as the cleaner gradually wears out the read/write heads. To clean a floppy disk drive you should use a special cleaning disk. The other methods listed may cause damage to the drive.

**39. B.** When finding a part wearing out you should tell the customer, and replace it if requested. Ignoring it or not telling the customer now because the part won't break until later does not build customer loyalty.

**40. B.** When using virus software, you must use the version for that operating system or you will damage your disk structure. The correct answer is Windows 95.

**41. B.** Electro-Static Discharge occurs when a static charge travels to a grounded object and is often produced by humans moving in dry areas.

**42. A.** The hard disk probably is badly fragmented. You need to run DEFRAG, which will run SCANDISK. CHKDSK is an old version of SCANDISK. As they are doing virus checks already, Norton Anti-Virus does not need to be run.

**43. A, D, E.** Electrostatic Discharge can harm circuit boards. High-powered devices such as monitors and power supply boxes are dangerous to work on, since the static that remains in them can be harmful.

**44. A, C, D.** These are the kinds of questions that you should really be watchful of. They usually concern the power box and other potentially dangerous items. Answer E is a typical A+ answer that you can rule out.

**45. B.** You can see the spark at 20,000 volts. Volts that are less than what you can feel (30,000 volts) can still damage equipment. This damage is tough to see and can cause components to mysteriously stop working.

**46.** **E.** The board has suffered from ESD, but now it is suffering from degradation. This is tough to track down. Many people in the field do not properly prevent ESD from occurring. They think that if they can't feel a shock then nothing can be occurring. Degradation can take a long time to surface, making the culprits of this poor practice even tougher to find.

**47.** **A.** Electro-magnetic Interference can cause magnetic fields that can damage components. Always remember all of the acronyms and their related full words. The A+ exam is notorious for asking for the full name of the acronym.

**48.** **D.** A noise filter stops noise that is present in electrical current. This noise causes electrical fields.

**49.** **A, E.** A screwdriver will not do the trick alone. It needs to be grounded. The jumper wire serves this purpose. Learn all the terminology surrounding this process and read each question carefully. An ESD strap is the last thing you want to use. In fact, you must take this off before performing this duty. In addition, this duty is reserved for experienced professionals.

**50.** **C.** Know your terminology if you want to pass the exam. Answers A, B, and D are all made up. The infamous "none of the above" will appear frequently on the exam.

**51.** **C.** A monitor can keep its charge for a long time. Don't work on it unless you are experienced.

**52.** **A, E.** Donations are always welcome in needy organizations. Selling the monitor to a resale shop is another good idea and you will end up with cash in your pocket. Most states don't allow monitors to be sent to landfills anymore.

**53.** **D.** Let common sense (and the law) be your guide. Answers A, B, and C are wrong and unlawful.

54. **B, C.** You cannot just simply throw them away. You may refill them, but there are many things to think about before doing this, namely a black powder all over your shirt, the printer, and the carpet if you are not careful.

55. **A.** This act was passed May 13, 1996. Since it was passed in Congress, this means that it is a Federal Law as opposed to a State Law. Federal Laws carry more weight than the State Laws.

56. **A.** The room has to be dust-less, dirt-less, and sealed, but these are not what these rooms are called.

57. **C.** Old hard disks actually require you to park the heads. This is usually a DOS command of PARK. Keep this in mind when you are working on these older PCs, especially if you are planning on moving the drive around and exposing it to vibration. You cannot oil it or open it under normal preventive maintenance duties. Low-level formatting is not good either, in terms of preventive maintenance. Incidentally, it is not a bad idea to back up and restore the drive every few years, since the drive is magnetic and it eventually will lose its charge over a long period of time.

58. **A, C, D, E.** The eraser can clean contacts, the rubber knife can get rid of sludge, and the vacuum and compressed air can get rid of dust. The soldering gun is not a part of preventive maintenance.

59. **C.** All of these actions are very dangerous and should not be attempted by the inexperienced. The reserved energy has enough power to kill you. Don't be foolish. Read the labels. When you see an international sign that means No Screwdrivers, pay attention.

60. **A, B, C, D, E.** Unfortunately all the answers are correct. I'm sure some tech of yesteryear had to learn some of these lessons the hard way. You are more

important than your job. Heed all warning labels, your common sense, and any accompanying literature.

**61.** **E.** When you absolutely need to prevent catastrophic equipment damage during a lightning storm, you must unplug the computer as well as the modem. With external modems you must unplug the modem power cord as well as the phone line. Even a machine that is turned off can get fried.

**62.** **C.** The other answers are all causes of downtime, but the question is asking for the best answer (which you can assume is the case when they are asking for one choice, even when two or more are correct).

**63.** **A, D, E.** Yes, it is true that the neighboring components can be affected by the component that has been affected by ESD. This is possible as long as the component is still in the machine.

**64.** **D.** Degradation is damage that may cause a component to function poorly. This type of damage is often caused by something like ESD or heat. The problem can be intermittent as well. Changing the suspected component should alleviate the problem.

**65.** **C.** You should never wear a wrist strap when working on any high-voltage system. Doing so is extremely dangerous. You might as well ground yourself and go stand in the middle of an open field during an electrical storm, or go fly a kite with a steel cable if you want some kick in your life.

**66.** **D.** Always check with your local government for disposal procedures when it comes to chemical waste. If you fail to do this, you are polluting our planet and risk some heavy fines if caught.

**67.** **D.** The dangerous part of a CD-ROM drive is the laser beam. It could blind you if you make eye contact with it. Normally it lives safely inside the case where it never focuses on anything but the CD-ROM media. If you decide to manually clean the laser lens, do it with the power safely turned off.

68. **D.** Whenever you encounter a new piece of equipment it is always best to consult the manufacturer's suggested preventive maintenance guidelines. Never assume you know something. Technology is always changing, usually for the better, but it is your responsibility to keep up on things.

69. **C.** A laser printer has a level 3 laser inside the protective chassis. This can be just as dangerous as the laser in a CD-ROM. Always use caution with laser printer service. Besides the dangers of the laser itself, there are components that get very hot, and there is high voltage in the laser printer as well.

70. **B.** Murphy's law states that, "Dropped tools and parts will always fall where they can cause the most damage." Therefore, we would first recommend that you shut the PC off immediately and retrieve the dropped screw. Telling anyone else about your dumb mistakes is purely a personal choice.

71. **B.** If a SIMM memory chip does not seem to fit properly, try reversing it 180 degrees so the notch on one end aligns properly with the SIMM socket. Never force anything when servicing a PC. Damage can occur easily and you could make a simple job become very difficult. In reference to choice D, I find that honesty goes a long way to building up a long-standing customer base.

72. **C.** The best place to store a PC card is in an anti-static storage bag. You can then place the component and bag in a cardboard box for more protection. Placing it in an unused slot can cause resource conflicts with other devices in the system. A lint-free cloth is a poor choice.

73. **B, C.** A UPS is designed to protect a PC from power surges, brownouts, and sudden power failures. I recommend a UPS to every customer I sell a

new PC to. Considering the cost of their investment, $150 is a pretty reasonably priced insurance policy.

**74. B.** EMI is an acronym for Electro-Magnetic Interference. This is noise and signals that can occur on an AC power line. Anything other than the 60-cycle AC current can be considered interference.

**75. A.** A UPS that has been stored offline for a long period of time may loose its battery charge. Before returning the unit to service, it should be recharged according to the manufacturer's guidelines, and thoroughly tested under load.

**76. B.** An environment that has humidity over 80 percent can cause condensation. Computers generally don't work well in moisture. Neither do monitors or any equipment that has high voltage, like laser printers.

**77. B.** When discharging a CRT, you should attach the ground end of the discharging device to a ground terminal on an electrical outlet.

**78. C.** A power supply that the fan has stopped working on can break down due to heat buildup. Power supplies, by their very nature, dissipate a lot of heat. In fact they usually disburse much more heat than the power they supply.

**79. B.** Always clean monitor screens with glass cleaner. Other cleaners may be too abrasive and could damage the screen. A clean monitor is a happy monitor. I always like to clean the screen of a PC I just serviced.

**80. C, D.** Preventive maintenance on a hard disk includes running the SCANDISK utility and running the DEFRAG utility. SCANDISK will check for and repair the disk file system integrity. DEFRAG will defragment the drive, which by nature tends to become fragmented. FDISK and formatting the drive will remove all existing data on that drive, which is generally not appreciated by your customer.

81. **A, B, D.** The 1.44 disk drive, 1.2MB disk drive, and the tape drive can usually be cleaned in the field. Hard disks are sealed and should not need to be cleaned, nor can they be opened except in a clean room.

82. **B.** When using new chemicals, always consult the warning label. It's nice to know the proper way to handle new chemicals. Many are very useful but can be volatile when combined with other chemicals or in an environment that is too hot or cold or close to a flame.

83. **B, D.** It is always best to recycle whenever possible. Donating a PC to a charitable organization is also good for a tax write-off. Scrapping a PC for parts can help keep another PC alive.

84. **B, C, D.** Electrical contacts are best cleaned with isopropyl alcohol or contact cleaner. The more stubborn items can be cleaned with an eraser if necessary. Soapy water can leave a residue and is not my recommendation.

85. **B, C.** It is your responsibility to know how harmful any chemicals you use are for yourself or the environment. The potential impact on the environment can affect you and your fellow workers. Knowing the proper disposal procedures for the empty container is also your responsibility.

# Motherboard/Processors/Memory

1. **B.** Very Large Scale Integration refers to a complex integrated circuit with thousands of devices, such as logic gates and transistors, placed on a semiconductor chip. A Central Processing Unit (CPU) is one example of VLSI.

2. **C, D.** The 486 and the 386DX CPU, a 32-bit register size, a 32-bit data bus, and a 32-bit address bus. The 386SX CPU came with a 16-bit data bus, a 24-bit address bus, and a 32-bit register size.

**3.** **C.** The 486SX came equipped with a 32-bit data bus, as well as a 32-bit address bus and 32-bit register. This is identical to the 386DX and 486DX processors.

**4.** **C.** The 286 processor came equipped with a 24-bit address bus, but only a 16-bit register and data bus. The only feature to increase in the newer 386SX processor was the register, which is 32-bit, as opposed to 24-bit.

**5.** **D.** Since a computer uses 1024 for a megabyte, the total amount of 16MB of physical memory would equal 16,777,216. 1024 is determined by raising 2 to the $10^{th}$ power. 16 times 1024 equals 16,777,216.

**6.** **A.** Static Random Access Memory chips (SRAM) do not need to be constantly refreshed, hence they are static. However, while they don't need a constant update, they do require a periodic update, and tend to use excessive amounts of power.

**7.** **B.** The motherboard is made of a fiberglass sheet that has miniature electronic circuitry embedded in it. This circuitry provides the pathways for electronic signals to flow between devices.

**8.** **C.** The EISA standard was developed to compete with IBM's Micro-Channel Architecture (MCA) devices, which increased their peripheral's bus size from a 16-bit bus to a 32-bit bus. However, the EISA standard was backward compatible with 16-bit ISA cards, and MCA was not.

**9.** **B.** The use of a DMA channel in Extended Capability Port printing speeds up data transfer rates by bypassing the processor and writing the data directly to memory.

**10.** **C.** The figure represented in the figure is a BIOS ROM chip, which is easily identified by the writing stamped on the chip, which represents the date and type of BIOS.

**11.** **C.** DRAM, rather than SRAM, abandoned the idea of using the unwieldy transistors and switches in favor of using the smaller capacitors that could represent 0s and 1s as an electronic charge.

**12.** **C.** Of the listed processors, the 486DX has a working math coprocessor. The 486SX has a math coprocessor. However, it was disabled at the factory to lower the price of the processor.

**13.** **B.** The capacity is the amount of data the card can hold, usually denoted in megabytes. However, the data bits determine if the SIMM utilizes parity. If the data bits equal 8 or 32, the SIMM does not use a parity bit, but a 9 or 36 will indicate that parity is in use (8 + 1 parity bit or 32 + 4 parity bits).

**14.** **B, C.** AT and ATX are types of motherboards. The AT motherboard actually comes in two different sizes: Full and Baby. The primary difference between the AT and the ATX is that the ATX defines a double height aperture to the rear of the chassis, which can be used to host a wide range of on-board I/O, and the AT does not.

**15.** **B.** The Video Electronics Standards Association (VESA) was formed to address compatibility problems with the local bus. VESA created the standards for the local bus architecture that were incorporated into the manufacturer's products.

**16.** **C.** The Dual Independent Bus Architecture allowed each processor inside the chip to execute instructions simultaneously and independently from the other, which is called parallel processing.

**17.** **B, C.** The 486SX chip did not increase the processor speed, which remained at 33 Mhz, or enlarge the bus size from 32-bit. It did introduce an on-board cache to the processor (an 8K cache), along with an on-chip math co-processor. Unfortunately, the math co-processor was disabled at the factory.

**18.** **D.** The data bus for the 80386DX processor was 32-bits, as well as the address bus. This was an improvement over the 80386SX processor, which had a data bus of 16-bits, and an address bus of 24-bits.

**19.** **B.** Whenever you receive the "Error loading operating system", or "Missing operating system" error, you should focus your attention on the hard disk. Most likely there is a hardware problem, such as an incorrect hard disk type in BIOS, or the hard disk is bad, or the cable is not firmly plugged in. Also, check that a floppy disk is not in the drive on boot.

**20.** **D.** When using an additional math co-processor with a 386DX processor, you need a 387DX processor. Math co-processors are easily recognized by their number, which is one number higher than the processor itself.

**21.** **C.** Only the 486DX chip includes an operational math co-processor that works with the processor to speed up math operations. The 486SX chip includes a deactivated math co-processor

**22.** **C.** When computers are sold, people express the memory size in the number of megabytes, not the actual number of bytes. Both numbers are correct.

**23.** **A, B.** The 8088 processor can run at 4.77 Mhz or 8 Mhz. The 484 processor may run at 66 Mhz and the Pentium processor may run at 133 Mhz.

**24.** **B.** When doing even parity checking, all the bits with a value of one in a byte are added. If the answer is an odd number, then one is put in the parity bit.

**25. A.** When doing odd parity checking, all the bits with a value of one in a byte are added. If the answer is an even number, then one is put in the parity bit.

**26. B.** The byte is probably correct, but if an even number of bits are wrong, it would show no error.

**27. B.** Serial ports transmit one bit of data over one conductor at a time.

**28. A.** Parallel ports transmit eight bits of data over eight conductors at a time.

**29. C.** The CMOS uses a low-voltage battery to retain the BIOS settings.

**30. B.** IBM introduced MCA (Micro Channel Architecture) to use with the IBM PS/2 computers. ISA (Industry Standard Architecture) was introduced with the IBM AT computer. The ISA companies developed EISA (Extended Industry Standard Architecture) to compete with MCA.

**31. A, C, D.** Floppy diskette drive standard types and sizes are: 5.25-inch, 360KB; 5.25-inch, 1.2MB; 3.25-inch, 720KB; 3.25-inch, 1.44MB; and 3.25-inch, 2.88MB.

**32. C.** Rings of concentric circles around a disk are called tracks. There is nothing on the disk called a slice. Combing the same track on each of the disks makes a cylinder. Sections on the disk shaped like pie slices are called sectors.

**33. B.** Combining the same track on each of the disks makes a cylinder.

**34. C.** A kilobyte contains 1024 bytes. It is thought of as containing approximately one thousand (1,000) bytes.

**35.** **D.** A megabyte contains 1,048,576 bytes. It is thought of as containing approximately one million (1,000,000) bytes.

**36.** **A.** The space for one character is called a byte, which is sometimes displayed as two hexadecimal numbers. The byte is made up of eight bits, which are binary digits.

**37.** **B.** SIMMs have memory chips that are embedded on one side of the card.

**38.** **C.** DIMMs have memory chips that are embedded on both sides of the card.

**39.** **A, C.** The sizes AT motherboards are produced in are AT (also called AT Full size) and Baby AT. ATX is the new style AT motherboard and requires an ATX type case.

**40.** **D.** Another terminology stickler. Beware of reasonable-sounding answers to questions. A good tip is, if you have never heard of an answer, then it is most likely there to throw you off.

**41.** **C, D.** If you have memorized all of these capabilities, these questions will mean a bunch of free points.

**42.** **D, E.** Be careful of this question. If you look at a chart of these attributes of CPUs, you will notice that the register and the data bus do not go in lock step in terms of the number of bits they support. Another thing to be careful of is the difference between an SX and a DX.

**43.** **B, E.** You should know the difference between the register and the data bus attributes for all these processors.

**44.** D. Don't be misled into thinking that it is 64-bit. Although the register and the data bus are 64-bit, the data bus is only 32. Beware of questions that use different terminology for these three attributes.

**45.** B. Bytes, kilobytes, and megabytes represent exponential increases, not mere multiplication. A computer that is said to have 64MB of RAM actually has more.

**46.** C. For these binary questions you can just memorize the amount of digits that each one has and the number associated with it. You may be asked how many megabytes in a gigabyte, or any other combination.

**47.** B. All the conversions among mega, giga, and terra are not multiples of 1000. This is due to the fact that you are dealing with a machine that likes to look at things in terms of 2, hence the 1024, which is 2 to the power of 10.

**48.** E. Answer A is close, but incorrect. The refresh is the ability of RAM to update. The rate at which chips are updated is called the refresh rate. This rate usually occurs in approximately 60–70 nanoseconds.

**49.** B. Know your terminology for all of these types of RAM, including the terminology for the acronym of RAM itself, which happens to be Random Access Memory.

**50.** E. Here is another typical A+ certification terminology question. Remember that a portion of the exam is exclusively terminology related.

**51.** A. This can be extremely confusing. Most people in the field use BIOS and CMOS interchangeably. The CMOS battery stores the BIOS, which is located in the CMOS. Remember also that the CMOS is a form of ROM.

**52.** **A, C.** EISA, which stands for Extended Industry Standard Architecture, was introduced to compete with IBM's MCA devices. If you have ever worked on an old IBM PC you will be very familiar with MCAs. They are very long boards that stretch across the unit. EISA is just Extended ISA. You mostly see these on later 386 and 486 computers.

**53.** **A.** Beware of plausible answers that sound right. Unless you know these terms cold, you will end up being fooled on the exam. There will most likely be a few questions on attributes and terminology.

**54.** **B.** They could only handle up to 16 bits until 1985. The PCMCIA in 1985 officially changed the name of these cards to PC cards, and they proposed a 32-bit card bus operation.

**55.** **D.** The VL-Bus stands for Video Electronics Standards Association Local Bus. The Video Electronics Standards Association acronym is VESA.

**56.** **D.** The Enhanced parallel port offers the same features of a bi-directional parallel port, but with the added benefit of the extended control code set.

**57.** **A.** Tracks are the circles that the disk is sub-divided into. A good way to remember this is to think of a running track, where the runners keep running around the track in the same lanes.

**58.** **B.** The piece of the track that is on the outside of the disk, subdivided into a sector, is equal in memory size to the inner track. This is a limitation of round disks. You can only fill them in as much as the inner disk allows.

**59.** **C.** View this as the cylinder that would be formed if you drew a line though all of the tracks. Once you know the track's cylinders and sectors, multiply these by the number of heads (the number of sides of data that can be read on a disk) to figure out the disk size.

60. **C, D, E.** Remember that the 80486SX had a co-processor, but it was not enabled. In terms of the A+ exam you should only choose those processors that had the math co-processor enabled.

61. **C.** The standard ISA bus runs at 8 Mhz. Even though processors soon ran at speeds much greater than this, the standard ISA bus still had the limitation of 8 Mhz data transfer speed.

62. **C.** The ECP, or Extended Capability Port, mode for parallel ports will use a DMA channel for data transfer. This greatly speeds up the transfer rate compared to a standard parallel port.

63. **B.** PCI is an acronym for Peripheral Component Interconnect. This is a 64-bit bus that is processor independent and also has its resources assigned through CMOS settings. It uses a special bridge circuit to accomplish this.

64. **B.** SIMM is an acronym for Single In-line Memory Module. This has been a standard that goes back to the 386 family of processor-based systems. SIMMs come in two sizes: 30-pin and 72-pin.

65. **C.** DIMM is an acronym for Dual In-line Memory Module. The DIMM chip has components on both sides and generally can be more populated with memory than a SIMM.

66. **C.** The DRAM type of memory requires a constant refresh rate. This is because it is made up of tiny capacitors that must be recharged at a regular rate to maintain the integrity of the data. Typical refresh speeds are 70 nanoseconds for these chips.

**67.** C. The EPP or Enhanced Parallel Port supports an extended control set. It is also a bi-directional port.

**68.** C. The 386SX processor uses a 16-bit data bus. This was the economy model at its inception. Its big brother, the 386DX processor, boasted a 32-bit data bus.

**69.** C. The 386SX processor had a 24-bit address bus. This was another compromising feature of the SX series at that time. The 386DX had a 32-bit address bus.

**70.** C. The 486DX had a 32-bit address bus. So did the 486SX. The economy model 486SX had the math co-processor disabled; otherwise the two 486 series chips were identical.

**71.** A. The 8088 processor had a 20-bit address bus. This was the first PC that hit the market. Who knew then, besides Bill Gates, where this would take us?

**72.** A. The Pentium processor uses a 64-bit address bus. It also has a 64-bit data bus and a 64-bit register. The Pentium chip actually combines two 486DX chips in one package and supports Dual Independent Bus Architecture.

**73.** B. The external clock speed of a 486DX4 chip is 33 Mhz. The clock speed is only internal to the processor. Externally, the chip appears to the rest of the PC as a 33 Mhz processor.

**74.** C. For a laptop computer the PCMCIA bus is the only show in town. There may be a PCI internal bus that supports the on-board EIDE controller but for external devices the PCMCIA slot is the way to go.

**75.** **C, D.** The Pentium family of processors work so hard that they require a heat-sink and/or a fan to keep them cool. I like my Pentium laptop in the winter. It keeps me nice and warm on my lap on the way to work in the bus.

**76.** **C.** The first thing to check when any port is not working on most modern computers is that port's CMOS settings that enable and disable the port. The other settings listed may enhance the performance of the port after it is enabled.

**77.** **A, C, D.** The three settings that need to be properly configured in CMOS for a hard disk to work properly are the HEADS, CYLINDERS, and SECTORS. The CMOS may display the drive SIZE based on those parameters, but in order for the geometry of the drive to be understood by the operating system, these three parameters must be set correctly.

**78.** **B.** The correct memory address for COM2 is 2F8 and IRQ3. To help you remember these, always remember that the odd IRQ goes with the even port. I also like to think of the addressing as being backwards. The ports 1–4 go backward address-wise: 3F8 2F8 3E8 2E8.

**79.** **B.** ISA is an acronym for Industry Standard Architecture. Remember this is a dual 8- and 16-bit bus that runs at 8 Mhz.

**80.** **D.** The EDO-RAM uses tiny capacitors to store data. EDO-RAM is a special type of DRAM that supports fast-page mode speeds 10–15 percent greater than standard SIMMs.

**81.** **D.** The simple solution is often the most common cure. The most likely cause of this error message is that the customer has inadvertently left a non-bootable floppy disk with his data files in the disk drive. If that is not the case, then answers A and C would be the other logical possibilities.

Viruses can destroy the boot sector of a hard disk. Corrupted CMOS settings could also render the hard disk unbootable until they were restored to the proper settings for the HEADS, SECTORS, and CYLINDERS for that particular type of hard disk.

# Printers

1. **B.** The main disadvantage of this type of printer is the amount of noise it creates from banging the characters against the page. Although measures have been taken in design to muffle the noise from these machines, they still remain the noisiest printers available.

2. **C.** When the solenoid is energized, the pin is forced away from the print head and impacts the printer ribbon and ultimately the paper, thus impressing the dot on the page.

3. **D.** The primary corona of a laser printer has the highest negative charge of any of the components in a laser printer. The primary corona is responsible for electrically erasing the photosensitive drum, preparing it to be written with a new image in the writing stage of the print process.

4. **B.** The heating element in the ink jet printer, in contact with the ink, heats up very quickly, causing the ink to vaporize, resulting in a build up of pressure in the chamber. This pressure forces the ink out the pinhole, forming a bubble of ink on the page.

5. **C.** Rather than the printer receiving instructions for each dot on the page, the PDL encoded in the printer receives commands from the computer on how to print the page. Using simple line drawing commands rather than printing each dot along that line greatly simplifies the instructions that must be passed to the printer.

6. **B.** This rubber blade extends the length of the photosensitive drum. It removes excess toner after the print process has completed and deposits it into a reservoir for re-use.

7. **C.** This highly negatively charged primary corona wire is responsible for electrically erasing the photosensitive drum, preparing it to be written with a new image in the writing stage of the print process.

8. **A.** The transfer corona contains a positively charged wire designed to pull the toner off of the photosensitive drum and place it on the page.

9. **B.** These rollers comprise the final stage of the electro-photographic (EP) printing process, bonding the toner particles to the page to prevent smearing. The roller on the toner side of the page has a non-stick surface that is heated to a high temperature to permanently bond the toner to the paper.

10. **D.** Before any image formation can occur, the photosensitive drum must be cleaned and electrically erased. For the photosensitive drum to be cleaned, a rubber blade extending the length of the drum gently scrapes away any residual toner left over from the previous cycle.

11. **C.** Once the image has been set in toner on the photosensitive drum, it must be transferred to the print medium, the paper. Because the toner is attracted to the drum, it must be pried away by an even stronger charge to get it to the paper.

12. **C.** Any light on the photosensitive drum will erase the image on it. This step ensures that the drum has been electrostatically erased so that it can receive a new image. Now the photosensitive drum is ready for the next step, charging.

**13. D.** The laser diodes of the laser printer will cause spots on the photoconductive drum that lose their charge. The laser is responsible for transferring the image to the drum, not transferring the image to the paper.

**14. B.** The fuser consists of three main parts: a halogen heating lamp, a rubberized pressure roller, and a Teflon-coated aluminum fusing roller. The fuser heats the fusing roller to anywhere from 165°C to 180°C. As the paper passes through the two rollers, the pressure roller forces the paper against the hot fusing roller, bonding the toner to the page.

**15. C.** The registration rollers synchronize the paper movement with the writing process inside the EP cartridge. The registration rollers do not advance the paper until the EP cartridge is ready to process the next line of the image.

**16. C.** A parallel cable consists of a male DB-25 connector that plugs into the computer and a male 36-pin Centronics connector that connects to the printer. The DB-25 connector has the same number of pins as the serial connector, but the gender is reversed.

**17. C.** The recommended length for a parallel cable is ten feet. Lengths any longer than ten feet run the risk of crosstalk, which causes signal degradation and causes communications to become unreliable.

**18. A, C.** Print heads and toner cartridges are just about the only FRUs that the printer manufacturer gives the end user responsibility for replacing. Most print quality problems can be remedied by replacement of these components.

**19. A.** If there's no toner in the cartridge, no images will be transferred to the page. If the transfer corona wire fails, no toner will be attracted from the photosensitive drum to the paper. If the high voltage power supply isn't providing the voltage necessary to either the primary corona or transfer corona, the printing process will not work correctly.

20. **D.** If an image smudges, then an element of the fusing process has failed. This could be a result of the halogen lamp burning out, failing to melt the toner to the page.

21. **A, B, D.** When you are storing printing paper, you must be aware of adverse conditions that may affect the quality of the paper, such as the temperature and humidity of the storage room, and whether the paper is being stored in an undesirable location, such as a very dirty warehouse.

22. **B.** Printers are classified as non-impact or impact. Laser and Ink Jet printers are non-impact. Dot Matrix and line printers are impact.

23. **C.** The process a laser printer uses to print is cleaning, charging, writing, developing, transferring, and fusing.

24. **A.** During the fusing step of the electro-photographic print process, the toner is permanently bonded to the paper.

25. **D.** The image is transferred to the paper during the writing step.

26. **D.** The HP LaserJet 5 printer will show a paper jam error if the back cover is not fully closed. Failure to close the cover will give a Cover Open error. The printer should not be reset after a paper jam, or data may be lost.

27. **A.** Parallel printer cables are normally 6 or 10 feet long. They are unreliable when longer than 10 feet.

**28.** **B.** Serial cables normally come in 10- and 25-foot lengths. They are not reliable when they are longer than 25 feet.

**29.** **D.** The message indicates the toner is low. Begin watching the output, and when the print gets light replace the toner cartridge. Normally, when this message appears you can print several hundred more copies. This is not a printer error, so no servicing is needed. Refilling the toner cartridge is not a user task.

**30.** **B.** A pin not printing will leave a white line and is fixed by replacing the print head.

**31.** **D.** A bad printer cable will cause wrong characters to print.

**32.** **A.** Parallel ports send data to the printer one byte, or eight bits, at a time.

**33.** **B.** The COM ports send data to the printer one bit at a time.

**34.** **A, B, C, D.** Printers may be connected to a computer via parallel cables, serial cables, and infrared and network connections.

**35.** **A.** The fact that there are two printers is the key. The customer has used the wrong printer driver to print to that printer. When choosing to print, choose the correct printer.

**36.** **D.** The printer to which the customer is sending the job is out of toner.

**37.** **C.** By turning off by the power strip, the printer is not going through power down, which is when it cleans the nozzles. The Ink Jet printer should always be turned off using the Power button on the printer.

**38.** B. Ink Jet printers do not have photosensitive drums. New ink cartridges include new nozzles and new ink.

**39.** A, C, D. Ink Jet, laser, and daisy wheel printers print letter quality. Dot matrix printers can print "near letter quality".

**40.** C. The problem stayed with the computer so it is not the printer. The printer cable on the first computer is probably bad. If replacing it with the second cable does not fix the problem then the computer is the problem.

**41.** D. A parallel cable has a male 36-pin Centronics connector that plugs in the printer. It is a bar type connector.

**42.** A. Toner cartridges may be replaced by the user. Normally this is not done by the manufacturer or a service technician.

**43.** A, B, C, D, E. All of these are components of a laser printer. Not only should you know these components, but also the components on an Ink Jet, thermal printer, daisy wheel, and Dot Matrix. You should also thoroughly understand the function and repair of all these major components.

**44.** C. The primary corona wire is negatively charged. It is in the writing stage that this occurs.

**45.** A, C, D E. You must know these processes thoroughly if you expect to pass the printing questions on the A+. Try to visualize the path of a sheet of paper going through each print process.

**46.** D. Try to think of a memorization technique for this order, since you will be heavily tested on it. I like **Clean Checks Will Develop Transferring Funds**. The test makers are well aware of memory tricks such as these and they will throw in a printing term that starts with the same letter in the correct order to throw you off, so make sure you know the terms. If you don't like this way of studying, then understand each step fully and the order will be obvious.

**47. B.** The second step is charging. Beware of similar sounding words that start with the same letter.

**48. B.** When the laser is hitting the drum, that means that the laser is in the On position. When the laser is in the Off position, the drum has a highly negative charge.

**49. E.** When the rubber blade is not cleaning the photosensitive drum correctly, you get residue from previous print jobs on your printouts. The rubber blade and an electronic erasure are part of the first step, which is the cleaning process.

**50. A, C, D.** A poorly formatted document, or one with complex formatting, could take too much memory to print. Low toner could also be a cause. Some of the newer laser jet printers will stop printing when the toner reaches a certain level, and the only solution is to replace it. The printer being offline is a very common problem.

**51. A, D.** What this question is really asking is: which of these are impact printers, and which are not? An impact printer impacts the page. Although you won't run into many daisy wheels on the job, it is still good to learn about them in case you do.

**52. A, B.** Beware of choices like answer C, "HPVS" failure. This would have been correct if it stated HVPS failure. HVPS stands for High Voltage Power Supply.

**53.** C. It is not acceptable to refill dry ink cartridges. The A+ exam wants to make sure that when you get rid of things, you do it in an environmentally responsible way. Learn what to do with all that you throw out and you will get several correct answers on the test.

**54.** A, C, D, E. The serial type of connection must be configured with the same types of things that modems do. Things such as bps, parity, and start and stop bits need to be set in the serial connection.

**55.** A, B C. Remember that the question asked you where can a serial printer be located, not what is the maximum distance.

**56.** A, B, C. Even though these ancient printers are practically obsolete, it is still important to know the terminology behind them. The electromechanical hammer, Solenoid, and Resistive Coil are all synonymous in the case of a daisy wheel printer. This process is very similar to a Dot Matrix printer and should be well understood.

**57.** B. This type of question gives you a 20 percent chance of answering it unless you have memorized these facts.

**58.** B, C. The output is usually more accurate to what the screen looks like, but the printing can be much slower. The font addressable printer can only hold whatever fonts you load into it.

**59.** A, B, C, D, E. The A+ exam will sometimes use terms that may not be familiar in this context. Chemistry, for example, would be an answer, and you would have to ask yourself does chemistry play a part in the laser printing process?

**60.** B, C, D, E. Don't be tricked by answer A, which sounds like something that you would find on a dot matrix printer. Unless you know the other four, you may pick a wrong answer.

**61. B, C, E.** These are the three motors found in printers. Know the reparability and replaceability of these, as well as all other parts of a printer.

**62. A.** In a dot matrix printer, the letters are usually printed partially as the printer head goes back and forth. If the ribbon is not advancing, it will hit the same area on the ribbon until it becomes light because of depleted ink.

**63. C.** You should never lubricate the printhead. The drivers actually were in the right place and the network was correct. The A+ exam will periodically throw in a Macintosh question. A superficial knowledge of Macintoshes is needed.

**64. B.** The best type of printer to print high-quality, black-and-white documents is a LaserJet. A Daisy Wheel printer will not print any graphics, so that is not as good a choice. If the requirement included the need to print multi-part forms, you would need to use an impact printer. Bubble Jet and LaserJet printers will not print multi-part forms.

**65. D.** An Ink Jet printer uses a pump and an inkwell. The print nozzle sprays the image onto the paper. An improved variation on this process is the Bubble Jet, which uses heat to cause the ink to bubble up, and creates pressure to spray the image onto the paper.

**66. B, C, D.** The Dot Matrix, Ink Jet, and Bubble Jet printers are considered line printers. These printers process the print job one line at a time. The LaserJet printer processes the entire page at once. This greatly increases the speed at which the LaserJet can print compared to a line printer.

**67. B.** The most likely cause of the smearing of LaserJet printed pages when touched is that the fusing process has failed. The fusing process uses heat to permanently bond the printed image to the surface of the paper. Without this process completing properly, the toner is merely laying on the paper, held in place only by a small static charge.

**68.** C. Always consult the manufacturer's guidelines before servicing any piece of equipment. We will usually browse through the information if it's available before going to perform a service call. That makes us look much more knowledgeable to our customer when we arrive on site. Some customers can get very nervous when they see you browsing through an instruction manual. New products often have new features and procedures. It is your responsibility to keep up to date on service information.

**69.** C. The easiest way to test a printer on a Windows 95 PC is to use the Print Test Page applet that is included in the Printers folder of My Computer for the printer in question. A working printer will print a test page with a graphical image and a list of the drivers that Windows 95 is printing. If the print job fails, then you have the option of using a print troubleshooting wizard to diagnose the problem.

**70.** D. A good test for the hardware connection to a printer is the DOS-based command sequence DIR > LPT$x$, with $x$ being the logical LPT port number. For example, to test the hardware connection to a printer connected to LPT2, you could enter DIR > LPT2. That will cause the directory listing to be re-directed to the printer port. This is a handy test, because it bypasses any printer drivers that could possibly be corrupted, causing other problems.

**71.** D. Corrupted printer drivers can cause print jobs to fail, but in this case the smaller jobs printed fine, so answer A is not the likely choice. Answer C is also incorrect. Most printers will notify you when they are out of ink. Empty ink cartridges or clogged print heads will generally print blank sheets or partially blank sheets. If that was the case you should use the print head cleaning utility that is normally built into the printer. Answer B is unlikely, because small jobs print. A bad printer cable would normally affect all print jobs. The correct answer is D, the hard disk is very low on space, and that would be the best place to begin troubleshooting. If the C:\TEMP directory is full of stale print jobs, then you should exit Windows and then delete all the files in the C:\TEMP directory first to free up hard disk space. If the system is using a permanent swap file, you may move it to another hard disk, if available, or reduce the size to free up disk space.

**72.** **A, C, D.** The potentially dangerous items in a LaserJet printer include: the heat fusion rollers, because they get very hot and you can burn yourself if you touch them without allowing time for them to cool down; the high voltage corona, which carries a charge of up to 5,000 volts; and the Class 3 laser beam, which can cause severe eye damage. Always consult the manufacturer's service manual for safe procedures for servicing these devices.

**73.** **C.** The third step of the LaserJet EP printing process is writing the image to the drum with the laser beam. Memorize the order of this process, as it will appear on the A+ exam.

**74.** **C.** The fifth step of the LaserJet EP printing process is transferring the image to the paper. In this part of the process the toner is transferred from the drum to the paper medium. Following this, it is fused to the paper, making the image permanent on the paper.

**75.** **B.** Prior to the EP process of writing to the drum, it must be charged to clear any old image left from the last page printed. The drum is charged by the primary corona wire to approximately -5000 volts. Don't be putting your fingers in there, or you will get an unpleasant surprise!

**76.** **A, C, D.** Printers that are normally capable of printing graphic images include dot matrix, LaserJet, and Bubble Jet printers. The daisy wheel printer can only print letter-quality type and has no way to print graphic images.

**77.** **A, B.** All printers must have a power supply. Each model of printer will usually have one specifically designed to provide the correct voltages for that printer. Another common mechanism is a paper-feeding mechanism. This is designed to move the paper from the supply through the printer and out the paper exit area. The type of feeding mechanism will vary from model to model, but they all must have some way to get the paper, print it, and deliver the finished print job to the user.

78. **B, D.** Two common types of printer ports are serial and parallel. Another specialized type of port you may encounter for plotters is a GPIB, or General Purpose Interface Bus. This will support plotters and other devices. Hewlett Packard has its own GPIB interface card known as the HPIB, or Hewlett Packard Interface Bus.

79. **A, B.** The standard printer cable has a DB-25 male (pins) connector on one end and a Centronics 36-pin (male) connector on the other end. This is an industry standard. A serial printer cable will use the DB-25 male (pins) and female (sockets) connector.

80. **D.** A printer indicating that it is out of paper when there is paper in the supply tray usually means that you should check the paper path and sensor switch. A bad cable might cause the PC to think the printer is out of paper because of a communication failure from the printer to the PC, but the indicator on the printer would not be showing an error in that case.

81. **A, B.** A printer cable longer than 10 feet may pick up noise and interference. We have also seen longer printer cables cause data skew.

82. **A.** A DIP switch is commonly found on many printers to control the options settings. This is normally the case on a Dot Matrix printer or a Bubble Jet or Ink Jet printer. Many modern printers, such as LaserJet Printers, use a soft set menu system built in to adjust printing parameters. To access the menu system, first consult the manufacturer's service or operations manual to determine the proper buttons and sequence to access, change parameters, and store them in the printer's memory.

**83.** **A, C, D.** The most common cause of a LaserJet printer that is printing blank pages is that the toner cartridge is empty. Other possible causes of this could be that the transfer corona has failed or the HVPS (High Voltage Power Supply) has failed.

# Portable Systems

**1.** **D.** Laptop computers are notorious for not adhering to computer industry standards, such as form factor components. When a component needs to be replaced or upgraded, it will most likely involve proprietary components from the original vendor. Of the listed components, though, the power supply (if external) is the most likely to be standard.

**2.** **D.** Active matrix displays are based on Thin Film Transistor technology (TFT). Instead of having two rows of transistors, active matrix displays have a transistor at every pixel. This allows much quicker display changes and produces display quality comparable to a CRT.

**3.** **D.** Without the use of a docking station, you cannot support PCI devices, which is an unfortunate drawback to laptop computers. However, PCMCIA devices are becoming capable of supporting more types of external devices, such as SCSI adapters.

**4.** **B.** Port replicators are the cheapest and simplest version of the three types of docking stations. Most portable computers have external VGA, keyboard, and serial connections. Port replicators simply provide a copy of the interfaces that already exist on the back of the portable computer.

**5.** **C.** Most portable computers at the time of this writing are shipping with 2.5-inch EIDE or UDMA hard disks. Manufacturers use different interfaces and different footprints that are not necessarily compatible. For this reason, it is necessary that a replacement hard disk be made for that particular computer.

**6.** **D.** PCMCIA actually refers to the Personal Computer Memory Card International Association, the non-profit organization that defines the specifications for these credit card-sized peripherals. PCMCIA was founded in 1989 by a consortium of vendors to create and maintain these standards and guarantee interoperability.

**7.** **D.** PCMCIA version 1.0 defined the 68-pin interface that we currently use as well as the physical specifications for the Type I and Type II cards.

**8.** **A.** Type I cards are the thinnest, measuring only 3.3 mm thick, Type II cards are 5.0 mm thick, and Type III cards are 10.5 mm thick.

**9.** **B.** Socket Services is a layer of BIOS-level software that isolates PC Card software from the computer hardware and detects the insertion or removal of PC Cards.

**10.** **B.** Card Services software manages the allocation of system resources automatically, such as memory and interrupts, once the Socket Services software detects that a card has been inserted in the PC Card slot.

**11.** **A.** The 1.0 version of the PCMCIA specification was released in June 1990 and was originally intended only for memory cards. PCMCIA version 1.0 defined the 68-pin interface.

**12.** **C.** Type III PC Cards are generally reserved for rotating mass storage, such as hard disks. Type III cards are 10.5 mm thick. Most portable computers now come with at least one Type III slot built in.

**13.** **B.** Type I cards are 3.3 mm thick. Type II are 5.0 mm thick and are generally used for I/O devices such as modems, network adapters, or SCSI adapters. Type III cards are 10.5 mm thick.

**14. C.** Generally, laptop computers have a higher resale value than desktop computers. This is due to a laptops' higher cost and complete package.

**15. C.** When a NiCad battery is recharged before it is fully discharged, the battery loses the ability to fully recharge again. Nickel/metal hydride, or NiMH, batteries offer several advantages over NiCad batteries, and are more commonly used today.

**16. C.** Although not as full-featured as a true docking station, an enhanced port replicator can add interfaces not available in the portable computer alone. Extended port replicators often add enhanced sound capabilities and more PC card slots.

**17. B.** Type 1 PC cards are the most flexible because they can fit into their own Type 1 slot and can also fit into a Type 2 slot. For this reason, most people have two Type 1 PC cards in a laptop system.

**18. B.** LiIon is the best choice if it is available, although it is slightly more expensive. NiMH is more common and less expensive, but is slightly heavier and produces less power. Stay away from NiCad batteries if at all possible.

**19. B, C.** Laptop computers usually have two areas that are accessible for memory upgrades: a proprietary expansion slot, and a PCMCIA memory card upgrade. Although PCMCIA memory upgrades are becoming less common, most laptop computers come equipped with an expansion slot that is easily accessible for RAM upgrades.

**20. B.** Operating systems such as Windows 95 and Windows 98 are very helpful for creating hardware profiles for laptop users who travel. This includes auto-detection of the docking station on startup, and hardware profiles to choose at startup for a specific configuration.

**21. B, C.** If you are using Windows NT on your laptop computer, Windows NT 4.0 currently does not support hot-swapping of PC card devices, like Windows 95 and Windows 98 can. You may have to shut down the computer, or use SUSPEND to insert the new PC card.

**22. A.** Portable computer batteries may be replaced by the user. Normally this is not done by the manufacturer or a service technician.

**23. A.** Type I cards are 3.3 mm thick.

**24. D.** PC cards are 54 mm wide.

**25. D.** PC cards are 85.6 mm long.

**26. C.** A portable computer requires a proprietary expansion card to add memory. Memory is added on desktop computers with either SIMM, DIMM, or memory chips.

**27. C.** A pointing stick is a small piece of rubber, a stick, in the center of the keyboard.

**28. D.** On a touch pad, you rub your finger over a small plastic square to move the pointer.

**29. B.** The 84-key keyboard is used with portable computers. The Dvorak keyboard features a different arrangement of the keys from the QWERTY keyboard. The separate numeric keypad is not on portable computers. The 101-key keyboard is used on desktop computers.

**30. B.** The first thing to do is to clean the contacts. If a problem still exists, check the AC converter.

**31. B.** An AC adapter converts either 110 Vac or 220 Vac to DC power. A computer does not use 110 Vdc power.

**32. A.** Passive matrix LCD displays are cheaper to buy and use less energy.

**33. B, C, D.** Active matrix LCDs display the superior image, are easier to see from an angle, and handle changing images better.

**34. C.** Alcohol, AJAX, and steel wool will destroy the surface. Use a damp cloth to clean the display.

**35. A.** The LCD display must be replaced as a whole. There are no serviceable parts.

**36. B.** If the power LED does not light, then the computer probably has a dead battery. If the hard disk or motherboard were bad, you would normally get a message.

**37. D.** If the power LED does not light, then you probably have a dead battery. If the LED lights, but nothing appears on the LCD, then the brightness is turned down. If the hard disk or motherboard were bad, you would normally get a message.

**38. D.** Type I, II, and III cards were developed by the Personal Computer Memory Card International Association. VESA sets standards for internal PC cards. MPEG and JPEG set video compression standards.

**39. A.** Failing to fully discharge a NiCad battery prior to recharging it causes a condition called memory effect. The battery is not dead, but must be replaced. The portable computer is not affected by this.

**40.** **D.** Having them move the mouse slowly would help, but is not a realistic solution. Adjusting the brightness will have no effect on the pointer on the screen. Changing the screen to an active matrix display is not an alternative without buying a new machine. The best solution is to set the trails option on for the mouse in Windows.

**41.** **E.** Remember that no battery in a computer can simply be thrown out. You must contact your state agency for proper disposal guidelines. You can replace all of these batteries with the same type, with the exception of a handful of manufacturers who have decided to weld the CMOS battery on to the motherboard. These will usually have an extra socket and a jumper switch to accommodate a new battery.

**42.** **D.** Checking whether the contacts are dirty is the first step to troubleshooting in this circumstance. Answer B is incorrect, since a plug cannot ever go into the wall backwards. Answers C and E are incorrect, because a memory problem like this would not happen so soon on a LiIon battery. There is no such thing as a POWER.DRV in the CONFIG.SYS.

**43.** **D.** A passive matrix has this function, as opposed to the active matrix which has a transistor at every pixel. A CRT, or Cathode Ray Tube, is obsolete technology and is not a flat screen like the LCD screens. An LED screen is actually the type of screen you see on a calculator and, on some of the newer laptops, you may see this feature above the keyboard as a status screen showing hard disk use and the like.

**44.** **E.** While all the others sound like the right answer, only Port Replicator is correct. Most people are satisfied with the basic feature of extending the ports and possibly having another power supply on this type of docking station.

**45.** **D.** Laptops not being seated are a big problem. Some docking station manufacturers have designed the station and laptop poorly. Many times you will find that they appear to be seated, but they are askew. Since not all systems support hot swapping, rebooting allows the computer to detect the modem. Checking compatibility is important. Even if they come from the same manufacturers, docking stations and laptops of different models may be incompatible.

**46. A.** The key to this question is the word "ensure". Since laptops are not standardized yet (and the hard disk is no exception), it is smart to use replacement parts from the same company and model that you are replacing. Many laptop companies use proprietary interfaces for these, and they do not necessarily work interchangeably.

**47. A.** Although the term Memory Card does not sound like what these cards do, this name came into being when memory was the purpose of these cards. Now they can function to help a vast array of peripherals to communicate with the laptop.

**48. D.** These mass storage devices are things like external hard disks. These happen to be the most common use of Type III cards. This is in contrast to Type II cards, which are generally used for modems and network adapters.

**49. B.** It would be a good idea to memorize the thickness of these cards. A Type I is 3.3mm thick, and a Type III is 10.5mm thick. They are all the same height and length, which are 85.6mm x 54mm.

**50. A, B, C.** These are all used today. Answer D is wrong. Let common sense be your guide on a question like this.

**51. A, C, D, E.** ZV is the acronym for Zoomed Video. Bus Mastering, DMA, and 32-Bit Card Bus operation were indeed in this specification.

**52. D.** This 68-pin interface is a carry-over from the PCMCIA Type I interfaces.

**53.** **A, B, C D.** This is a terminology question. A pointing stick is used on laptops. It resembles the head of an eraser and is replaceable.

**54.** **A.** The Power applet in the Control Panel is the place where you change all the settings for the battery, There are no tabs or buttons to go to advanced screens on the standard Windows 95 load. It is part of being a good technician to understand intimately where everything is on the major operating systems.

**55.** **E.** These services isolate the PC card software from the computer hardware. All of the other choices are invalid in the context of this question. Realize that Windows 95 recognizes insertion and removal of PC cards, and Windows NT generally does not.

**56.** **B.** NiCad is limited to about 1000 recharges. These are the earliest batteries for laptops and are now obsolete. These batteries also had memory problems. The memory stayed in the battery if you did not fully discharge the battery before recharging. This memory can diminish battery lifetime quite substantially.

**57.** **B.** This service manages the allocation of memory and interrupts once the Socket Services have done their job. Hardware Manager sounds like Device Manager, which you find in Windows 95, but this question is asking about operating systems in general.

**58.** **B.** These are very common on laptops. In order to use them, you put your finger under the arrow and pull out. Then you press in and the PC card will eject. When you put a PC card in, this will be in the unlatched position; press on the end of the piece where the arrow is pointing, and secure this piece so that it is flush with the side surface of the laptop.

**59.** **A, B.** Usually the power supply button is on the front of the docking station, but you will find some very well hidden on the side. Laptop ejects can either be a lever, which you pull to manually eject the laptop, or a button that automatically ejects the laptop for you.

**60.** **C.** The correct answer to this is Windows 95. Windows NT will ask you when you boot if you are stationed in a docking station or not. Windows 3.1 and DOS were made before docking stations gained any popularity.

**61.** **A, B, C, D, E.** This is on a full-feature docking station. Most users nowadays do not have all these capabilities, since most of them are using Port Replicator types of docking stations. Even if they are using Enhanced Port Replicating docking stations, they do not have these features, since these usually just add PCI support.

**62.** **B.** Because of the proprietary nature of laptop computers, it is often difficult to upgrade them. We have even found that some PCMCIA cards will not work properly in some models of laptop. Our experience proves it is always best to check with the manufacturer before trying to upgrade a laptop PC.

**63.** **A.** The NiMH or nickel/metal hydride battery is the most popular battery for laptops today. It is generally less susceptible to memory effect than the nickel cadmium and contains less harmful chemical, so it is a bit safer environmentally.

**64.** **B, D.** If the major requirement for a laptop is battery life, then the combination of using a Lithium Ion battery and a passive matrix screen will give the longest period of usage between charging. Another good recommendation in this case might be to order a second battery.

**65.** **C, D.** If the customer's primary concern is to have a clear screen for his laptop, you should recommend an active matrix screen. A second recommendation could be to purchase an external VGA monitor that could be used when working at home with the system. Most laptops include an external VGA connector to facilitate such an option.

**66.** **B.** If a customer wishes to have extra features for a laptop in the office, then the correct recommendation would be to purchase a docking station and monitor for use in the office. This will allow the customer to use many standard desktop PC peripherals, as well as have the portability of the laptop.

**67.** **D.** Most laptops manufactured today come with a Touch Pad. This pointing device has almost no mechanical parts except for the two click buttons, and is generally much more failure-proof than a trackball.

**68.** **A, D.** Some of the advantages of owning a laptop include small size and portability, and better resale value. Laptops are generally more expensive than desktops, so their resale value is slightly higher as well. As for the portability, try putting a handle on a Gateway 2000 with a 17-inch monitor and taking it on the bus!

**69.** **D.** A laptop battery that will only run the PC for a short period of time has suffered from memory effect. This is usually caused by recharging the battery before it has had a chance to fully run down. Most manufacturers suggest that when you purchase a new laptop, run the battery down and recharge it fully 3 or 4 times to burn in the memory. This helps greatly in avoiding this problem. A battery with memory effect has to be replaced.

**70.** **C.** A Type III PC card is 10.5mm thick. These devices are usually hard disks. That is why they are so thick. You should memorize the PCMCIA specs, as there will be questions about them on the A+ exam.

**71.** **C.** Eating fried chicken and using a trackball will surely foul up the trackball mechanism. Normally the oil in your fingers is enough to foul it up over time. Clean the trackball with a damp cloth to alleviate this situation and avoid fried chicken and other greasy food. It's bad for you, anyway!

**72.** **C.** A type I PC card measures 85.6mm x 54.0mm x 3.3mm. Most of these will be memory expansion cards.

**73.** **C.** To change a PC card in a Windows 95 laptop the preferred method is to use the remove card applet by clicking on the icon in the lower right task bar. Windows will then prompt you with a dialog box to confirm removal. This is the best method because if you are using a device such as a network card it will allow the operating system to update and disk cache to write before disconnecting from the network.

**74.** **B.** To run a laptop on land power (120VAC) you need an AC power adapter. Normally one will come with a new laptop. Usually this device also doubles as the battery charger.

**75.** **D.** The most common device interface to add features to a laptop is the PCMCIA socket. You should consult the manufacturer of the laptop on compatibility issues.

**76.** **A, C.** Of the three most common pointing devices for a laptop, the ones noted here are the Trackball and the Touch Pad. The third possibility, not given as a choice in this question, is the Pointing Stick.

**77.** **C.** One of the pitfalls of a passive matrix is that the screen refresh is not as fast as an active matrix. One of the results of this is that when you move the mouse it may be difficult to see. That is why Microsoft has added mouse tails as an option in the Mouse Control applet, located in Control Panel.

**78.** **A, B, D.** Using a docking station with a laptop will normally allow the use of PCI-based cards, ISA-based network cards, and other ISA cards as well. Most laptops have an external VGA connector, but the docking station makes the implementation of External Monitors easier.

**79.** **B, D.** Some disadvantages of owning a laptop when compared to a PC include higher cost of ownership (although the gap has closed considerably in the last few years), and the fact that the laptop is easily dropped and damaged. Compatibility with peripheral devices is not nearly so much of an issue as in the past, because of the increased availability of PC cards and docking stations.

**80.** **B.** A PCMCIA card has a 68-pin/socket interface. This allows quite a variety of devices, because of the number of physical connections that are possible.

**81.** **B.** Release 2.*x* of the PCMCIA standards included the specifications for the Type III card. These cards include modems, network interface devices, and SCSI interfaces, to name a few.

**82.** **B, C, D.** In 1995 the PCMCIA standards included specifications to support Zoomed Video, 32-bit bus support, and 33 Mhz transfer speed. The PCMCIA specification has come a long way in a few short years. Laptops are now capable of supporting so many devices through this standard that you can find almost anything that you would want for a desktop PC in the PC card catalog.

# Basic Networking

**1.** **B.** Unshielded twisted pair is the most commonly used networking cable today, because of its low cost. It's used with the very popular Ethernet Star topology, which uses shorter lengths of UTP cable to attach to central hubs.

**2. B.** 10BaseT does not use coaxial cable. 10BaseT uses twisted-pair cabling, not coaxial. Although not a type of cable, BNC refers to the connector associated with the coaxial cable.

**3. C.** The cable presented in the diagram is coaxial, or ThinNet. Physically, coaxial cable consists of a central wire that is surrounded by a screen of fine wires.

**4. C.** Fiber optic cabling is much more resistant to Electro Magnetic Interference (EMI) than any other cable type. Fiber optic cable is much less susceptible to these environmental difficulties because it uses light signals rather than electrical signals.

**5. A.** Although twisted-pair is more common than coaxial cabling, it suffers from attenuation after 100 meters, whereas coaxial cable begins to suffer from attenuation after 185 meters.

**6. B.** Carrier Sense Multiple Access/Collision Detection (CSMA/CD) is a network access method used with the Ethernet technology to maintain control over who uses the network and when they use it.

**7. B.** When using a Token Passing network access method, a device that wishes to communicate must seize the token, which can take longer on a small network. However, Token Ring is more efficient on a large network than CSMA/CD.

**8. D.** TCP/IP stands for Transmission Control Protocol/Internet Protocol. This protocol is the foundation of the Internet, as every device on the Internet requires a unique address called an IP address.

**9. C.** Although NetBEUI is the fastest and easiest-to-configure networking protocol, it cannot be routed. This means your network cannot be separated into smaller networks by using routers.

10. **C.** NetBEUI is extremely easy to configure. Just install the protocol combined with a functioning network adapter and it's done. However, you do not have much control over locating computers by unique address and using diagnostic utilities to contact computers, like you do with TCP/IP.

11. **B.** Network interface cards are by far the most popular method of connecting computers to the network. Modems are also quite common for connecting users, especially remote users, to the network.

12. **D.** When using 10BaseT, which is using twisted-pair cabling, nothing will need to be terminated. Coaxial cable in a bus topology commonly requires termination.

13. **C.** The connector in the diagram is a BNC T-connector, used to connect a workstation to the coaxial backbone, while still maintaining the link.

14. **D.** Fiber optic cable has a range up to 3,000 meters when LEDs are used, and up to 30Km when laser diodes are used. This is due to the use of light rather than electricity, but also due to networking devices along the way that can extend the distance.

15. **C.** RJ-45 refers to twisted-pair cabling, which can either be unshielded or shielded. Shielded twisted pair is less susceptible to interference than unshielded twisted pair, and also has a greater cable distance.

16. **A.** The 2 in 10Base2 refers to 200-meter maximum cable distance, which is actually closer to 185-meter maximum cable distance. In 10Base5, which is thick coaxial cable, the 5 represents 500 meters for the maximum cable distance.

17. **B, D.** Since coaxial and ThinNet cabling are the same, both of these types of cable are most commonly used in a bus topology. Bus topologies,

however, are not the most common form of network today. Star topology with twisted-pair cabling is the most popular.

**18.** **C.** When configuring network cards, you have to specify an IRQ that is not in use, as well as an I/O memory address that is not overlapping with another device in the system. Many times, you also need to configure the duplex type, the interface being used (Coax, TP, or AUI), and the transmission speed.

**19.** **A, B, C, D.** All of the answers are common network problems that can slow down a network, prevent connection for only a specific computer, or even worse, prevent connection to all computers on the network, which is the effect when a terminator is missing on a bus topology.

**20.** **B.** 10Base5, thick coaxial uses a bus topology, just like thin coaxial uses. Every device must connect to the network backbone. However, these devices do not use a BNC connector to connect to the main backbone in 10Base5.

**21.** **C.** When two stations attempt to transmit at the same time on a CSMA/CD network, they will retransmit after waiting a random period of time. If the time period was a fixed duration, and not random, these stations would continually attempt to transmit simultaneously.

**22.** **A, C, D.** Telephone cable is not good enough to handle data. Network cable may include twisted pair, coaxial, and fiber optic.

**23.** **C.** UTP is an acronym for unshielded twisted pair.

**24.** **C.** STP is an acronym for shielded twisted pair.

**25.** **A.** Each end of a coaxial network must have a 50-ohm terminator. Devices connect to a coaxial network via a T-connector.

26. **B.** Devices connect to a coaxial network using a T-connector. RJ-45 connectors and splices are used with twisted pair cables. There is no 50-ohm connector.

27. **B.** The maximum length for coaxial cable is 180 meters.

28. **C.** There is no maximum length for fiber optic cable.

29. **A.** A network interface card (NIC) is required to connect a personal computer to a network. A docking station may include a NIC. A portable computer may have a NIC PCNCIA card. A hard disk is not required to attach to a network. T connectors are used to hook the NIC to the coaxial cable.

30. **C.** The server and software will not affect the speed of the token ring network. At least one card is running at 4 Mbps. A token ring network runs at the speed of the slowest card.

31. **A, C.** CSA/USA is not a method of network access. Some of the common ones are CSMA/CD, CSMA/CA, and token passing. Baton passing occurs in track and field.

32. **A.** A break in the fiber optic cable will disable all users on the token ring network for network activity.

33. **C.** The picture is of the ring architecture. Ethernet is a network topology and may use ring or star architecture.

34. **B.** The picture is of the bus architecture. Ethernet is a network topology and may use ring or star architecture.

**35.** **A.** The picture is of the star architecture. Ethernet is a network topology and may use ring or star architecture.

**36.** **A.** If the server goes down in a star network, the entire network is down.

**37.** **B.** The server is not accessible.

**38.** **B.** If the server goes down in a ring or bus network, only the server is not accessible.

**39.** **D.** The first thing to check is whether the network is working. If it is, check the physical connection from the PC. The power cord is not the problem, since the client did not report the computer as not working. If no changes in the machine were reported, it is probably not an IRQ conflict.

**40.** **B.** Since the client can still use Netscape, you know that the NIC is fine and the network is operational. If the company uses a network version of WordPerfect, and the client has it installed, the problem is that the server for WordPerfect is down.

**41.** **A.** The order of cable susceptibility to interference, from least to most, is: fiber optic, coaxial, STP, UTP.

**42.** **C.** Coaxial cable uses the 50-ohm terminators. You would never connect the shield to the wire and fiber optic has neither. You install special transceivers at both ends.

**43.** **B.** 25 ohms is not the right size terminator. Bad ground is not the problem, because there are grounds on each side of the backbone. The backbone is thicknet, and so 190 meters is not too long. For the exam, you should be able to recognize the symbol for ground, and you should know that you need one, as well as a terminator, on each end.

**44.** **A, B, C, D.** NIC cards and network adapter cards are the same thing. This is just another example in computers of having two terms for the same thing. NIC is used more often in the real world. A PC Card, if it is a modem or a NIC, can connect to the network. A modem can connect by dialing up, but it can be extremely slow. Jet Direct cards are used to connect network printers to the network.

**45.** **C.** Both consist of a central wire, a mylar plastic surrounding, a mesh of wires, and finally a rubber outside. Thicknet is just a larger gage than thinnet. These are both types of coaxial. On a TV cable, the end connector twists on to an adapter that looks like a screw. Computer wire uses a BNC connector that twists on about a quarter turn and is locked.

**46.** **A.** Broadband is the type of communication that coaxial uses. Broadband uses analog communications. Fiber uses baseband, which is a digital form of communications.

**47.** **A, D, E.** Remember, 100 meters = 328 feet. Learn all metric conversions for any topic that you are studying on A+. It would be a shame to miss a question just because you could not convert to metric, even though you understood what the question was asking.

**48.** **A, B.** Coaxial has a limitation of 180 meters. Just multiply 3.28 by the number of meters and you will get the amount of feet. (You may be wondering how cable TV companies span large distances. They use amplifiers.)

**49.** **A.** This question is asking about the most common speed that is used for fiber optics, not the maximum. Fiber optics travel at the speed of light, since they use pulses of light to communicate digitally. The problem is that the NIC cards cannot handle that much information at once. A circuit speed will never be equal to the speed of light. 100 megabits is the most common speed today. In the future expect to see quantum leaps in this realm of networking.

**50.** **B.** The four workstations connected to the hub would lose network connectivity. The whole network wouldn't go down unless the server running the other computers was on the bad segment. A segment is a portion of a network that is divided by routers, gateways, and bridges.

**51.** **B.** A LAN is Local Area Network. A WAN is a Wide Area Network. Answers A and C represent a WAN. A LAN is local by definition. At a minimum, it is two computers connected by a network wire, using some sort of protocol to communicate.

**52.** **E.** DHCP will automatically enter all of this information once it is enabled. In DHCP, the D stands for dynamic, which means automatic. If you enter static entries, they will always override dynamic when using DHCP.

**53.** **D.** 10baseT is for a twisted pair. Memory trick: T is for twisted.

**54.** **A, B, C, D.** Yes, network cards can have different adapters on them. The most common are 10Base2 and 10BaseT. Answers A and B are the same as answers D and C, respectively. These have a RJ-45 port and a BNC connector.

**55. A, D.** Token Ring networks are becoming obsolete. In order for a token passing scheme to work, the network must be a loop. Since a bus is a straight line, it is not a token passing network.

**56. A, B, C, D, E.** The DLC protocol seems to be thrown into many questions. Just understand that it is a valid protocol and you should be fine. The IPX/SPX is for Novell, and TCP/IP is the protocol of the Internet.

**57. A.** First of all, TCP/IP is great for connecting non-homogenous computers together. Second, by binding it first, it is the first protocol that will be used on the computer.

**58. A.** A packet is unit that is transferred on a network. A packet contains detailed information such as the destination and source of the packet, error-checking information, and various other types of information for each level of the protocol stack.

**59. A, E.** The question actually defines network access. CSMA/CD and CSMA/CA are examples of this.

**60. B, C, D.** Most network cards require these three items. The driver is usually included with the card. The IRQ and IO memory address should not conflict with other peripherals. The DMA channel is used on high performance NIC cards.

**61. C, D.** Dissimilar networks can not be simply connected into. The only way that different topologies can be connected is by a router or bridge, to keep each type in its own segment.

**62. A.** Twisted cable is the cheapest cable. UTP and STP are both twisted cables. One is Shielded Twisted Pair and the other is Unshielded Twisted Pair. Shielded Twisted Pair Cable actually has a shield wrapped around the pair of wires, thus making it more expensive that the UTP.

**63.** C. This is a bus network. This is not fiber, because it has 50-ohm terminators. A star network actually looks like a star, with cables coming out of a hub. A star bus is a hybrid of several star networks connected by a bus. A token ring requires a loop.

**64.** B. The main reason that twisted pair cable is constructed with each pair tightly twisted together is to reduce interference. This is known as common mode rejection. UTP has two categories, Category 3 and Category 5. The physical difference between the two is in the tightness of the twisting. Category 5 will support 100 Mbps while Category 3 is only good up to 10 Mbps.

**65.** C. The least expensive network cabling is unshielded twisted pair. ThinNet coax is more expensive per foot, and fiber optic is the most expensive per foot.

**66.** C. UTP is the correct acronym for unshielded twisted-pair cable. STP was used in early token ring networks, and FDDI is for fiber optic cable.

**67.** C. The correct impedance of a ThinNet coaxial network is 50 ohm. Nothing else will work. It's that simple. This is set up that way to reduce reflections on the LAN. Each end of the coaxial cable must be properly terminated or it won't work.

**68.** A. In a coaxial ThinNet network, each workstation will use a BNC T-connector to connect to the LAN. Remember that each end of this type of network must be terminated with a 50-ohm resistor, and one of the terminators MUST be a grounded type.

**69.** A. An ethernet network uses CSMA/CD, or Carrier Sense Multiple Access/ Collision Detection, for access control. Each NIC card listens for activity first before transmitting packets. When a collision is detected, both NIC cards stop transmitting and use a random timeout period before attempting to re-transmit.

**70.** **D.** The Granddaddy Protocol of them all, TCP/IP, requires that each host (PC) have a unique IP address. This address is assigned by a network administrator and requires additional configuration for this Internet-routable protocol to work.

**71.** **C.** The native Novell NetWare protocol is IPX/SPX. This is a routable protocol and is generally easier to configure than TCP/IP.

**72.** **B.** The de facto protocol for the Internet is IP, or Internet Protocol. It is commonly referred to by its proper long name of TCP/IP or Transport Control Protocol/Internet Protocol.

**73.** **B.** This NetWare protocol, IPX/SPX, stands for Internetwork Packet Exchange/Sequenced Packet Exchange. This is actually two protocols that work together. You can use either or both, depending on the requirements of the particular network application.

**74.** **C.** The NetBEUI protocol was designed for small office LANs. It is not routable but it has a very low overhead and is pretty responsive to traffic demands. This is the simplest protocol to configure. It is common on Microsoft networks.

**75.** **C.** A dial-up networking connection could be considered a WAN type of connection. This is commonly used when you connect to your ISP to browse the web. Dial-up networking is included in Windows 95 as an applet to control the modem and have it emulate a PPP connection to the Internet.

**76.** **D.** A requirement to connect two network nodes with a length of 1000 meters should be accomplished using fiber optic cable. You will need to use special termination equipment, transceivers, on each end of the fiber link to make this work. Transceivers usually attach to an AUI port on a Hub.

**77. A.** An ethernet Network Interface Card requires a Frame Type and IRQ. Some require a DMA channel, but those are generally considered to be high performance types of NIC cards and are usually found in a server rather than a workstation. Most NIC cards will also require an IO address.

**78. B, D.** The two common speeds for a Token Ring network are 4 Mhz, the older standard, and 16 Mhz, the newer standard. 10 Mhz and 100 Mhz are ethernet speeds.

**79. C.** Always respect the turf of the Network Administrator when you are working on a LAN for a business. You are a guest, so abide by the house rules regarding the LAN. This can be a great help to make your job go a lot smoother!

**80. B.** A small network with several workstations and no dedicated server is called a Peer to Peer network. Each workstation can share files and printing services with the rest of the LAN. Security and permissions are maintained individually on each workstation. This is also known as Share Level Security.

**81. A, C, D.** Common network problems include damaged cable, excessive traffic, and missing terminators. A fragmented hard disk is strictly a performance issue for the affected PC.

**82. C.** An Ethernet network uses Carrier Sense Multiple Access/Collision Detection (CSMA/CD) to sense for network activity before attempting to transmit a packet of data.

**83. B.** NetBEUI is an acronym for NetBIOS Extended User Interface. This is a simple, non-routable protocol designed for use on small office LANs.

**84. A, D.** The two common native NetWare frame types are Ethernet 802.2 and Ethernet 802.3. Oddly enough, the .3 version is actually the older of the two. Ethernet 802.2 is the default for Novell 3.12 – 4.11 systems.

# Customer Satisfaction

1. **C.** When repairing a computer, let the user explain the problem fully before starting to work on it. Many times the exam takes into account exceptions that the technician would run into if they did not listen fully to the customer and ask pertinent questions.

2. **A.** Look for nonverbal cues to help you know how to handle each situation. For example, if you are in a situation where you've been working on a PC for a long time, the user might just want you to leave and fix it the next day.

3. **C.** The relationship between you and the user is more important than a printer. Inform the user it's not the first time a printer has been broken. You shouldn't inform the user's boss.

4. **C.** After you have determined what the problem is by asking the customer, you should ask her what has changed with the computer since it was last working. Your questions may be answered right here. She may say, "It was working until a bolt of lightning hit it…"

5. **B.** When you have asked all of your questions, paraphrase what the user has said and say it back to him. Then ask him if this is what he said. This can be a question such as, "Just to make sure I understand the problem fully, let me say it back to you." Then state the problem and ask, "Is this what is actually happening?"

6. **B.** If you are calm about a situation, it calms the user. Reassure him. For example, if his problem is hardware related, let the user know that you have a part that you can swap for them and will be back later in the day to swap it. A calm user is a satisfied user.

**7.** **C.** Make sure that you are projecting the type of cues that you want the user to see. If you look anxious, then the user will start to feel anxious, because she thinks you might not know what you are doing. Users are already worried about their computers, and they don't need to get more worried about your skill.

**8.** **A.** Do you remember when you were not very experienced, and some techie was talking about EMS, HIMEM, and MSCDEX? No one likes to feel dumb, so put yourself in the user's shoes and treat him as you would like to be treated.

**9.** **C.** Take the extra time and give them hints if time permits. Try to explain the big picture to them. Show them how the directories are structured. These short lessons can save you and your company time in the long run. This may result in fewer phone calls to you, and more work getting done for the company.

**10.** **C.** When the customer views you as a person with whom they have a good rapport, they are less likely to withhold important information from you, and they will be more likely to cooperate with you. If you become their friend, then they will be more likely to cooperate with you.

**11.** **B.** What swearing tells people is that the technician has a bad attitude. They assume the technician is incompetent at fixing PCs. If you find yourself getting angry on the job and venting, you'd better ask yourself: Why am I being so negative?

**12.** **A, B, C.** Users are not very productive when you are working on their PCs. If they have work to do, you should consider rescheduling your visit. Also, make it a point not to appear as if you are eavesdropping on the user, and certainly don't interrupt a meeting to talk to the user.

13. **B.** If you have not worked with the user, or if you have any reservations about entering the workspace, then by all means don't go in. Try to contact them another way. This is to avoid working on the wrong computer, or violating someone's personal space, or even worse, maybe getting accused of stealing something.

14. **C.** Never do anything that even appears to be compromising in terms of integrity. Obey all software copyright laws. Never try to break into anything you should not be getting into. If a person tracks the files that you have opened, and you are going into confidential files, you will not have a fun time explaining yourself.

15. **C.** Although in some situations it may be wise to confront the user first, it is your job to notify management about the games without mentioning specific users. If you are found withholding information, you will look bad.

16. **B.** I know it is difficult, but you should give these users as much or more attention than the rest of the users. Quickly responding to their requests before they get angry is key to resolving disputes with these users.

17. **D.** Although you can save a lot of time by just fixing problems quickly and leaving, we need to make the users feel like we have tended to their needs, especially when they are visibly upset.

18. **C.** When working phone tech support, it is common to get an angry customer who is complaining about being transferred too many times, or being on hold too long. You must apologize for any inconvenience the customer may have experienced. This is the first step in calming an irate customer. Now that you have soothed the angry customer, you can begin by asking what you can do for the customer.

**19.** **A.** It is quite common to work on PCs that someone has accidentally misconfigured. Mistakes happen. If a computer was improperly configured by a technician in your department, insist it was a mistake, and apologize for the inconvenience. You do not want to leave the impression with the user that your department is not competent in what they do.

**20.** **A.** I have found that users don't mind calling in the troops to help with a problem. This makes the user feel you are trying to solve the problem quickly and get the user back up and running. Often, the user is missing valuable work time.

**21.** **B.** After introducing yourself, have the user explain the problem. Often he will explain something that reveals the problem, or eliminates the need for several tests. Then tell the user what you are going to do. Take your break before coming to the user.

**22.** **C.** You should ask the user about changes to the machine and the environment. The changes may well have caused the problem. Then explain the changes you are going to do and start. Always attempt to fix it in some way and, if you are stumped, tell the user that you are going to research the problem and when you plan to return.

**23.** **B.** You should summarize the problem the user has stated and then state your possible solution. After you have finished work, you can discuss the ball game.

**24.** **B.** You should first establish whether power is coming to the PC. Asking about the LED is a good way. Then ask the user to check if the computer may have been unplugged by accident, or the power strip turned off by accident.

**25.** **C.** You should always assume nothing about your customer's technical knowledge. Find out from them and use this information to help solve the problem.

**26.** **C.** Even if someone talks a lot about computers, he may only have a reading knowledge of the subject. Talk with him to establish his knowledge level. If he knew how to fix the computer, he would not have called you.

**27.** **B, D.** Always have the user confirm you have fixed the problem and then ask about any other problems. If there are any, fix them or note to yourself to return later. You should never leave without at least being civil. If it was a problem the user could fix, make sure he now knows how.

**28.** **B, D.** You should always own up to your errors. Customers know you are human and do not expect perfection, but do expect you to admit your errors and correct them.

**29.** **A.** You should always present a neat and clean appearance. Your customers choose the technician they use based not only on his knowledge, but also on how comfortable they are with him around.

**30.** **C, D.** The customers will treat you much better and be more likely to call you in the future if you are friendly and have a concern for their business. Although you may do the best job fixing a problem, if your attitude is bad, they do not want you around.

**31.** **B.** When arriving and seeing him on the phone, wait at the door and let him see you. Then back off where you are not eavesdropping.

**32.** **A, C.** If you run into a problem you cannot solve (and you will), you should tell the customer you need to research it. Talk to other technicians. They may know the solution instantly. Also, go read up on it. No one knows everything about PCs. Do not blame a previous technician, especially if you can't solve the problem.

**33. A, B.** You should never tell the user to leave. She may not be comfortable with you there. Let her know what you will do and whether you need her to leave the desk (not the office) or if you can work around her.

**34. B, D.** You should answer the question. Give pros and cons of both products and state your personal preference.

**35. B, D.** Show respect for this new user. Since no one showed him how to start the computer correctly, take time to make sure he can do it now. Speak in a language he understands. Your title already shows you are an expert.

**36. C.** You should allow the customer to explain the problem, then fix the problem. If it is still bad, get another monitor. Treat the customer with respect.

**37. A, C.** You should attempt to finish the job. If it gets too bad, get another technician to finish the job.

**38. B.** Removing the FORMAT command is not a good idea, as the customer will still need to format floppy diskettes. You should explain to the customer what happened and how it happened, and then fix it. Do not try to place blame.

**39. C.** You should follow company policy. Tell him it is against policy and do not fix it. Do not delete the files without allowing him to save his files first.

**40. A, C.** You should check if she has an Office Professional license. If so, install it. If not, tell her that company policy does not allow unlicensed software to be installed. As she has an Office license, do not uninstall it.

**41.** **D.** You should finish the repair and tell the user that they need a license for Office. If you erase the folder you may erase legitimate files.

**42.** **B, D.** Do whatever is in your power to not lay blame but to try to resolve the issue. UNDELETE is good for finding deleted files. The file search is great if the file got inadvertently moved to another directory. Look in the Recycle Bin, as well as on a floppy in the A: drive, as these are common hiding places for files.

**43.** **E.** This customer will understand that you have a page and will realize that he has to wrap things up. If he notices that you do not even look at the number, he will feel important. When he has finished explaining his problem, politely ask to use the phone. Let the people who page you page twice in an emergency situation. If it rings a second time, then you should look at the number and determine if it is appropriate to interrupt the customer.

**44.** **A.** Hearing the customer out is always the best solution. When taking the exam, if you see an answer that stresses listening to the customer, it is probably the right answer.

**45.** **E.** It would be best to find a cart, especially if the distance was long. This is one of those questions that those who have not been in the real business world will have no clue about. Those who have see all the other answers as ludicrous.

**46.** **E.** You save the customer embarrassment by not accusing him of anything. Also, the fact that this is company policy shows that your organization is prepared to act upon various potentially embarrassing situations.

**47.** **D.** Asking appropriate questions will show the user that you are taking interest in the problem at hand and will gain you the information you need to solve it.

**48.** **E.** The user wants to learn how to make a shortcut, not just have you create one for her. If you go too fast or use obscure shortcuts, the user will get lost. Try to discern the user's level of knowledge, and talk at a pace that she will understand.

**49.** **E.** You don't know that the person who asks you to repair the laptop is the person who spilled the coffee. Answer E is the best solution, since it does not blame the user and it accommodates him in the interim.

**50.** **A.** Your goal in terms of customer satisfaction is to have the customer confident and delighted. The other answers may be suitable for many situations, but this section of the exam is asking for the best answer.

**51.** **B.** It's best to come back at the customer's convenience. Sometimes users will allow you to stay late. You should then evaluate whether you should go the extra mile and get the thing working, or come back another day.

**52.** **C.** You should not try to get involved in conflicts. You should not involve your boss unless you have to, nor should you play detective, unless this is part of your job duties.

**53.** **B.** Telling someone to calm down may make him even more upset. Listen to what the customer has to say. YOU are the crisis specialist.

**54.** **C.** You should try to go that extra mile (or in this case, 10 miles) to satisfy the customer. You have to be flexible.

**55.** **C.** Correct answers are those that make the customer happy. Integrity is why A is wrong. Answer E is a company policy issue, which the exam is not testing you on.

**56.** C. While being late is sometimes unavoidable, you should leave a note to let the customer know you at least made a good faith effort to be there on time. If you page him/her, they may be in a meeting or in their car. Of course you should never be in this situation to begin with. If you know you are going to be late, let the customer know with a phone call ASAP.

**57.** C, D. Never promise anything that you are not absolutely sure you can deliver on. Show empathy, establish rapport, and report back to the user on what you have found out.

**58.** B. Answer B is nonchalant and does not clue the user in to the fact that you are watching his behavior. It does show that you appreciate that his time is valuable.

**59.** D. Use a repair visit as an opportunity to instruct the user. The user should be grateful, because you are empowering him.

**60.** A. The customer is always right. In this case it is possible that the user is right because he may be running some program that heavily taxes the computer's resources, and which no one but the user can see.

**61.** B. When answering any question that has anything to do with a customer's state of being, choose the answer that will leave them in the best state.

**62.** A, B, C, D, E. If you do not understand this, you may want to re-read the chapter in the companion Study Guide.

**63.** A, C, D. Most PC users in the workplace fit into one of these three categories. They may be intimately familiar with their own workstation, but most likely do not fully understand the operating system intricacies. Most do not fully understand things like DOS commands, or may know only a few basic ones, such as COPY or the DIR command. You have to be patient when assisting them with operating system commands, especially on a tech support issue over the telephone. They understand the particular business software package that they use everyday—probably better than you would—but they know little about their LAN. The network resources just magically appear via a logon script that they probably know nothing about. They can easily become frustrated when their daily work routine is interrupted or hindered by PC problems.

**64.** **C, D.** Setting up an on-site trouble log for a customer's LAN is a good idea because it shows the customer that you are genuinely concerned with their system and can also aid in working out difficult or intermittent problems. If you have several network accounts, it is difficult to remember what you did where last. A trouble log can also have a place for entries from the LAN users and can often give unique clues when viewed over a period of time. A log can also save you time and the customer money, especially if more than one technician is involved in a particular incident.

**65.** **B.** No matter how much experience we have "in the trenches", there is always the possibility that we will encounter a problem that seems to defy logical explanation. The clock is ticking and the customer is pacing the floor. The best procedure in this case is to explain the difficult nature of this problem to the customer and suggest that you research this issue with the proper manufacturer and return at a later date to finish the repair. Business customers never like to see a workstation leave the office, because that means a loss of productivity. Working for hours on end when you've run out of ideas usually results in unbillable hours and unhappy clients.

**66.** **A, B, D.** After listening to a customer's explanation of a particular PC problem, without interrupting, ask questions that demonstrate your concern and attentiveness to the customer's needs. The answers can be invaluable in troubleshooting the situation.

**67. B, C.** When you get an interruption such as a page or a telephone call, it is important that the customer you are working for does not feel put aside. If you get a page, check the number on the pager and try to determine if it can wait a few minutes. Try to finish up the part of the procedure you are working on and ask the customer if you could use the telephone. Never help yourself to someone's phone without asking first. Another tip that we use is to leave the beeper on vibrate mode. It is less disturbing to those working around you, and your client won't even know that you are being interrupted when you're working on their time. Explaining another customer's problems to your present customer will not benefit him in any way.

**68. B, C.** If you are working on a PC and the normal user is not there, ask to speak with his or her supervisor and try to confirm the reason for the service call. Never assume to know the problem without speaking to someone about it first. It is also a good idea to leave a note for the person who is absent, explaining what you did, along with a telephone number or pager number for them to contact you if they have any questions or problems. Never rearrange anyone's desk. People can get very territorial about their workspace.

**69. B, C.** If you need to work on a workstation that someone is using, it is always best to politely ask that person if he could save his work and let you sit down and work on that PC for a while. If he is trying to get something done under a deadline, you might ask if he is planning on taking a break soon and offer to come back at that time. Everybody has a job to do. Your job is no more important than your clients' work.

**70. A, C.** Working on a LAN system has special requirements and responsibilities. Maintaining the security of the LAN should be paramount in your duties. Never change anyone's password without specific instructions from the LAN Administrator. It is also prudent to maintain a friendly working relationship with the LAN Administrator. Request an Administrator- or Supervisor-level password, if necessary, for your own use, and maintain that security. Don't give your Supervisor password to anyone.

**71. C.** Office gossip and politics are definitely not part of your job description. Always try to avoid getting involved in such matters. It is unprofessional and will come back to haunt you or cost you a client.

**72. C, D.** It is not uncommon to show up on location to make a simple repair and get hit with a barrage of requests from office workers to help them with their other problems. Consider it a compliment to your skills when this happens. Listen carefully to the other issues to see if any of them may relate to the task at hand. There may be some valuable troubleshooting clues there. Most importantly though, work on what you came to do first. Try not to get distracted. Then get permission from the office manager before addressing the other issues mentioned.

**73. D.** Non-verbal communication can account for 80 percent of the message. Learn to read your customers and watch your own non-verbal messages.

**74. B, D.** Sometimes a temporary fix can be the best thing. Office workers often have deadlines, and if you can help get the work out then you can be a hero. If they have interoffice e-mail, a second choice might be to e-mail the report as an attachment to someone else on the LAN so that person can print it out.

**75. B, A, C, D.** The four levels of user competency listed in the correct order would be: novice, casual user, power user, and administrator. Watch out for the power users. They can be as much a problem as a help. Administrators usually have some LAN certification behind them. Be patient with the novices and frank with the casual users.

**76. B, C, D.** When someone has misconfigured a PC system, never say anything to make him feel stupid. His honesty could be important to your efforts to undo his mistake. Share some of your experience in this same area with the customer. Correct the errors, and while doing so, try to explain how to avoid these problems in the future.

**77. A, B.** Good rapport with a customer will result in the customer being more honest with you when he knows that he did something wrong. This will make it easier for you to fix the problem. Customers are more likely to trust your abilities as a technician when they like you.

**78. B.** Talking with customers about things other than PCs gives them a chance to shine in their own light and feel good about themselves. They will view you as someone other than a PC nerd. It helps to break the ice and build a good rapport.

**79. B, C.** The workplace is a good place to build professional relationships and gain referrals to other potential customers. Word of mouth is your best form of advertisement.

**80. A.** To maintain a professional appearance you should avoid wearing heavy cologne. Save it for the nightclubs. Taking showers regularly is a better solution than the cologne. Keeping a your hair trimmed, and wearing neat clothing, will gain you respect.

**81. B, C, D.** Blaming other people, or getting angry at inanimate objects, shows poor character. If you are having a difficult time, take some time out to reassess the situation.

**82. C, D.** After an upgrade has been performed on a customer's PC, the old parts still belong to them. Offer the customer or business for which you are working a trade-in credit for these parts against the bill. Another option would be to suggest to the customer that they might use the parts on another PC at their business. This could generate more business for you!

**83. A, B, D.** Before leaving the job site, it is always a good idea to demonstrate to the customer that the problem you were called to fix is repaired.

Cleaning up your mess will ensure that you don't make any enemies. Asking if there is anything else to repair is good business.

**84.** **A, B, C.** If you at least take the time to listen to the problem, then the customer won't feel slighted. Sometimes your next appointment may not be ready yet, and you can take care of the additional issue on the spot, and save a return trip.

# Part 2

## Windows/DOS

# Practice
# Questions

*Q & A*

T he A+ question pool is very large and you never know what kind of questions will be on the exam. The questions in this book are meant to help you determine what you still need to study. They cover all the subject areas that CompTIA has said are relevant. By looking at these questions as a way to alert you to what you need to study further, you will end up being a much better technician than if you just memorized the questions and answers.

The style of the A+ exam is very similar to what follows. You may find that there are more single-answer choices on the exam. The rationale behind having more multiple answers in these questions is to try to prepare you for the worst that the exam will throw at you. The exam makers claim that there are no trick questions. Be on your guard, though, for tricky questions or questions that, if you do not read them carefully, you might misread. Always think of what they are trying to test you on. Chances are they will be asking you about things that commonly occur, as opposed to some obscure exception to the rule that was not covered in the literature. Watch out for acronyms and terms that you have never heard before.

# Function, Structure, Operation, and File Management

1. Which file is COMSPEC specified in?

   A. CONFIG.SYS

   B. COMMAND.COM

   C. AUTOEXEC.BAT

   D. SYSTEM.INI

2. Which of the following is not required for operating system startup?

   A. IO.SYS

   B. MSDOS.SYS

   C. COMMAND.COM

   D. CONFIG.SYS

**3.** Which of the following files displays the DOS prompt?

A. IO.SYS

B. COMMAND.COM

C. MSDOS.SYS

D. AUTOEXEC.BAT

**4.** Which of the following are Windows 3.*x* system files? (Choose all that apply.)

A. GDI.EXE

B. USER.DAT

C. WIN.INI

D. SYSTEM.INI

**5.** Which of the following files no longer contains system code when used with Windows 95?

A. IO.SYS

B. COMMAND.COM

C. MSDOS.SYS

D. GDI.EXE

**6.** Windows 95 only runs in _____ mode, so there is only one kernel.

A. Protected

B. User

C. Real

D. Virtual Real

**7.** When you use the FORMAT C: /S command, DOS formats the C: drive and places the system files on the hard disk. Where is the pointer placed to find these system files?

A. On the boot partition

B. In the boot sector

C. In the boot record

D. In the BOOT.INI file

8. In the following table, insert the required parameter for the ATTRIB command:

| | |
|---|---|
| R | Read Only file attribute |
| A | Archive file attribute |
| S | System file attribute |
| H | Hidden file attribute |
| | Processes files in all directories in the specified path |

A. /P
B. /D
C. /S
D. /A

9. You do not need to specify the extension when executing which types of file? (Choose all that apply.)

A. BAT
B. COM
C. SYS
D. EXE

10. If I have three files in the same directory called GO.BAT, GO.EXE, and GO.COM, what is the hierarchy in which they will be executed?

A. BAT then COM then EXE
B. COM then EXE then BAT
C. EXE then COM then BAT
D. BAT then EXE then COM

exam
ⓦatch    **COMMAND.COM displays the DOS prompt.**

**11.** Rather than putting all available functions into a single huge executable file, most DOS developers create library files with what extensions?

A. .BIN and .TMP

B. .OVL and .DLL

C. .BIN and .OVL

D. .TMP and .DLL

**12.** What does the CTRL-ESC keystroke combination do in Windows 95?

A. Opens My Computer

B. Opens the Start menu

C. Opens Network Neighborhood

D. Opens Explorer

**13.** A user is complaining that his hard disk appears to be getting slower. You sit down at his computer, which is running DOS 5.0 and Windows 3.*x*, and open a command prompt window. What will happen when you try to run DEFRAG?

A. You cannot run DEFRAG in a DOS box

B. You must change to the DOS directory first

C. DEFRAG is not compatible with Windows 3.*x*

D. DEFRAG is not available with DOS 5.0

**14.** What will happen when SCANDISK encounters a bad cluster during a scan?

A. Nothing

B. SCANDISK will repair the cluster

C. SCANDISK will attempt to save the information from the cluster, and mark the cluster as bad.

D. SCANDISK will attempt to save the information from the cluster, and attempt to fix the cluster.

15. Program Manager in Windows 3.*x* stores information concerning the program groups in files with what extension?

    A. PRG
    B. GRP
    C. PRO
    D. GRO

16. Where are the individual groups to be loaded by Program Manager located?

    A. USER.DAT
    B. PROGMAN.DAT
    C. PROGMAN.INI
    D. WIN.INI

17. What type of multitasking requires that an application voluntarily relinquish control of the CPU?

    A. Non-preemptive
    B. Preemptive
    C. Linear
    D. Cooperative

18. In the following table, fill in the missing shortcut.

|        | Print |
|--------|-------|
| CTRL-X | Cut   |
| CTRL-C | Copy  |
| CTRL-V | Paste |

    A. CTRL-F5
    B. CTRL-F1
    C. CTRL-P
    D. CTRL-L

**19.** How many files can be held in the DOS root directory?

A. 128

B. 256

C. 512

D. 1024

**20.** Text-based operating systems for PCs include:

A. DOS

B. Windows 95

C. Windows 3.1

D. UNIX

**21.** There are a number of 32-bit operating systems. These systems include:

A. DOS

B. OS/2

C. Windows NT

D. Windows 3.1

**22.** Which of the following files are required to start DOS?

A. AUTOEXEC.BAT

B. COMMAND.COM

C. CONFIG.SYS

D. IO.SYS

**23.** The customer calls and complains about his DOS prompt. He wants you to change it. In what file do you put the change?

A. AUTOEXEC.BAT

B. COMMAND.COM

C. CONFIG.SYS

D. SYSTEM.INI

**24.** In DOS, what actually displays the DOS prompt?

    A. AUTOEXEC.BAT

    B. COMMAND.COM

    C. PROMPT

    D. CONFIG.SYS

**25.** A customer has a hard disk that was a slave drive and now is a master drive. She cannot get the system to start. Without erasing the hard disk, what command should she use to get DOS to start on it?

    A. FORMAT C:/S

    B. FDISK

    C. SYS

    D. This cannot be done

**26.** In DOS, filenames are limited to a length of:

    A. 254 characters

    B. 8 characters

    C. 8 characters period 3 characters

    D. no limit

**27.** You have a new, right-out-of-the-box hard disk. To use that hard disk you must perform what steps first?

    A. FDISK, FORMAT

    B. FORMAT, FDISK

    C. It is ready to use

    D. FDISK

**28.** To copy all the files and subdirectories from one directory to another use the _____ command.

A. XCOPY /S

B. XCOPY

C. COPY

D. COPY /S

**29.** Internal commands are part of _____.

A. AUTOEXEC.BAT

B. COMMAND.COM

C. CONFIG.SYS

D. IO.SYS

**30.** DOS chooses the file to run by its extension in the order of:

A. .BAT, .COM, .EXE

B. .COM, .BAT, .EXE

C. .BAT, .EXE, .COM

D. .EXE, .BAT, .COM

**31.** A customer calls and says he used XCOPY to copy the files on his disk. However, the new file names are shorter, and many have tildes in them. What happened?

A. DOS does not copy Windows 95 long file names

B. He should have used Windows 95 to copy the files

C. He is looking in the wrong place

D. File names cannot contain tildes

**32.** In DOS the command to list the directory of files is called:

A. DIR

B. DIRECTOR

C. TREE

D. LD

**33.** When you are changing floppy disks in Windows 95, and you want to update the directory on the screen, press the _____ key.

A. F1
B. F5
C. F10
D. Can't be done

**34.** Directories were examined in Windows 3.1 by using File Manager. Windows 95 allows you to use:

A. File Manager only
B. Windows Explorer only
C. File Manager and Windows Explorer
D. Internet Explorer

**35.** While Windows 95 is running, a task locks up. To shut down the task you may:

A. Restart the computer
B. Press ALT-CTRL-DEL and end the task
C. The task cannot be ended
D. CTRL-C

**36.** All directory entries are stored in the _____ on the disk.

A. File Allocation Table (FAT)
B. File directory
C. File Assistance Tab (FAT)
D. Root directory

**37.** Entries that control how the desktop looks in Windows 3.x are located in the _____ file.

A. WINDOWS.INI
B. SYSTEM.INI
C. WIN.INI
D. CONFIG.SYS

**38.** Four of the attributes that are stored on a file in DOS are:

A. Read, system, read/write, share

B. Read, write, system, hidden

C. Read, write, hidden, archive

D. Read, system, hidden, archive

**39.** Plug and Play means that:

A. Solitaire is available when the machine starts

B. Windows 95 recognizes and installs new devices

C. The computer can be plugged in and run

D. When a CD is placed in the CD drive, it plays automatically

**40.** Which of the following are located in the root directory?

A. IO.SYS

B. MSDOS.SYS

C. HIMEM.SYS

D. ANSI.SYS

E. CONFIG.SYS

**41.** What displays the DOS prompt?

A. IO.SYS

B. MSDOS.SYS

C. PROMPT.EXE

D. COMMAND.COM

E. None of the above

**42.** Where does Windows look for the device driver KEYBOARD.DRV?

A. WIN.INI

B. AUTOEXEC.BAT

C. CONFIG.SYS

D. SYSTEM.INI

E. ANSI.INI

**43.** Where do you load the MOUSE.COM?

A. WIN.INI

B. AUTOEXEC.BAT

C. CONFIG.SYS

D. SYSTEM.INI

E. ANSI.INI

**44.** Where is the DEVICE=C:\WINDOWS\HIMEM.SYS line located?

A. AUTOEXEC.BAT

B. CONFIG.SYS

C. WIN.INI

D. SYSTEM.INI

E. None of the above

**45.** On a 486DX Windows computer the Expanded Memory is controlled by:

A. EMM386.EXE

B. EMM486.EXE

C. PAGEFILE.SYS

D. HIMEM.SYS

E. LOADDOS HIGH command

**46.** Smartdrive is a program that is used by:

A. Hard disk caching

B. CD-ROM caching

C. Windows 95

D. DOS

E. Universal drivers used on generic peripherals

**47.** You want to rename a file in DOS from C:\A to C:\B. Which of these commands will work?

A. RENAME C:\A C:\B
B. COPY C:\A C:\B then press ENTER and type **DEL C:\B**
C. RN C:\A C:\B
D. ATTRIB C:\A C:\B
E. REN C:\A C:\B

**48.** What is the effect of typing **ATTRIB -R C:\A** at the DOS prompt? ("A" is a read only file.)

A. It stays read only
B. It changes to not read only
C. Nothing, since the command has the wrong switch
D. The file is hidden
E. None of the above

**49.** What DOS command can be used to detect the presence of hidden files?

A. DIR
B. SCANDISK
C. CHKDISK
D. DRWATSON
E. ATTRIB

**50.** If you want to copy a whole hard disk to another, which of the following commands will work?

A. XCOPY /E /H
B. XCOPY /S /E /H
C. XCOPY /S /E /W /H
D. XCOPY /S /E /C /H
E. XCOPY /S /E /C /Y /H

**51.** If you have just formatted a floppy and you want to make it bootable, what can you do?

A. Start | Control Panel | Add/Remove Software | Startup Disk | Create Disk
B. Type SYS C: at the DOS prompt
C. Copy AUTOEXEC.BAT to the disk
D. Copy IO.SYS to the disk
E. Copy COMMAND.COM to the disk

52. Where can Buffer= and Files= be found?

    A. AUTOEXEC.BAT
    B. CONFIG.SYS
    C. WIN.INI
    D. SYS.INI
    E. SYSTEM.INI

53. Which of the following are DOS system files?

    A. MSDOS.COM
    B. COMMAND.COM
    C. HIMEM.SYS
    D. EMM386.EXE
    E. ANSI.SYS

54. Where is LOAD HIGH used?

    A. CONFIG.SYS
    B. SYSTEM.INI
    C. WIN.INI
    D. AUTOEXEC.BAT
    E. SYS.INI

55. A user has locked the screen saver with a password, quit his job, and left town. You reboot to DOS and edit which file to reset the password?

A. AUTOEXEC.BAT

B. CONFIG.SYS

C. SYSTEM.INI

D. WIN.INI

E. SCRSVR.BAT

**56.** The bulk of the Windows 95 file is in the:

A. SYSTEM.INI

B. SYSTEM.DAT

C. CONFIG.SYS

D. WIN.INI

E. USER.DAT

**57.** In Windows 95, how do you get to the screen shown here?

A.  CTRL-ESC | SETTINGS | CONTROL PANEL | PASSWORDS

B.  Start | Settings | Control Panel | Passwords

C.  Start | Settings | Control Panel | Network

D.  Start | Settings | Control Panel | Network | Protocol | Properties

E.  Start | Settings | Control Panel | Passwords | Protocol | File and Print Sharing

**58.** What is the extension of the Windows 95 shortcuts shown here?

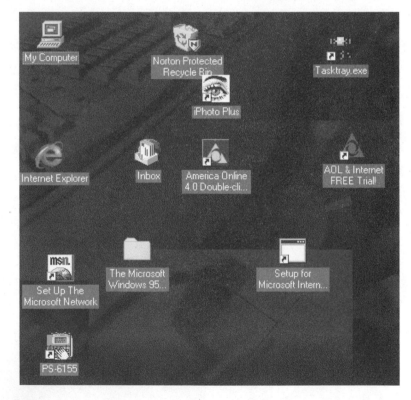

A.  TIF

B.  LNK

C.  SCT

D.  EXE

E.  SHC

**59.** What are the main functions of an operating system? (Choose all that apply.)

A. Defines input and output devices

B. Creates a document

C. Provides instructions for the CPU to operate on data

D. Creates a spread sheet

**60.** DOS consists of two basic types of commands. What are they?

A. Executable

B. Internal

C. Compiled

D. External

**61.** The processor in the Macintosh is based on the _____ family of processors known as the _____ series.

A. Intel

B. Motorola

C. 80x86 series

D. 680XX series

**62.** With the development of the 80386 chip, the processor and system memory are able to read and write how many bits of data per clock cycle?

A. 16

B. 8

C. 32

D. 64

**63.** Which file attribute prevents a file from being deleted? (Choose all that apply.)

A. -H

B. +S

C. +R

D. D +A

**64.** Which of the following is an example of an internal DOS command? (Choose all that apply.)

A. EDIT

B. DIR

C. COPY

D. FDISK

**65.** Which DOS system files are NOT required for system startup? (Choose all that apply.)

A. COMMAND.COM

B. HIMEM.SYS

C. IO.SYS

D. AUTOEXEC.BAT

**66.** Which two Windows 3.*x* system files are ASCII files and may be edited with a text editor if necessary?

A. GDI.EXE

B. WIN.INI

C. WIN.COM

D. SYSTEM.INI

**67.** Which Windows 3.*x* file configures specific hardware devices and their associated settings?

A. WIN.INI

B. SYSTEM.INI

C. PROTOCOL.INI

D. API.INI

**68.** Which two Windows 95 files remain mainly to satisfy backwards compatibility with 16-bit Windows 3.*x* applications?

A. USER.DAT

B. SYSTEM.DAT

C. WIN.INI

D. SYSTEM.INI

**69.** Which leftover file in Windows 95 no longer contains system code, but allows for special system settings to be user defined?

A. IO.SYS

B. MSDOS.SYS

C. ANSI.SYS

D. HIMEM.SYS

**70.** You need to run Windows 3.*x* in standard mode, so you enter the command WIN /S at the DOS prompt. You receive an error message stating that a file is missing. Which file is most likely missing when you receive this error message?

A. WIN386.EXE

B. HIMEM.SYS

C. DOSX.EXE

D. WIN.COM

**71.** You are working on a customer's Windows 3.*x* PC and you notice that the Main program group is missing several applets. How can you easily repair this problem?

A. Using the customer's Windows disk, set Reinstall Windows

B. From Program Manager click File Run and enter **SETUP /P** to restore the default program groups

C. Copy all of the *.GRP files from another PC to this one

D. Edit the SYSTEM.INI file

**72.** You encounter a hard disk that will no longer boot. After booting with an emergency boot floppy and running an anti-virus program, you successfully remove the virus that infected the boot sector of the hard disk. What command could you use to restore the boot record of the hard disk?

A. FORMAT

B. FDISK /MBR

C. MIRROR

D. RESTORE

**73.** You wish to partition a hard disk. After carefully backing up all the data on the drive, which DOS command would you use to create a primary and secondary DOS partition?

A. FORMAT /U

B. FDISK

C. SYS

D. SCANDISK C:

**74.** You want to set up a PC so it automatically starts Windows 3.*x* upon bootup. Which lines should you be sure are in the AUTOEXEC.BAT?

A. PATH C:\DOS;C:\WINDOWS

B. LOADHIGH WINDOWS

C. WIN

D. EXEC WIN.COM

exam
ⓦatch    *Familiarize yourself with the networking capabilities of each of the OSs, as there are invariably questions about this on the exam.*

**75.** A customer claims that he cannot print large print jobs using Windows 3.*x* Print Manager. You note that his C: drive only has about 5MB of available space on it, but he has a D: drive with over 200MB of space available on it. What two things should you do to give Windows Print Manager more room to spool print jobs?

A. Create a new directory located at D:\TEMP
B. Tell the customer you have to format the C: drive to get more space for the print spooler
C. Edit the AUTOEXEC.BAT file so the line SET TEMP=D:\TEMP replaces the old TEMP variable line
D. Edit the WIN.INI file to modify the print spooler path

**76.** You need to copy the entire contents of a floppy disk to a directory on a hard disk called LANCARD. What would be the best command and syntax to use to accomplish this task?

A. COPY *.* A: C:\LANCARD
B. XCOPY A\*.* C\
C. XCOPY A:\*.* /S C:\LANCARD
D. XCOPY A:\*.* /S /E C:\LANCARD

**77.** If you wanted to protect a file from being overwritten, what command and syntax should you use?

A. ATTRIB -R <filename>
B. ATTRIB +R <filename>
C. ATTRIB -A <filename>
D. None of the above

**78.** A customer complains that whenever he holds down the arrow to navigate along text lines on his Windows 95 PC, there is a delay before it moves.

The repeat function needs to be adjusted. What should you adjust in the applet shown here?

A. The Repeat Delay
B. The Repeat Rate
C. Both the Repeat Delay and Repeat Rate
D. None of the above

**79.** Referring to the following illustration, which tab should you click to see a display showing a tree of devices in the Windows 95 system?

A. Hardware Profiles

B. Device Manager

C. Performance

D. None of the above

# Memory Management

**1.** Basically, all memory above the 1024KB line is considered _____.

A. Expanded memory

B. Extended memory

C. High memory

D. Reserved memory

**2.** Where can a portion of the DOS operating system be loaded?

   A. Expanded memory

   B. The high memory area

   C. Extended memory

   D. Reserved memory

**3.** What became known as "upper memory"?

   A. The first 64KB of the high memory area

   B. The first 384KB of extended memory

   C. The reserved 384KB of the first 1024 of memory

   D. The last 64KB of reserved memory

**4.** Expanded memory swapped portions of memory called _____ in and out of upper memory.

   A. Frames

   B. Pages

   C. Registers

   D. Segments

**5.** What are the two functions of EMM386.EXE? (Choose all that apply.)

   A. Enables expanded memory

   B. Controls extended memory

   C. Enables the use of the high memory area

   D. Enables the use of upper memory as system memory

**6.** How can you force EMM386 to use specific regions of upper memory?

   A. Specify the area of memory with the INCLUDE switch

   B. Specify the area of memory with the FORCE switch

   C. Use HIMEM.SYS

   D. Use FCBS

**7.** How can you tell whether a specific driver is being loaded in conventional or upper memory?

    A. Type the MEM command

    B. Type the MEM /P command

    C. Type the MEM /C command

    D. Type the MEM /D command

**8.** You are called out to troubleshoot a user's system that receives an Illegal Operation error after a few minutes in the operating system. What is most likely the problem?

    A. Bad memory module

    B. Parity error

    C. Application error

    D. Expanded memory paging error

**9.** Which of the following is the extended memory manager?

    A. HIMEM.SYS

    B. EMM386.EXE

    C. HIMEM.EXE

    D. EMM386.SYS

**10.** What information will you see when you type the MEMINFO command in DOS 5.0?

    A. Amount of conventional memory

    B. Amount of reserved memory

    C. Number of drivers loaded into memory

    D. Nothing. There is no such command.

**11.** Based on the following excerpt from a CONFIG.SYS file, what appears to be the problem?
DEVICE=C:\DOS\EMM386.EXE
DEVICE=C:\DOS\HIMEM.SYS

DOS=UMB,HIGH
DEVICEHIGH=C:\Display\DISPLAY.SYS

A. The DOS=UMB,HIGH command will not work

B. HIMEM.SYS is being loaded after EMM386.EXE

C. The DEVICEHIGH line is incorrect

D. HIMEM does not have the proper parameter to load DOS into the high memory area

12. What are two features of HIMEM.SYS? Choose two from the following:

A. It is the expanded memory manager

B. It can create the high memory area

C. It is the extended memory manager

D. It can create the high memory area from the last 64KB of reserved memory

13. Which of the following attributes lead you to believe you have more hard disk space on your computer than you do?

A. Read-only

B. System

C. Hidden

D. System

14. What is one advantage of using SCANDISK rather than CHKDSK?

A. SCANDISK can repair errors on floppy drives

B. SCANDISK can repair physically bad clusters on a hard disk

C. SCANDISK can correct lost clusters on a compressed drive

D. SCANDISK can repair lost partitions

15. Which of the following is the upper memory manager?

A. MEMMAKER
B. HIMEM.SYS
C. EMM386.SYS
D. EMM386.EXE

**16.** What is the name for a memory resident program that stays in memory, even when not being used?

A. MEM
B. TSR
C. OVL
D. TMP

**17.** Virtual memory refers to what process?

A. The process of swapping data in and out of reserved memory
B. Using a file on the hard disk to simulate RAM
C. Swapping memory from extended to expanded
D. Using extended memory to simulate expanded memory

**18.** How can the AUTOEXEC.BAT file be used to decrease the amount of conventional memory used?

A. You can load some drivers from the AUTOEXEC.BAT instead of the CONFIG.SYS
B. You don't have to specify the use of the AUTOEXEC.BAT, which frees up conventional memory
C. You can load software in the AUTOEXEC.BAT file to force programs into high memory
D. None of the above

**19.** The first 640KB of memory are referred to as:

A. Conventional memory
B. Upper memory
C. Extended memory
D. High memory area

20. When installing SIMM memory modules you can determine the correct direction to install the modules by:

A. Notches in the chips
B. Notch in the middle of the pins
C. Notch on one end of the module
D. They can be installed either way

21. You are looking at a memory module thought to be a DIMM module. How many pins would be on a DIMM module?

A. 30 pins
B. 72 pins
C. 168 pins
D. 16 pins

22. You are working on an older PC and discover it is using a RAMDRIVE. A RAMDRIVE is:

A. The same as virtual memory
B. Memory that works like a hard disk
C. Used to permanently store information
D. A hard disk that appears to be RAM

23. Checking the hard disk while running Windows 3.1, you discover a very large file called 386SPART.PAR. What is this file?

A. Windows temporary swap file
B. Windows permanent swap file
C. A temporary file created when installing Windows 3.1
D. A temporary file created when installing DOS

**24.** When checking virtual memory on Windows 3.1 on a machine that does not seem to run Windows as fast as it should, you notice it has a temporary swap file. Should you change it?

A. Yes, a permanent swap file runs Windows faster

B. No, a temporary swap file runs Windows faster

C. Yes, a permanent swap file is removed at the end of Windows

D. No, a temporary swap file is removed at power down

**25.** To install DIMM modules into the motherboard you will:

A. Place the module at a 45 degree angle in the socket, then bring it to a vertical position

B. Line up all the metal tabs and press straight down

C. Line the module straight over the socket and press down

D. Lay the module in position and screw it down

**26.** The system BIOS and ROM chips are called:

A. Software

B. Hardware

C. Firmware

D. Bootware

**27.** Which of the following operating systems use conventional, upper, and extended memory?

A. Windows 95

B. DOS

C. Windows NT

D. Windows 3.1

**28.** Memory chips that are pressed individually into the motherboard are:

A. DIP

B. SIMM

C. DIMM

D. ROM

29. A customer calls and says he needs some SIMM modules. What type processor should he have?

A. 486

B. 386

C. Pentium

D. Pentium Pro

30. The computer runs for various periods of time before giving an "out of memory" message. The possible reason is:

A. Bad hard disk

B. Badly seated memory chips

C. Bad power supply

D. Virus

31. You have a 486 PC. You have bought SIMM modules for it. When you attempt to install them you discover they do not fit. What is the problem?

A. 486s do not use SIMM

B. You have the wrong type of SIMM (30- or 72-pin)

C. You are installing in the wrong socket

D. You cannot add RAM to a 486

32. The Microsoft program that allows you to display various reports of memory usage is:

A. MEMMAKER.EXE

B. MSD.EXE

C. QEMM.EXE

D. MEM.EXE

**33.** The Microsoft program that displays information about various items of the system and shows memory conflicts is:

A. MEMMAKER.EXE

B. MSD.EXE

C. QEMM.EXE

D. MEM.EXE

**34.** What is the program that fixes disk errors caused by files that were left in an open status?

A. DEFRAG

B. SCANDISK

C. FAT

D. MEMMAKER

**35.** What program made by Microsoft is similar to SCANDISK in fixing disk errors?

A. CHKDSK

B. MEMMAKER

C. QEMM

D. DEFRAG

**36.** The customer reports that he is at a DOS prompt and cannot start Windows 3.1. Windows was working an hour ago. What is the problem?

A. Windows not on machine

B. They have gone to the Windows DOS prompt

C. Windows is damaged

D. Virus

37. You are getting memory errors and you think that it is because your software is conflicting with your motherboard. What should you do first to solve the problem?

A. Contact the vendor for updates and patches

B. Test the motherboard with Norton Utilities

C. Swap out the motherboard with an identical PC

D. Low-level format your drive

E. Run MEM /C /P /Z

38. What is XMS?

A. Incorporates DPMI and VCPI to work harmoniously

B. A form of EMS

C. Non-volatile

D. Expanded Memory

E. Extended Memory

39. What is EMS?

A. Incorporates DPMI and VCPI to work harmoniously

B. A form of XMS

C. Non-volatile

D. Expanded memory

E. Extended memory

40. What does EEPROM stand for?

A. Electronically Executable Programmable Read Only Memory

B. Electronically Erasable Programmable Read Only Memory

C. Extended Erasable Programmable Read Only Memory

D. Expanded Erasable Programmable Read Only Memory

E. Expanded Executable Programmed Read Only Memory

**41.** If you want to load DOS high what should you do?

A. Include DOS = High in the CONFIG.SYS

B. Include DEVICE=HIMEM.SYS in the CONFIG.SYS

C. Add stacks = 9526 in the CONFIG.SYS

D. Include DOS = High in the AUTOEXEC.BAT

E. Include DEVICE=HIMEM.SYS in the AUTOEXEC.BAT

**42.** Which of the following is the fastest?

A. IDE

B. EIDE

C. PCI

D. ROM

E. RAM

**43.** If you want to force EMM386 to stay out of a specific region of upper memory, what would you do?

A. Use Virtual Memory settings in the 386 enhanced applet

B. Run MEMMAKER

C. Use the INCLUDE switch in the CONFIG.SYS

D. Change this setting in MSD

E. Use the EXCLUDE switch in the CONFIG.SYS

**44.** The LIM memory specification renamed system memory to:

A. Standard

B. Expanded

C. Extended

D. High

E. Conventional

**45.** You have formatted a hard disk and just loaded Windows 95 and Microsoft Word. You are getting an insufficient memory message in Microsoft Word when you open it for the first time to create a new document. What should you do?

A. Start | Control Panel | System | Virtual Memory

B. Start | Control Panel | System | Performance | Virtual Memory

C. Run MSD

D. Run MEMMAKER

E. Buy more RAM

**46.** What are the two major functions that EMM386.EXE performs?

A. Enables and controls XMS

B. Enables and control EMS

C. Enables the upper memory as system memory

D. Enables the conventional memory as system memory

E. Dynamically avoids memory errors

**47.** If you get an illegal operation, what is recommended after rebooting?

A. Run SCANDISK

B. Run CHKDSK

C. Run DEFRAG

D. Re-install software

E. Increase swap file size

**48.** Where is conventional memory located?

A. Up to 640KB

B. Above 1040KB

C. Between 640KB and 1024KB

D. Above 1024KB

E. Above 384 and below 1024KB

**49.** Where is extended memory located?

A. Up to 640KB

B. Above 1040KB

C. Between 640KB and 1024KB

D. Above 1024KB

E. Above 384 and below 1024KB

**50.** Where is upper memory located?

A. Above 384 and below 1024KB

B. Up to 640KB

C. Above 1040KB

D. Between 640KB and 1024KB

E. Above 1024KB

**51.** Where is HMA located?

A. Above 1040KB

B. Between 640K and 1024KB

C. 1024KB through 1088KB

D. Above 1040KB

E. Between 640KB and 1024KB

exam

ⓦatch

*Physical memory consists of the hardware that handles memory in a PC. This memory is stored in chips that are either: ROM—read only memory chips, or RAM—random access memory.*

**52.** Memory that is getting paged to a hard disk is called:

    A. Virtual Memory

    B. Extended Memory

    C. Upper Memory

    D. High Memory

    E. Cached memory

**53.** Almost all Pentium series contain _____ -pin SIMMs.

    A. 30

    B. 36

    C. 56

    D. 64

    E. 72

**54.** How do you get to the screen shown here?

A. Start | Settings | Control Panel | System | Memory

B. Start | Settings | Control Panel | System | Performance

C. Start | Settings | Control Panel | System | Performance | Virtual Memory

D. Start | Settings | Control Panel | System | Performance | Advanced

E. Start | Programs, then right-click MS-DOS prompt | Properties

**55.** As shown here, what command was just run?

A. MEM /D

B. MEM /F

C. MEM /M

D. MEM /S

E. MEM /T

**56.** Which type of memory can be considered to be volatile memory?

A. SRAM

B. DRAM

C. ROM

D. None of the above.

57. What types of RAM need to be refreshed at a regular rate? (Choose all that apply.)

A. SRAM

B. DRAM

C. EDO RAM

D. ROM

58. What type of ROM can be reprogrammed? (Choose all that apply.)

A. DRAM

B. ROM

C. EPROM

D. FLASH RAM

59. In a DOS-based PC, the memory is addressed using what two forms of addressing?

A. direct

B. offset

C. simple

D. segment

60. In a PC, the first 1MB of memory is divided as follows: The first 640KB is system memory. The additional 384KB is known as:

A. Upper memory

B. Lower memory

C. Basic memory

D. Reserved memory

**61.** The LIM memory specification was developed by which three major manufacturers?

   A. Lexmark, Intel, and Microsoft
   B. Lotus, Intel, and Microsoft
   C. Lotus, Intuit, and Microsoft
   D. Lotus, IBM, and Microsoft

**62.** The original 808x processor could only access how much RAM?

   A. 1024KB
   B. 8MB
   C. 16MB
   D. 640KB

**63.** All memory above the 1024KB border is considered _____ memory.

   A. Extended
   B. Expanded
   C. High
   D. Conventional

**64.** DOS, version _____ and above can load part of its system code above the 1024KB area.

   A. 3.2
   B. 5.0
   C. 6.0
   D. 6.22

**65.** Microsoft developed the DOS Protected Mode Interface (DPMI) for XMS management. What other XMS system, developed by Phar-Lap Corp., used to be available?

A. XPMS
B. VPMS
C. VCPI
D. PLMS

66. Upper memory would include the area between _____ and
_____ .

A. 640KB and 1024KB
B. 1024KB and 1082KB
C. 0KB and 640KB
D. 1082KB and above

67. You wish to take advantage of the upper memory area to load device
drivers. Which line must you have added to your CONFIG.SYS to allow
this feature?

A. DEVICE=HIMEM.SYS
B. DEVICE=EMM386.EXE
C. DEVICE=DOUBLESPACE
D. DEVICE=DRIVESPACE

68. You need to make use of memory above 1024KB in an 80386 PC. What
must you add to the CONFIG.SYS to allow the use of page frame
swapping?

A. DEVICE = C:\DOS\HIMEM.SYS
B. DEVICE = C:\DOS\EMM386.EXE
C. DEVICE = SMARTDRVE.SYS /XMS
D. None of the above

69. According to the screen display shown here, which devices are loaded in the
upper memory area?

```
Modules using memory below 1 MB:
Name          Total              Conventional        Upper Memory
--------   ----------------    ----------------    ----------------
MSDOS        33,856  (33K)       33,856  (33K)           0    (0K)
TEAC_CDI      7,344   (7K)        7,344   (7K)           0    (0K)
HIMEM         1,120   (1K)        1,120   (1K)           0    (0K)
DBLBUFF       2,448   (2K)        2,448   (2K)           0    (0K)
IFSHLP        2,864   (3K)        2,864   (3K)           0    (0K)
SETVER          832   (1K)          832   (1K)           0    (0K)
WIN           3,744   (4K)        3,744   (4K)           0    (0K)
Vmm32         5,216   (5K)        5,216   (5K)           0    (0K)
COMMAND       8,560   (8K)        8,560   (8K)           0    (0K)
Free        589,104 (575K)      589,104 (575K)           0    (0K)
Memory Summary:
Type of Memory      Total          Used          Free
----------------   -----------   -----------   -----------
Conventional         655,360        66,256       589,104
Upper                      0             0             0
Reserved             393,216       393,216             0
Extended (XMS)    40,894,464       180,224    40,714,240
----------------   -----------   -----------   -----------
Total memory      41,943,040       639,696    41,303,344
Total under 1 MB     655,360        66,256       589,104
Largest executable program size           589,088   (575K)
Largest free upper memory block                 0     (0K)
MS-DOS is resident in the high memory area.
```

A. TEAC_CDI.SYS

B. IFSHLP

C. SETVER

D. None of the above

**70.** If you load part of the DOS operating system high, where in memory does it load?

A. Above 640KB

B. In the first 64KB above 1024KB

C. In the upper 64KB of low memory

D. None of the above

**71.** You get a new NIC card to install in a customer's PC. The card has no jumper or switch settings on it. How would you set the resources for this device?

    A. Solder in a DIP switch and set it to the address you need

    B. Check the CMOS settings in the PC for conflicts

    C. Use the soft set utility disk that came with the card to set resources

    D. Nothing, it must be a plug and play card if it has no DIP switches or jumpers

**72.** When installing an EISA network card, how would you set the resources to avoid a memory conflict?

    A. Set the jumpers on the card to plug and play mode

    B. Use the EISA utility that came with the PC, adding the correct configuration file that came with the card

    C. Set the CMOS peripheral device settings as specified by the PC manufacturer

    D. Install a diagnostic utility to resolve the conflict

**73.** You have to install a PCI-based NIC card in a workstation. Where can you set the resources for this card's IRQ setting?

    A. With the utility disk that came with the card

    B. In the CMOS PCI Settings screen

    C. Use the DIP switch settings on the card

    D. They cannot be set; it must be plug and play compliant

exam
ⓦatch

*DIP chips are physically soldered to a motherboard. SIMMs are chips that are soldered to a small board that is installed into a slot on the motherboard. Using SIMMs allows the memory to be easily replaced.*

# Installation, Configuration, and Upgrading

**1.** What happens when Windows 95 detects a new device on your computer but does not have a driver for the device?

    A. Windows 95 will not load a driver, and you will have to return to Device Manager to configure the device

    B. Windows 95 will install the closest driver for the device

    C. Windows 95 will ask you for the name of the device so it can search for the driver

    D. Windows 95 will ask you for the driver

**2.** What is the utility for partitioning disks with Windows 95?

    A. FDISK

    B. Disk Administrator

    C. WINDISK

    D. MSD

**3.** What is the maximum size of a partition in Windows 95?

    A. 1GB

    B. 2GB

    C. 2.5GB

    D. 4GB

**4.** Which little-known internal utility can you use to help load device drivers in DOS?

    A. DRIVLOAD

    B. EDLIN

    C. ANSI.SYS

    D. There is no such utility

**5.** Which of the following files is required for Windows 95 to load properly?

A. CONFIG.SYS

B. AUTOEXEC.BAT

C. SYSTEM.DRV

D. None of the above

6. Once you have installed Windows 95, how can you boot straight into DOS mode?

A. Configure the CONFIG.SYS

B. Configure the AUTOEXEC.BAT

C. Press F8 on system startup

D. Press F5 on system startup

7. You have just formatted a computer and installed DOS 6.22 and Windows 3.*x*. When you restart the computer, it boots up into DOS. What appears to be the problem?

A. You did not have a successful install of Windows 3.*x*

B. Windows 3.*x* does not start by default

C. You need to configure the BOOT.INI to load Windows 3.*x* on startup

D. You need to press F8 on system startup to start Windows 3.*x*

8. Which of the following does Windows 95 Plug and Play automatically configure and track resources for? (Choose all that apply.)

A. DMA channels

B. Port identifiers

C. IRQ assignments

D. I/O Memory addresses

9. Windows 3.*x* will not run unless:

A. HIMEM.SYS has been loaded

B. EMM386.EXE has been loaded

C. Expanded memory is made available

D. Memory has been reserved

**10.** Which Windows 95 CONFIG.SYS settings have been incorporated into the IO.SYS? (Choose all that apply.)

A. FILES=

B. DOS=HIGH

C. SHELL=COMMAND.COM

D. HIMEM.SYS

**11.** Look at the following excerpt from a Windows 95 file. What file are these from?

Logo=1

BootMenu=1

BootMulti=0

A. IO.SYS

B. MSDOS.SYS

C. SYSTEM.INI

D. BOOTLOG.TXT

**12.** When Windows 95 is installed and a SYSTEM.INI is detected, the settings will be migrated to the Registry, and the SYSTEM.INI will be renamed to what?

A. SYSTEM.W95

B. SYSTEM.BAK

C. SYSTEM.WIN

D. The SYSTEM.INI file will not be renamed

**13.** What do both DOS and Windows 3.*x* require in order to boot?

A. A temporary swap file

B. A permanent swap file

C. They both need to be booted from the first partition of the master hard disk

D. They both need secondary partitions set to active

**14.** What is the purpose of the EBD.SYS file?

A. A driver for booting in Safe Mode

B. It makes a startup disk

C. It is a universal display driver

D. It is the driver used during the detection phase in setup

**15.** What is one advantage of Windows 3.1 running in 386 Enhanced mode?

A. You can run more than one application at a time

B. Drivers are not required for system-level devices

C. You can emulate 386 hardware-based processing activity

D. You can run DOS applications that are not compatible with Windows

**16.** Examine the following excerpt from a Windows 95 file. What is this excerpt from?

Loadsuccess=c:\windows\himem.sys

loadsuccess=c:\windows\setver.exe

loadsuccess=c:\windows\dblbuff.sys

A. DETLOG.TXT

B. BOOTLOG.LOG

C. BOOTFILE.TXT

D. BOOTLOG.TXT

**17.** Which of the following commands is not commonly found in the CONFIG.SYS file?

A. SHELL

B. PATH

C. LASTDRIVE

D. SET

**18.** Of the following, which is not an option for controlling the boot process when using DOS 6.2?

A. F5

B. F8

C. F4

D. CTRL-F5

**19.** If you were to configure CONFIG.SYS with the following entries listed below in the diagram, what would happen on startup?
[MENU]
MENUITEM=GAMES
MENUITEM=NOGAMES
MENUDEFAULT=WORK,10

A. Nothing. This is invalid because NOGAMES is not accessible.

B. DOS will default to the WORK configuration after 10 seconds if a choice is not made.

C. DOS will start the GAMES configuration.

D. Nothing. This is invalid because another parameter required for [MENU] is not specified.

**20.** You have a hard disk that is not bootable. What option is available to make it bootable?

A. Since the drive was not originally made bootable, it never can be

B. Use FORMAT with /S

C. Use SYS command

D. Use BOOT command

**21.** You have a new hard disk. You need to set up the partitions on it. To do the partitioning you will use which utility?

A. PARTITION

B. FDISK

C. FORMAT

D. SETUP

**22.** When DOS is installed, how are device drivers installed?

    A. Manually adding them to AUTOEXEC.BAT and CONFIG.SYS

    B. Automatically detecting and loading drivers for all devices

    C. Using a setup program supplied by the device manufacturer

    D. Automatically adding them to AUTOEXEC.BAT and CONFIG.SYS

**23.** When Windows 95 is installed, how are device drivers installed?

    A. Manually adding them to AUTOEXEC.BAT and CONFIG.SYS

    B. Automatically detecting and loading drivers for all devices

    C. Using a setup program supplied by the device manufacturer

    D. Automatically adding them to AUTOEXEC.BAT and CONFIG.SYS

**24.** When preparing to install Windows 95, what hardware would fit the requirements? (Choose all that apply.)

    A. Pentium processor with 16MB of memory

    B. 486DX processor with 4x2MB of memory

    C. Cyrix 586 processor with 4x16MB of memory

    D. AMD K6 processor with 16MB of memory

**25.** When a PC starts up, what is the standard sequence of events?

    A. Attempt to boot the floppy drive then the hard disk

    B. Attempt to boot the hard disk then the floppy drive

    C. Always only boot from the floppy drive

    D. Always only boot from the hard disk

**26.** During the startup of Windows 95, what mode will Windows 95 start up in to allow you to correct configuration errors?

    A. Normal mode

    B. Safe mode

    C. DOS mode

    D. Windows 95 mode

**27.** When using Plug and Play in Windows NT 4.0, what resources are configured by Windows 95 for new devices?

A. IRQ

B. IO memory addresses

C. Plug and Play is not supported

D. DMA addresses

**28.** When Windows 95 is installing a device using Plug and Play, where does Windows 95 look for the drivers, and in what order?

A. Windows 95 library of drivers, Windows 95 source disks, user supplied disks

B. User supplied disks, Windows 95 source disks, Windows 95 library of drivers

C. Windows 95 library of drivers, user supplied disks, Windows 95 source disks

D. Windows 95 source disks, Windows 95 library of drivers, user supplied disks

**29.** When a device is not operational in DOS, where do you look to see if the device drivers are installed?

A. COMMAND.COM

B. AUTOEXEC.BAT

C. IO.SYS

D. CONFIG.SYS

**30.** When you are attaching a printer to Windows 95, you should:

A. Run the Printer wizard

B. Run the Add New Hardware wizard

C. Run the Add/Remove Software wizard

D. Use the Control Panel

**31.** You are working with Windows. You decide that there is something that needs changing in the AUTOEXEC.BAT or CONFIG.SYS file. Can this be done?

A. Both files are user changeable

B. Both files are system encrypted

C. Both files have no user information

D. Only the AUTOEXEC.BAT file is user changeable

**32.** When working with a new disk drive on a personal computer, using DOS, Windows 3.*x*, or Windows 95A, what is the maximum partition size?

A. 8 gigabytes

B. 6 gigabytes

C. 2 gigabytes

D. 500 kilobytes

**33.** A customer reports that she cannot get out on the network in Windows 95. Everything appears fine to her, and she reports that even Windows 95 says it is safe to use. What is the problem?

A. Bad network card

B. Started in Safe mode

C. Started in Normal mode

D. Bad CONFIG.SYS file

**34.** What files are required in the root directory to start DOS?

A. COMMAND.COM

B. CONFIG.SYS

C. AUTOEXEC.BAT

D. WIN.COM

**35.** After going through the Windows 95 installation, Windows 95 restarts the computer, then:

A. Windows 95 is ready

B. It sets up Plug and Play devices

C. It has you edit the AUTOEXEC.BAT and CONFIG.SYS files

D. Prompts you for the CD key

**36.** When upgrading from Windows 3.1 to Windows 95, Windows 95 will do what with your previously installed software?

A. Erase all Windows 3.1 software

B. Set the software to run in Windows 95

C. Display a list of all the software the user must reinstall

D. Notify the user that Windows 3.1 software must be upgraded to the Windows 95 version

**37.** Before doing an operating system upgrade, what should you always do?

A. Back up the hard disk

B. Format the hard disk

C. Buy new versions of all software

D. Destroy all copies of the old operating system

**38.** On a machine that uses Windows 3.*x*, what happens after DOS loads to cause Windows 3.*x* to load?

A. Windows 3.*x* automatically loads

B. Windows 3.*x* loads if it is in the AUTOEXEC.BAT file

C. Windows 3.*x* loads if it is in the CONFIG.SYS file

D. Windows 3.*x* loads when directed by the user

**39.** What does Microsoft say are minimum requirements for running Windows 95?

A. 386SX-20

B. 386DX-20

C. 386DX-25

D. 486SX-25

E. 486DX-33

**40.** Which operating system will support FAT32?

    A.  DOS

    B.  Windows 95

    C.  Windows 95b

    D.  Windows NT 3.51

    E.  Windows NT 4.0


**41.** What is the maximum partition size under DOS?

    A.  540MB

    B.  1GB

    C.  1.2GB

    D.  2GB

    E.  3GB


**42.** You want to dual boot Windows 3.11 and Windows 95. What file would you modify?

    A.  BOOT.INI

    B.  AUTOEXEC.BAT

    C.  IO.SYS

    D.  MSDOS.SYS

    E.  WIN.INI


**43.** You have a video game that will not run under Windows 95 and you want to try it under DOS. You press the Start button and choose Restart in MS-DOS Mode. What else is this mode called?

    A.  DOS Mode

    B.  Virtual DOS

    C.  DOS Compatibility Mode

    D.  Conventional DOS

    E.  Real Time DOS

**44.** What is the same as typing FORMAT C: /S?

A. SYS C:

B. FORMAT /A /C

C. FDISK /FORMAT /S

D. All of the above

E. None of the above

**45.** If you want to check the partition for errors, which format switch should you use?

A. /A

B. /B

C. /C

D. /D

E. /E

**46.** In Windows 95, what can you edit the AUTOEXEC.BAT and the CONFIG.SYS with?

A. Notepad

B. Wordpad

C. Microsoft Works

D. Shell out to DOS and run EDIT

E. Choose Run: SYSEDIT

**47.** Which of the following files are in SYSEDIT?

A. PROTOCOL.INI

B. SYS.INI

C. WIN.INI

D. AUTOEXEC.BAT

E. CONFIG.SYD

**48.** What is the first step to solving printing problems?

A. Change the spooler settings
B. Delete and re-install the drivers
C. Use the Print Troubleshooter
D. Clean the printer
E. Swap printer cables

49. What is the command to upgrade Windows 3.1 to Windows 95?

A. INSTALL
B. SETUP
C. UPGRADE
D. RUN
E. None of the above

50. You have a SCSI chain with a non-system hard disk on 001 and 110. When will a drive with the ID of 010 boot in relation to a normal boot process?

A. First
B. Second
C. Third
D. Fourth
E. Fifth

51. What is the correct sequence to re-install all of your programs and operating systems, while deleting your old files?

A. FORMAT, FDISK, SYS C:, install operating systems and software
B. FDISK /S, FORMAT, install operating systems and software
C. FDISK, FORMAT /S, SYS C: /E, install operating systems and software
D. FDISK, FORMAT C: /S /C, CHKDSK /F, install operating systems and software
E. FDISK, FORMAT, SYS C:, install operating systems and software

52. How many different primary modes will Windows start in?

A. 1
B. 2
C. 3
D. 4
E. 5

**53.** Windows 95 Plug and Play configures and tracks the following resources:

A. DDE
B. OLE
C. MAPI
D. IO Memory
E. DMA addresses

**54.** If you are having problems with a piece of hardware, which of the following is the best fix?

A. Go to the Device Manager, look at the IRQs, DMAs, and memory addresses and see if any are conflicting. Delete the culprit, reboot, accept the new hardware if correct.
B. Decompile the driver and re-write it to your liking
C. Change the bus that they are in
D. Spray the contacts with denatured alcohol
E. All of the above are good techniques

**55.** You install an old DOS program, but the program made no icon. What should you do if you want an icon?

A. Right-click Desktop, choose New | Shortcut, then command line
B. Install the program from Add/Remove Programs in Control Panel
C. Right-click and drag and drop the program from Explorer
D. Go to Start | Settings | Taskbar | Start Menu
E. Right-click result of answer D and drag onto desktop, then choose Create Shortcut

**56.** As shown here, what does the exclamation point by the Communications Port signify?

A. Bad driver

B. IRQ conflict

C. Memory problem

D. Disabled hardware

E. Not enough information to answer this question

**57.** What file is shown here?

```
;SYS
[Paths]
WinDir=C:\WINDOWS
WinBootDir=C:\WINDOWS
HostWinBootDrv=C

[Options]
BootMulti=1
BootGUI=1
Network=1
;
;The following lines are required for compatibility with other programs.
;Do not remove them                be >1024 bytes).
;xxxxxxxxxxxxxxxxxxxxxxxxxxxxxxxxxxxxxxxxxxxxxxxxxxxxxxxxxxxxxxxxxxxxxxxxa
;xxxxxxxxxxxxxxxxxxxxxxxxxxxxxxxxxxxxxxxxxxxxxxxxxxxxxxxxxxxxxxxxxxxxxxxxb
;xxxxxxxxxxxxxxxxxxxxxxxxxxxxxxxxxxxxxxxxxxxxxxxxxxxxxxxxxxxxxxxxxxxxxxxxc
;xxxxxxxxxxxxxxxxxxxxxxxxxxxxxxxxxxxxxxxxxxxxxxxxxxxxxxxxxxxxxxxxxxxxxxxxd
;xxxxxxxxxxxxxxxxxxxxxxxxxxxxxxxxxxxxxxxxxxxxxxxxxxxxxxxxxxxxxxxxxxxxxxxxe
;xxxxxxxxxxxxxxxxxxxxxxxxxxxxxxxxxxxxxxxxxxxxxxxxxxxxxxxxxxxxxxxxxxxxxxxxf
;xxxxxxxxxxxxxxxxxxxxxxxxxxxxxxxxxxxxxxxxxxxxxxxxxxxxxxxxxxxxxxxxxxxxxxxxg
;xxxxxxxxxxxxxxxxxxxxxxxxxxxxxxxxxxxxxxxxxxxxxxxxxxxxxxxxxxxxxxxxxxxxxxxxh
;xxxxxxxxxxxxxxxxxxxxxxxxxxxxxxxxxxxxxxxxxxxxxxxxxxxxxxxxxxxxxxxxxxxxxxxxi
;xxxxxxxxxxxxxxxxxxxxxxxxxxxxxxxxxxxxxxxxxxxxxxxxxxxxxxxxxxxxxxxxxxxxxxxxj
;xxxxxxxxxxxxxxxxxxxxxxxxxxxxxxxxxxxxxxxxxxxxxxxxxxxxxxxxxxxxxxxxxxxxxxxxk
```

For Help, press F1

A. COMMAND.COM
B. MSDOS.SYS
C. IO.SYS
D. BOOT.INI
E. CONTROL.INI

**58.** In order for a hard disk to be bootable it must have what type of partition?

A. Passive
B. Large
C. Symmetric
D. Active

**59.** Windows 95 OSR2 (aka Windows 95B) will support hard disks larger than 2GB, because it uses a:

A. 16-bit FAT system
B. 32-bit FAT system
C. DoubleSpace
D. DriveSpace

**60.** You need to make a hard disk bootable but do not want to loose the data on the drive. What command can you use to accomplish this?

A. FDISK
B. FORMAT /S
C. SYS
D. SCANDISK

**61.** Most devices used with a PC require a:

A. Serial number
B. User interface
C. Device driver
D. All of the above

**62.** In DOS, device drivers are loaded in the:

A. AUTOEXEC.BAT
B. CONFIG.SYS
C. MSDOS.SYS
D. COMMAND.COM

**63.** You are having problems getting a Windows 95 machine to boot. What key can you press when Starting Windows 95 appears on the screen, to temporarily modify the startup options?

A. F9

B. F8

C. F3

D. F2

**64.** To start DOS in interactive mode, you can press what key when the screen displays Starting MS-DOS?

A. F5

B. F3

C. F8

D. None of the above

**65.** To add new devices in Windows, which icon shown here would you click?

A. Add/Remove Software

B. Display

C. Add New Hardware

D. See if the device is listed, and click the appropriate icon

**66.** You need to set some of the configuration settings for Windows 95. Which of the icons shown here would you click to start that process?

A. The C: Drive icon

B. The Printers folder

C. The Control Panel folder

D. The Dialup Networking folder

**67.** Windows 95 Plug and Play will automatically track which resources of devices? (Choose all that apply.)

A. IRQ settings

B. DMA settings

C. Base addresses

D. All of the above

**68.** To install a new device in Windows 95, a file is usually required that describes that device to the operating system. What type of file is required?

A. CNF

B. INF

C. COM

D. CFG

**69.** A device listed in Device Manager with a ! next to it means what? (Choose all that apply.)

A. The device is excited

B. The device driver has failed to load properly

C. There is a resource conflict between that device and another one

D. The device driver is corrupted

**70.** Windows 3.x will not run without which DOS driver?

A. ANSI.SYS

B. HIMEM.SYS

C. EMM386.EXE

D. KBD.SYS

**71.** What command in Windows 95 allows easy access to most of the text-based configuration files?

A. SYSEDIT

B. REGEDIT

C. EDIT

D. CONTROL PANEL

**72.** When modifying a WIN.INI file, Fred deleted a line that he thought was causing a problem. Now Windows won't run at all. What would have been a better method for him to use to modify the suspect line in the configuration file?

A. Copy the entire file to another file name for backup

B. Re-Install the operating system to correct the original problem

C. Comment out the suspect line rather than deleting it

D. FDISK the drive first

**73.** If you want to comment out a line in the WIN.INI. What character should you use?

A. :

B. ;

C. #

D. !

**74.** To format a floppy disk and make it bootable, you must use which of the following command syntaxes?

A. FORMAT /U

B. FORMAT /L

C. FORMAT /S

D. FORMAT /Q

**75.** In order to run older DOS programs it may be necessary to do what? (Choose all that apply.)

A. Edit the properties for the icon shortcut

B. Run Windows 95 in DOS mode

C. Set up a dual boot PC with Windows 95 and DOS

D. All of the above

**76.** To set up Windows 95 on a Microsoft network, what do you need to purchase? (Choose all that apply.)

A. A NIC

B. Network cabling

C. Network software

D. All of the above

# Diagnosing and Troubleshooting

**1.** What can you do as a workaround to the "Incorrect DOS version" error?

A. Start up the computer with a boot disk that disables the VER feature

B. Enter the SETUP utility to disable ROM shadowing

C. Use SETVER to disable the VER feature in BIOS

D. Use SETVER to report another version of DOS

**2.** How do you remedy the problem of a corrupt swap file in Windows 3.x?

A. Delete the PAGEFILE.SYS file from the root directory and reboot the computer

B. Go to the 386 Enhanced section of the Control Panel and remove the swap file

C. Go to the Virtual Memory section of the Control Panel and remove the swap file

D. Delete the PAGEFILE.TMP from the root directory and reboot the computer

**3.** What are two causes for the "Missing or Corrupt HIMEM.SYS" error in Windows 95?

A. The operating system is corrupt, because Windows 95 does not need HIMEM.SYS

B. Your CONFIG.SYS may be referencing a missing HIMEM.SYS file

C. The HIMEM.SYS file may not be in the correct directory

D. The HIMEM.SYS file is from another version of DOS

**4.** What mode allows execution of some older MS-DOS applications that are not capable of running in Windows 95?

A. Real

B. Vitual Real

C. MS-DOS Compatibility

D. Protected

WINDOWS/DOS QUESTIONS

**5.** Which icon in the Control Panel do you use to create a Windows 95 startup disk?

    A. System

    B. Add/Remove Programs

    C. Devices

    D. You do not create a Windows 95 startup disk from the Control Panel

**6.** What can you do to fix a print spool that's been stalling?

    A. Restart the computer

    B. Delete the print job

    C. Stop and restart the printing service

    D. Restart the print spooler

**7.** What is the most common cause of a printer printing garbled characters after being installed?

    A. The print processor or print driver is not correct

    B. The printer cannot handle the speed of the print job

    C. The printer is set to uni-directional

    D. The printer was not installed correctly

**8.** Mary, the receptionist, was able to log on to the network yesterday, but today she cannot. She insists nothing has changed since yesterday. Which of the following is most likely NOT the problem?

    A. The network is down

    B. Mary has loaded the wrong network driver

    C. A cable may be damaged or broken

    D. Mary's password may be expired or her account is locked out

**9.** Ron is having trouble with a new device on his Windows 3.1 computer. You need to quickly determine his system settings. Which is the quickest and most detailed means of gathering this information?

A. The Control Panel

B. CMOS Setup

C. MSD

D. File Manager

10. What can you do if you are infected with a boot record virus?

A. Run SCANDISK

B. Type FDISK /MBR

C. Run CHKDSK

D. Run FDISK /BR

11. What is the difference between the Windows-based SCANDISK and the DOS-based SCANDISK?

A. The DOS version could not check for lost clusters

B. The Windows version can automatically fix problems

C. The DOS version could not fix cross-linked files

D. The Windows version can stop lost clusters before they happen

12. How can you configure a DOS application to use more memory?

A. Using the MEM command

B. Adjusting the shortcut for the application

C. Using the Control Panel

D. Specifying an entry in the AUTOEXEC.BAT

13. What is the most difficult virus to remove from a computer?

A. CMOS virus

B. Memory virus

C. FAT virus

D. Boot Sector virus

**14.** What is the easiest way to fix a startup or boot problem?

    A. Inspect the boot sector

    B. Rerun the Setup program that came with the operating system

    C. Use the FDISK /MBR command

    D. Repair the boot sector with the SYS command

**15.** What is the purpose of dynamic memory allocation?

    A. To use just enough memory to boot your computer

    B. To optimize the extended memory by paging it to disk

    C. To give enough memory to applications, and take memory away when not needed

    D. To assign memory addresses to device drivers that do not have onboard memory

**16.** You are trying to run a DOS application that frequently causes illegal operations errors. What should you do to get the application running correctly?

    A. Modify the FILES= line in the CONFIG.SYS

    B. Force the application to run in MS-DOS mode

    C. Give the application more memory

    D. Configure the application to use the Windows 95 swap file

**17.** Which utility can speed up the performance of your machine?

    A. MSD

    B. SCANDISK

    C. DEFRAG

    D. CHKDSK

**18.** Which type of virus may cause you to lose data? (Choose all that apply.)

A. FAT virus

B. CMOS virus

C. Boot sector virus

D. Macro virus

**19.** You received an error when trying to use the modem on your computer. How can you quickly determine the port that the modem is connected to?

A. Use MSD

B. Use CMOS Setup

C. Use the PORT command

D. Use the MODE command

**20.** You are attempting to run an older software package. You get the message "Wrong Windows Version". What is the problem?

A. Program is designed to run only in DOS

B. Program is designed to run on a different version of DOS

C. Program will run only on Windows 95

D. Program cannot be used on this PC

**21.** The program you want to run requires DOS 4.0 but you are using DOS 6.22. What command will fix this problem?

A. SCANDISK

B. DEFRAG

C. COMMAND.COM

D. SETVER

**22.** You get the message "Error in CONFIG.SYS line 20". To correct this error you should:

A. Check that the driver on line 20 is present

B. Fix the CONFIG.SYS file

C. Remove the CONFIG.SYS file

D. Run SCANDISK

23. When attempting to run Windows 3.1 you get a message saying, "HIMEM.SYS is not loaded". What file should you look in to see if HIMEM.SYS is loaded?

A. AUTOEXEC.BAT

B. CONFIG.SYS

C. COMMAND.COM

D. WIN.INI

24. During the startup of Windows 95, what mode will Windows 95 start up in to allow you to Run older DOS games?

A. Normal mode

B. Safe mode

C. DOS mode

D. Windows 95 mode

25. A customer reports he cannot get out on the network in Windows 3.1. He saw some error flash by as the machine started. What is the problem?

A. Bad network card

B. Started in Safe mode

C. Started in Normal mode

D. Bad AUTOEXEC.BAT file

26. What Microsoft program allows you to set and display the attributes for files in DOS?

A.  FDISK
B.  DEFRAG
C.  ATTRIB
D.  MSD

**27.**  Computer viruses are:

A.  Always destructive
B.  Always hoaxes
C.  May be destructive
D.  May be hoaxes

**28.**  What Microsoft program is used to check disk drives for errors and can fix them in DOS?

A.  FDISK
B.  DEFRAG
C.  SCANDISK
D.  ATTRIB

**29.**  What Microsoft program do you use to create and delete partitions on a hard disk?

A.  FDISK
B.  DEFRAG
C.  ATTRIB
D.  MSD

**30.**  What Microsoft program is used to check disk drives for errors and can fix them in Windows?

A.  FDISK
B.  DEFRAG
C.  SCANDISK
D.  ATTRIB

**31.** In Windows 95, the settings for the system are entered where?

A. CONFIG.SYS

B. Registry

C. AUTOEXEC.BAT

D. SYSTEM.INI

**32.** A customer who just bought a computer from you yesterday calls frantically. He tells you the computer says he performed an illegal operation. What do you tell him?

A. Bring the computer in for repair

B. Choose OK and restart the program

C. Explain that one of the programs told the CPU to do something it can't

D. Explain that he told the CPU to do something that the CPU can't do. Tell him not to do it again.

**33.** Which of the following are Windows-based tools?

A. SCANDISK.EXE

B. DEFRAG.EXE

C. SYSEDIT.EXE

D. Control Panel

E. System General Properties

**34.** What is the right context to correct an "incorrect version" error message and make a file named C:\WRONG, which is in version 6.0, think it is in DOS 6.22?

A. SETVER COMMAND.COM 6.22 C:\WRONG

B. SETVER. 6.22 C:\WRONG

C. SETVER. C:\WRONG 6.22

D. SETVER. C:\WRONG /6.22

E. SETVER. C:\WRONG 6.0 6.22

**35.** Windows 3.*x* needs which of the following to load?

A. DEVICE=C:\WINDOWS\HIMEM.SYS in the CONFIG.SYS

B. DEVICE=C:\WINDOWS\HIMEM.SYS in the AUTOEXEC.BAT

C. HIMEM.SYS in the Windows directory

D. Buffers = 9256

E. Files = 40

**36.** If you get the error message "operating system not found," what are the first three things you should do?

A. Check the power cord to the hard disk to see if it is loose.

B. Check the network cable

C. Run the setup disk to troubleshoot

D. Run SYS C:

E. Test the hard disk to see if it is working

**37.** You get a VFAT initialization failure in Windows 95. What should you do?

A. Load DOS high

B. Run FDISK /MBR

C. Run the setup disk

D. Reboot with Safe Mode

E. Run SCANDISK

**38.** Which of the following are ways to make a startup disk with utilities on Windows 95?

A. Through the online help

B. Start | Settings | Control Panel | Windows Setup

C. Format A: /S

D. Start | Settings | Control Panel | System | Startup Disk

E. Start | Settings | Control Panel | Add/Remove Programs | Startup Disk

**39.** On a Windows 95 machine, you find that the spooler is stalled. What should you do?

    A. Turn it back on through the Registry

    B. Change the print driver to the correct one

    C. File | Properties | Restart Printing from the Printer window after highlighting the printer

    D. Restart the spooler services in the SERVICE directory

    E. Reboot and resubmit the print job

**40.** If you type format A: /S, what files will you have on your floppy?

    A. COMMAND.COM

    B. MSDOS.SYS

    C. IO.SYS

    D. DRVSPACE.BIN

    E. CONFIG.SYS

**41.** What is the best solution to the problem of having a bi-directional driver and printer, but a uni-directional cable?

    A. Disable bi-directional printing in the CMOS

    B. Disable bi-directional printing in the printer setup

    C. Disable bi-directional printing in the printer itself

    D. Get a bi-directional cable and install it

    E. None of the above

**42.** An incorrect printer driver can be changed from:

    A. Detail tab of the Printer Properties dialog box

    B. Control Panel | Drivers

    C. Control Panel | Printing

    D. A download file

    E. None of the above

**43.** You are trying to run a program and it will not load. What should you do?

    A. Reboot

    B. Re-install the application

    C. Check the network connections

    D. Uninstall the old application

    E. Save customized settings and put them in the newly installed program

**44.** What is the most important thing to remember about FDISK?

    A. Not to use the /MBR switch on older machines with drives larger than 540MB

    B. That your needed data is backed up

    C. To format the disk after using it

    D. To run SYS C:

    E. To use the right filing system

**45.** You suspect errors on a Workgroup for Windows (WFW) dual boot Windows 95b machine. Which of the following should be run from WFW?

    A. CHKDSK

    B. SCANDISK

    C. DEFRAG

    D. MEMMAKER

    E. None of the above

**46.** You have just installed a new piece of hardware. You boot up and Windows 95 detects a conflict. What program is automatically started?

    A. Conflict Troubleshooter

    B. Device Manager

    C. Hardware Wizard

    D. DOS

    E. Safe mode

*The Microsoft Diagnostics utility can be used to provide information about the system. This information can be valuable in determining if a workstation is capable of being upgraded.*

**47.** How do you get into the Registry in Windows 95?

A. REG.EXE

B. REGEDIT.EXE

C. REG32.EXE

D. REGEDT.EXE

E. WINREG.EXE

**48.** Which of the following viruses are usually not spread by themselves, but with other viruses?

A. FAT

B. Macro

C. Memory

D. Hoax

E. Boot Sector

**49.** In Windows 95, the concept of giving one program memory when needed, while taking it away from another, is:

A. 32-bit Memory Addressing

B. Plug and Play

C. Dynamic Memory Allocation

D. Static Memory Allocation

E. None of the above

**50.** How do you get to the helpful screen shown here?

**Computer Properties** ? X

View Resources | Reserve Resources |

○ Interrupt request (IRQ)    ○ Direct memory access (DMA)
○ Input/output (I/O)    ○ Memory

| Setting | Hardware using the setting |
|---------|---------------------------|
| 00 | System timer |
| 01 | Standard 101/102-Key or Microsoft Natural Keyboard |
| 02 | Programmable interrupt controller |
| 03 | Sierra 28800 PnP SQ3465 |
| 04 | Communications Port (COM3) |
| 05 | MPU-401 Compatible |
| 05 | YAMAHA OPL3-SA Sound System |
| 06 | Standard Floppy Disk Controller |

OK    Cancel

A. Device Manager | Computer | Properties

B. Device Manager | View Device by Contention

C. Device Manager | I/O Devices | Computer Properties

D. Device Manager | right-click My Computer | Properties

E. Device Manager | MSD32

# QUESTIONS AND ANSWERS

| To make the file . . . | I would use the command . . . |
|------------------------|-------------------------------|
| C:\AUTOEXEC.BAT hidden and read-only | attrib c:\autoexec.bat +h +r |
| C:\AUTOEXEC.BAT unhidden | attrib c:\autoexec.bat –h |
| C:\AUTOEXEC.BAT system, read-only, not hidden, and archive | attrib c:\autoexec.bat +s +r -h +a |
| All files in the C:\INFO directory read-only | attrib c:\info +r |
| All files in the C:\INFO directory and all subdirectories | attrib c:\info +r /s |

**51.** In the window shown here, what is the choice for Spool Data Format by default?

**Spool Settings**

- ⊙ Spool print jobs so program finishes printing faster
  - ○ Start printing after last page is spooled
  - ⊙ Start printing after first page is spooled
- ○ Print directly to the printer

Spool data format: RAW ▼

- ○ Enable bi-directional support for this printer
- ○ Disable bi-directional support for this printer

[ OK ]  [ Cancel ]  [ Restore Defaults ]

A. EDS
B. EDP
C. PPS
D. EMF
E. EPP

**52.** You are troubleshooting a PC by using your own boot disk that you carry in your service kit. After booting from that floppy disk, you change directory to C:\DOS successfully and try to run a DOS command. You receive the error, "Incorrect DOS version." What is the cause of this?

A. A virus has infected the C:\DOS directory
B. The boot sector on your floppy disk is corrupted
C. The version of DOS on the customer's PC is different from the one on your boot floppy
D. MSDOS.SYS is corrupted on the customer's PC

**53.** A customer's PC keeps getting an "out of environment" error. He cannot run specific programs because of this. What line can you add to his CONFIG.SYS to correct this problem?

A. COMSPEC=C:\DOS\COMMAND.COM

B. SHELL = C:\DOS\COMMAND.COM /P /E:1024

C. SHELL = C:\DOS\COMMAND.COM /E:512

D. None of the above

**54.** The most likely cause of the error "Bad or missing COMMAND.COM" is which of the following? (Choose all that apply.)

A. The boot sector has been destroyed by a virus

B. COMMAND.COM has been deleted from the hard disk root

C. The C:\DOS directory contains a different version of DOS than the root DOS files

D. The shell command is pointing to the wrong path for COMMAND.COM

**55.** Which statements are true about a Windows 3.*x* swap file?

A. It is automatically deleted when Windows 3.*x* exits

B. It is a hidden system file

C. It requires a contiguous block of space on the hard disk

D. It has the file extension .PAR

**56.** To set up the swap file in Windows 3.*x* you would:

A. Manually create a file called 386SPART.PAR

B. Use the Control Panel 386-enhanced applet

C. Add a second hard disk and make it active

D. Add a C:\TEMP directory to your PATH statement

**57.** You are working on a customer's Windows /DOS 3.*x* PC. You have just upgraded the video card and driver. When you try to re-start Windows you get the following error message, "Unable to initialize display adapter." Windows will no longer run. How can you correct this problem?

    A. From a DOS prompt edit the C:\WINDOWS\WIN.INI file with a text editor

    B. From a DOS prompt edit the C:\WINDOWS\SYSTEM.INI file with a text editor

    C. From the C:\WINDOWS directory, run SETUP. Then change the display adapter type

    D. None of the above

**58.** Upon attempting to start Windows 3.*x* you find that you receive an error pointing to a line in the WIN.INI file. How can you troubleshoot and correct this error? (Choose all that apply.)

    A. Copy the WIN.BAK file to WIN.INI

    B. Copy a WIN.INI file from any other PC to the broken one

    C. Use a text editor to correct the line in WIN.INI

    D. Check for the presence of the path and file mentioned in the troublesome line in the WIN.INI

**59.** In order for Windows 95 to correctly load HIMEM.SYS, which line must be located in the CONFIG.SYS file?

    A. DEVICE=C:\WINDOWS\HIMEM.SYS

    B. DEVICE=HIMEM.SYS

    C. DEVICE =C:\WINDOWS\COMMAND\HIMEM.SYS

    D. None of the above. Windows 95 loads HIMEM.SYS automatically.

**60.** A customer calls you and complains that his Windows 95 PC is running in safe mode. He has just added a new device to his system. What could be the cause of the problem?

A. The customer has inadvertently installed a virus on his system. Run an anti-virus program to correct the error

B. The customer's WIN.INI configuration file has been corrupted

C. Windows cannot load a critical device driver and has automatically started in safe mode

D. None of the above

**61.** Windows 95 reports a bad or missing COMMAND.COM. What could be the cause of this error?

A. A path statement in the AUTOEXEC.BAT file has been added that does not include C:\WINDOWS\COMMAND in the path

B. The COMSPEC line in CONFIG.SYS is incorrect

C. The SHELL command line in the CONFIG.SYS does not point to the correct path for COMMAND.COM

D. All of the above

**62.** To create an emergency boot disk in Windows 95, which of the icons shown here would you click to start the process?

WINDOWS/DOS QUESTIONS

A. Accessibility

B. Add New Hardware

C. Add/Remove Programs

D. Find Fast

63. What is the easiest method to troubleshoot a printer in Windows 95?

A. Make sure the cable is connected to the printer

B. Be sure the printer is online

C. Use the Printer Troubleshooting wizard in Help

D. Call the printer manufacturer tech support line

64. You need to enable bi-directional support for a new printer you are installing in a Windows 95-based PC. Where would you enable the bi-directional support for the parallel port?

A. Windows Control Panel | System

B. The Printers folder

C. The Print Troubleshooting wizard in Help

D. The PC CMOS settings | peripheral device settings

65. You are troubleshooting a printing problem in Windows 95. The Printer icon is grayed-out in the Printers folder. What does that mean? (Choose all that apply.)

A. The printer drivers are corrupt

B. "Use printer offline" has been selected

C. The network path to that printer is not available

D. The print spool has become corrupted

66. After changing the settings for a printer port from SPP to ECP or EPP, what should be done to ensure that Windows 95 recognizes the new features properly?

A. Use the Add New Hardware applet to update the port settings

B. Edit the Registry to change the port settings

C. Edit the WIN.INI file to update the port settings

D. Reinstall Windows 95

**67.** You have a customer who calls you to ask for help with his Windows 95 PC. He has just gotten the message "PAW4.EXE has performed an illegal operation and will be shut down." What should you advise the customer to do first?

A. Re-boot the system and see if the problem continues

B. Reinstall the application

C. Call the application vendor's technical support line

D. Call the Microsoft technical support line

**68.** If a GPF fault continues to occur within a specific application, which two of the following would be the best way to resolve the problem?

A. Call that application's technical support

B. Search the web for an updated version of that application

C. Uninstall and reinstall the application

D. Back up critical data, then uninstall and reinstall the application

**69.** If you suspect that the hard disk has some corruption of files on it, what is the best thing to do first to try to correct the problem?

A. Run the FDISK utility

B. FORMAT the hard disk

C. Perform a low-level FORMAT on the drive

D. Run the SCANDISK utility

**70.** A handy utility that comes built into MS-DOS for troubleshooting system resource problems in a DOS/Windows PC is:

A. FDISK
B. SCANDISK
C. DEFRAG
D. MSD

# Networks

1. Which of the following operating systems are capable of sharing files with other users on a network? (Choose all that apply.)

A. DOS
B. Windows 3.1
C. Windows 3.11
D. Windows 95

2. Which of the following is not true regarding e-mail?

A. The messages can be stored temporarily on many different computers over the course of their journey
B. E-mail takes less time to deliver than regular postal e-mail
C. E-mail can be assigned priority, just like postal mail
D. E-mail must maintain a connection to the destination computer while the message is being sent

3. The following text is an example of what?

```
div.Offscreen      { display:none }
span.Offscreen     { display:none }
span.BulletNumber { font-size: x-large; font-weight: bold; color:
#66ccff }
span.BulletText    { font-size: x-small; font-weight: bold; letter-
spacing: -1pt; text-align:center}
</style>
<body LINK=#FF0000 VLINK=#4E4E4E>
```

A. HTTP

B. HTML

C. A Mime e-mail attachment

D. An e-mail header

**4.** MGET, APPEND, LCD, and MKDIR are examples of what?

A. HTTP remote copy utilities

B. HTML-based metafiles

C. FTP commands

D. Telnet commands

**5.** What is used to resolve a name such as comptia.com to an IP address?

A. Domain Resolving Protocol

B. Domain Name Service

C. Domain Resolution Service

D. Domain Name Resolution System

**6.** Your boss would like you to research what would be involved to have dial-up access to the Internet for some of the employees of the firm. Which of the following do you not need to research?

A. Modems

B. ISPs

C. Microsoft's Internet Information Server

D. Web browsers

exam
ⓦatch    *Whenever installing network drivers, installing network cards, or configuring file and printer sharing, the manufacturer's procedures should be followed.*

7. Which of the following is not correct when configuring your Internet connection?

    A. Receiving TCP/IP configurations from a server when you dial into the ISP
    B. Using the modem manual to find your unique address for your computer on the Internet
    C. Manually configuring your software from settings received from your ISP
    D. Having your modem configured with the TCP/IP protocol

8. Your boss asks you to do some research on connecting workstations at the firm to the Internet. There are 15 users on the network. What is the most logical type of connection in this situation?

    A. Modems for all 15 users on their individual workstations
    B. A private bank of modems called a modem pool
    C. One 28.8 direct-dial phone line
    D. A high speed T1 line

9. You are in charge of creating a web site for your company's internal network. You created a web page that serves as the jump station for each department. How should you use this jump station?

    A. You should e-mail it to all users, and instruct them to place the HTML file in the directory of their choice
    B. You should cover the HTML file as a MIME type, and the web browser will convert the file to a user's home page
    C. You should make this HTML file the default home page for the users
    D. You should place this HTML file in the STARTUP folder of the department's file server

10. Which of the following are commonly entered when configuring a user's e-mail connection? (Choose all that apply.)

A. The user's password

B. The POP3 or SMTP server

C. The username

D. The user's e-mail address

11. How should you configure your workstation if you use the IPX/SPX protocol to connect to a server on the local area network, and TCP/IP to connect to the Internet?

A. Configure the computer to use both protocols. When you need to use one protocol, you will have to instruct the computer to begin using that particular protocol.

B. Bind IPX to the NIC and bind TCP/IP to the modem

C. Bind IPX to the NIC and bind both TCP/IP and IPX/SPX to the modem

D. You cannot do this without configuring the protocol redirector software for the adapters

12. Which of the following are possible when accessing the files that your DOS computer has shared on the network? (Choose all that apply.)

A. Reading a document

B. Adding a file

C. Deleting a file

D. No access

13. You are having trouble accessing the Internet on your computer. Which of the following do you not have to check in order to get the connection up and running again?

A. The IP address of your computer

B. The modem speed

C. The hardware (physical) address of your computer

D. The protocol being used for the connection

14. Which will you never have to specify when configuring a user's web browser?

A. E-mail address
B. Internet Service Provider's name
C. Default home page
D. Dial-up networking software

**15.** Which of the following technologies is probably not in use while you are connected to the Internet?

A. FTP
B. SNMP
C. SMTP
D. DNS

**16.** Which of the following is not common with both network adapter cards and modems?

A. They both usually have IRQs that need to be configured
B. You can configure parity on both
C. They both usually have I/O addresses that need to be configured
D. They both can be used to access the Internet

**17.** What is the difference between configuring a network card in Windows 3.*x* and Windows 95?

A. The card will need a special hardware address added when used with Windows 3.*x*
B. The card does not require an IRQ or I/O address when used in Windows 3.*x*
C. The card does not use any resources when used with Windows 95
D. None of the above

**18.** You have just purchased a new modem for your computer so you can access the Internet. What software do you need to install before you can begin cruising the Internet?

A. Modem driver

B. Serial port driver

C. Protocol software

D. Networking software

**19.** The Domain Name Service (DNS) is used to resolve domain names to
_____ that the computer is able to understand.

A. NetBIOS names

B. WINS names

C. IP addresses

D. Hardware addresses

**20.** You have just configured a user's dial-up connection for her computer at
work. The modem is working correctly, and you leave her to enter the
phone number for her Internet Service Provider. She calls you back a few
minutes later and says the number dials, but she doesn't hear the computer
connecting. What is most likely the problem?

A. She has not configured auto-dial, which will begin communicating with
the computer once the remote phone answers

B. She does not have the correct modem speed set

C. She may not be dialing 9 first to get out of the office

D. The connection cannot initialize, because TCP/IP has not been
configured correctly

**21.** The basic net topologies are:

A. Ethernet

B. Ring

C. Star

D. Bus

**22.** Cable that is used for ThickNet is:

    A. 10BaseT

    B. 10Base5

    C. 10Base2

    D. 10BaseFL

**23.** A collision on a network is:

    A. When multiple computers send data at one time

    B. When multiple networks send data at one time

    C. When one computer receives two messages at one time

    D. When two different wires are attached on a network

**24.** The NAUN on a token ring network is the:

    A. Nearest Active Unknown Neighbor

    B. Nearest Active Upstream Neighbor

    C. Nearest Access Unknown Neighbor

    D. Nearest Access Upstream Neighbor

**25.** You install a 16 Mbps token ring card on a computer in a network to replace a 4 Mbps token ring card. You then measure the speed again. It is 4 Mbps. What happened?

    A. Bad network card

    B. Wrong settings set

    C. There is still a 4 Mbps card on the network

    D. Token ring networks can only be run at 4 Mbps

**26.** The maximum number of nodes you can put on a token ring network is:

    A. 500

    B. 260

    C. 1024

    D. 100

**27.** The maximum number of nodes you can put on a ethernet network is:

A. 500
B. 260
C. 1024
D. 100

**28.** Listed from the bottom to the top, the seven layers of the OSI reference model are:

A. Application, Presentation, Session, Transport, Network, Data Link, Physical
B. Physical, Data Link, Network, Transport, Session, Presentation, Application
C. Presentation, Data Link, Network, Transport, Session, Physical, Application
D. Transport, Physical, Data Link, Network, Session, Presentation, Application

**29.** In order to sign on as a UNIX terminal on a network, you use the _____ service to connect.

A. HTTP
B. FTP
C. Telnet
D. OSI

**30.** In order to transfer files from one computer to another on a network you use the _____ service.

A. HTTP
B. FTP
C. Telnet
D. OSI

**31.** IP addresses as used on the Internet consist of _____-bit addresses.

WINDOWS/DOS QUESTIONS

A. 4
B. 8
C. 32
D. 64

32. Class B IP addresses range:

    A. From 0.___.___.___ to 126.___.___.___
    B. From 128.0.___.___ to 191.255.___.___
    C. From 192.0.0.___ to 254.255.255.___
    D. From 192.168.0.0 to 192.168.255.255

33. When assigning IP addresses, you can assign a temporary number to the machine from a server using:

    A. PPP
    B. DHCP
    C. InterNIC
    D. ISP

34. The URL for a web page consists of the:

    A. Path and/or file name
    B. Domain name
    C. Protocol
    D. Computer name

35. To map a drive on the host computer to the client computer in Windows 95, you can:

    A. Right-click the Network Neighborhood
    B. Left-click the Network Neighborhood
    C. Choose Tools in Window Explorer
    D. Go to Dial-Up Networking

**36.** A customer says when he uses the computer and modem in his office, the modem drops at irregular intervals. The customer does not have call waiting on the line. When you test it in your office, it performs the same way. What is the probable source of the problem?

A. Bad modem

B. Bad phone line

C. Call waiting not deactivated

D. Bad cable

**37.** The transmission standard to use a modem at 33.6 Kbps is:

A. V.90

B. V.34

C. V.32

D. X2

**38.** The CCIT transmission standard to use a modem at 56 Kbps is:

A. V.90

B. V.34

C. V.32

D. X2

**39.** You have a user who reports that she cannot send e-mail through Eudora 3.0. It was working, but now it is not. She also comments that the computer is saying the date is 1/5/2098. What is the problem?

A. Eudora has been badly installed

B. Y2K problem

C. Eudora 3.0 will not work after 2034

D. Wrong IRQ

**40.** Which of the following are forms of ISPs?

A. Dialing CompuServe

B. Dialing AOL

C. Your corporate Internet access through a phone bank

D. A connection through a digital leased line to the Internet through a company that offers the Internet

E. All of the above

**41.** The Internet is:

A. A WAN

B. An internetwork of computers

C. A LAN

D. Private

E. Public

**42.** Which of these would be the IP address of a web site?

A. HTTP:\\www.microsoft.com

B. HTML:\\www.microsoft.com

C. 207.68.156.61

D. FTP:\\www.microsoft.com

E. 255.255.255.0.0

**43.** Which of the following are Domain names?

A. ftp.microsoft.com

B. www.microsoft.com

C. 207.68.156.61

D. microsoft

E. 207.68

**44.** Say that you want to share out your phone directory to people to be able to open and print, but you want them not to delete or change it. What privileges do you assign them?

A. No access

B. Read

C. Write

D. Change

E. Delete

**45.** If you connect two computers together, which of the following can be true?

A. One is a client and one is a server

B. Both are servers only

C. Both are clients only

D. Both can be both clients and servers

E. None of the above

**46.** Which of the following can be shared devices?

A. Modem

B. File

C. Folder

D. Printer

E. Three of the above

**47.** If you know exactly where your file is, what is the fastest way to transfer it?

A. HTTP

B. HTML

C. FTP

D. Gopher

E. WWW

**48.** You have set up an Internet dial-up on your Windows 95 computer with a proprietary ISP. You have set the modem up with the right settings for the ISP, but you don't get a dial tone. What is probably wrong? (Choose the best choice.)

A. The phone line is not plugged in

B. You did not follow the manufacturer's installation guidelines

C. Your IRQs are not set up in Windows 95 correctly

D. Your COM port is not set up in Windows 95 correctly

E. A and B

**49.** Which of the following operating systems are capable of connecting to a shared device?

A. UNIX

B. DOS

C. WFW

D. Windows 3.1

E. Windows 95

**50.** How do you find out your POP3 when setting up a browser?

A. Use SMTP

B. Check the properties of your browser

C. From your ISP

D. It's your full user name

E. It is your e-mail address

**51.** Which of the following are necessary to be on a network?

A. Network card

B. Network card drivers

C. Network cable

D. Network protocol installed

E. All of the above

**52.** Which of these can involve downloading?

A. Cruising the Internet

B. Reading an attachment to an e-mail

C. Slaving hard disks

D. Copying a floppy disk

E. Processing a logon batch file

**53.** You have set up an online service on a new computer and have been cruising the Net for about a year and have not downloaded any programs. You have not even used the floppy drive or other input, such as network drives. You have only made three small text files. All of a sudden, you can't print. What is the problem?

A. Virus

B. Out of hard disk space

C. Printer offline

D. Paper jam

E. All of the above

**54.** This resolves Domain Names into IP addresses:

A. A Domain Name Server

B. The Domain Name System

C. POP3

D. SMTP

E. SNMP

**55.** Which of the following can be used to upload?

A. E-mail

B. HTTP

C. FTP

D. HTML

E. Shared drive

**56.** What are the ways to share a file on Windows 95?

A.  Through My Computer

B.  Through the Control Panel

C.  Through the Network applet

D. Through Windows Explorer

E.  All of the above

**57.** When you are setting up TCP/IP for use on your LANlan, what should you fill in on the window shown here?

A.  Disable DNS

B.  Enable DNS

C.  Host

D. Domain

E.  DNS server search order

**58.** What does the screen shown here represent?

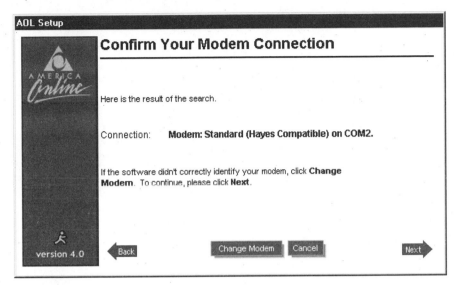

A. An ISP

B. Dial-up networking

C. A GUI

D. None of the above

**59.** To connect your PC to a Network you will need a:

A. Credit card

B. Network interface card

C. Serial port

D. USB port

**60.** A workstation on a network uses _____ software to communicate with the server.

A. Application

B. Utility

C. Client

D. Server

**61.** To install a network card you usually need which resources to be available in the client PC?

A. IRQ

B. Base memory address

C. MAC address

D. Serial port

**62.** To access a mail server on the Internet you need which of the following to be configured? (Choose all that apply.)

A. Username

B. Password

C. Mail server name or IP address

D. Mouse

**63.** Which of the following is not a valid Internet e-mail address?

A. www.joesmith.com

B. joesmith@ingress.com

C. johndoe@faysonlakes.com

D. ftp.joepc.com

**64.** Which is the proper format to access a web page?

A. HTTP://www.microsoft.com

B. HTML://www.microsoft.com

C. HTML:/www.microsoft.com

D. HTML.microsoft.com

**65.** What must every PC on the Internet have in order to communicate?

A. Serial number

B. Unique IP address

C. IPX address

D. NetBIOS name

**66.** TCP/IP is considered a _____ network protocol.

    A. Foolproof

    B. Routable

    C. CRC

    D. Virtual

**67.** To set up dial-up networking in Windows 95, which desktop icon shown here would you click to begin setting up the connection to an ISP?

A. The Internet

B. My Computer

C. Network Neighborhood

D. None of the above

68. A customer is trying to connect to your ISP service. He has a modem installed but doesn't have dial-up networking installed. Which of the following would you instruct him to do to install the Windows 95 Dial-up Networking applet?

A. Go to Control Panel | Add New Hardware

B. Go to Control Panel | Add/Remove Software

C. Click the Windows Setup tab and highlight the Communications icon

D. Check the Dialup Networking check box and click OK

69. Referring to the following illustration, what can you tell about the Communications group of software applications for this PC?

A. None of the communications applications is installed

B. Some, but not all of the communications applications are installed

C. All of the communications applications are installed

D. None of the above

**70.** Microsoft Internet Explorer version 3.*x* can do which of the following? (Choose all that apply.)

A. Download from an FTP site

B. Upload to an FTP site

C. Browse a web site

D. All of the above

**71.** You are configuring a LAN-based customer for Internet access through their LAN. The administrator of that LAN instructs you to use DHCP. What does DHCP stand for?

A. Dynamic Host Communications Protocol

B. Dynamic Host Configuration Protocol

C. Dimensional Host Communications Protocol

D. None of the above

**72.** DHCP can provide which of the following TCP/IP parameters for a client PC? (Choose all that apply.)

A. IP address

B. Gateway address

C. DNS address

D. All of the above

**73.** For a WFW 3.11 PC to access the Internet, you will need to install:

A. IPX/SPX

B. TCP/IP 32

C. NetBEUI

D. None of the above

WINDOWS/DOS
QUESTIONS

**74.** If you connect to the Internet through a proxy server, what must you do to configure Internet Explorer?

   A. Nothing. It will work without changing any settings.

   B. Set the web caching for a minimum of 10MB

   C. Set the Properties | Connection setting for proxy server, and enter the correct parameters for the proxy server connection

   D. Contact your LAN Administrator

**75.** To enable Internet e-mail for Microsoft Exchange clients, what services will need to be set up? (Choose all that apply.)

   A. Personal folders

   B. Internet mail

   C. Personal address book

   D. Microsoft Mail

**76.** A customer complains that he has received a returned e-mail stating that the address cannot be found on the host mail server. What is the most common cause of this problem?

   A. The user does not exist on that system

   B. The e-mail address was typed incorrectly

   C. The intended receiver does not have a valid e-mail account

   D. The mail server is down

**77.** To access Internet news servers, what is required? (Choose all that apply.)

   A. An ISP account or other Internet access

   B. An account on a news server

   C. A web browser

   D. An FTP application

# Answers

Q & A

The answers to the questions are in boldface, followed by a brief explanation. Some of the explanations detail the logic you should use to choose the correct answer, while others give factual reasons why the answer is correct. If you miss several questions on a similar topic, you should review the corresponding section in the *A+ Certification Study Guide* (Osborne/McGraw-Hill) before taking the A+ Certification test.

# Function, Structure, Operation, and File Management

1. **C.** COMSPEC is used to set up the DOS environment, and therefore it is placed with the other environment modifiers, in the AUTOEXEC.BAT.

2. **D.** The three files, IO.SYS, MSDOS.SYS, and COMMAND.COM, are the heart of the DOS operating system, and are required to operate system startup. CONFIG.SYS and AUTOEXEC.BAT are not required to start the operating system.

3. **B.** COMMAND.COM is the DOS command interpreter, and is responsible for displaying the DOS prompt. This file is also a required operating system component; the DOS system cannot start without it.

4. **A, C, D.** GDI.EXE, WIN.INI, and the SYSTEM.INI are all Windows 3.*x* system files. USER.DAT is a Windows 95 system file, which holds Registry settings.

5. **C.** Because Windows 95 no longer relies on a separate copy of DOS, the fundamentals have changed. While IO.SYS and COMMAND.COM remain for compatibility reasons, MSDOS.SYS no longer contains system code, but allows for special system settings to be user-defined.

6. **A.** Windows 95 now runs in protected mode, whereas Windows 3.*x* and previous operating systems ran in real or protected mode. Protected mode, as the name implies, is much more stable.

**7. B.** DOS puts a pointer in a special location, known as the boot sector, which is located in the first cluster on the boot partition. This pointer tells the processor exactly where to find the system files.

**8. C.** Specifying the /S switch when using the ATTRIB command will adjust the attributes for every file in the path specified, which is usually an entire directory's contents. This is very useful for adjusting a number of files at once.

**9. A, B, D.** When executing any .BAT, .COM, or .EXE file, the extension may be dropped. Be aware, however, that there is a hierarchy to execution if multiple commands with the same extension are in the same directory.

**10. B.** DOS looks first for .COM files, then .EXE files, then .BAT files. If you ever execute a command and get strange results, be sure to check for the presence of another command with the same name, but a different extension.

**11. C.** These library files usually have a .BIN or .OVL extension. Windows took this one step further and developed Dynamic Linked Libraries (.DLL files). These overlays have the additional benefit of being sharable by all of the applications loaded in Windows.

**12. B.** The CTRL-ESC keystroke combination will open up the Start menu in Windows 95, Windows 98, and Windows NT 4.0.

**13. D.** DEFRAG is not available with DOS 5.0, so you will not be able to run the command. DEFRAG, as well as SCANDISK, became available with DOS 6.0.

**14. C.** When SCANDISK encounters a bad cluster, it will attempt to save the information from the cluster, and mark the cluster as bad. These clusters are physical defects and cannot be repaired.

**15. B.** When Program Manager in Windows 3.*x* saves information about the program groups on your computer, this information is stored in a file with the GRP extension. These files can be used to save your program group information when migrating to Windows 95.

**16. C.** The individual groups to be loaded by Program Manager are listed in the PROGMAN.INI file. The GRP file contains the program group content information, while the PROGMAN.INI file contains the list of individual groups to be loaded at startup.

**17. D.** Cooperative multitasking, the least efficient of the two types of multitasking, requires that an application relinquish control of the CPU. If an application failed to relinquish control of the CPU, the whole system could hang.

**18. C.** CTRL-P is the shortcut key to print. Rather than just printing immediately to the default printer, a Printers dialog box will appear, where you can choose which printer to print to, and configure the print properties.

**19. C.** 512 files can be placed in the root directory, which is normally not a concern. However, long filenames generate two files, and can fill the root directory twice as fast if they are stored there.

**20. A, D.** UNIX and DOS are text-based operating systems. Windows 95 is a GUI-based operating system, and Windows 3.1 is an operating environment that runs on DOS.

**21. B, C.** OS/2 and Windows NT are 32-bit operating systems. DOS is a 16-bit operating system, and Windows 3.1 runs on DOS.

**22. B, D.** IO.SYS and COMMAND.COM are required to start DOS. If AUTOEXEC.BAT and CONFIG.SYS are present, they are processed at startup.

**23. A.** The change will be put in the AUTOEXEC.BAT file. The PROMPT tells how to display the prompt. The COMMAND.COM file actually displays the prompts. SYSTEM.INI is a Windows file

**24. B.** The COMMAND.COM file actually displays the prompt. The PROMPT command, which may be in the AUTOEXEC.BAT file, shows the appearance for the prompt.

**25. C.** If you use FDISK or FORMAT, you will erase the hard disk. The SYS command will transfer system files to the disk.

**26. C.** Windows 95 allows filenames to be 254 characters long. DOS allows file names that are no longer than eight characters before a period, and three characters after.

**27. A.** A new drive must have FDISK run on it to partition it and then the drive must be formatted using FORMAT.

**28. A.** COPY will not copy subdirectories. XCOPY with the /S switch will copy subdirectories.

**29. B.** Internal commands are part of COMMAND.COM and are loaded at startup. AUTOEXEC.BAT, CONFIG.SYS, and IO.SYS are files that are run at startup.

**30.** **A.** The order DOS looks at extensions to choose the file to run is .COM, .EXE, .BAT, .COM, .EXE.

**31.** **A, B.** The customer is using Windows 95. When copying with a DOS command (XCOPY), DOS uses only the DOS version of long filenames and drops the long filename. The DOS version of long file names often includes tildes (~).

**32.** **A.** The command to list a directory is DIR. TREE lists the directory structure (directories). LD and DIRECTOR are not command names.

**33.** **B.** The F5 key will update the window. F1 activates help and the F10 key activates the menus.

**34.** **C.** In Windows 95 you can use File Manager or Windows Explorer. Windows 98 includes Internet Explorer as a file manager, also.

**35.** **B.** CTRL-C will sometimes stop a DOS task. By pressing ALT-CTRL-DEL you will get a task manager window in which you can end the task.

**36.** **A.** Directory entries on a disk are stored in the File Allocation Table (FAT).

**37.** **C.** The entries that control the desktop appearance are stored in the WIN.INI file.

**38.** **D.** The only four file attributes that DOS has are Read, System, Hidden, and Archive.

**39.** **B.** Solitaire comes with Windows, but may be installed or uninstalled. Plug and Play means when a new device is attached to a PC running Windows 95, the operating system recognizes and installs the device with minimal input from the user. The CD drive can be set to auto run CDs when they are inserted.

**40. A, B, E.** IO.SYS and MSDOS.SYS are hidden from view.

**41. D.** The COMMAND.COM displays the DOS prompt. You can change the attributes of the DOS prompt. The standard attribute is P$G$.

**42. D.** The keyboard can exist in quite a few different files and you need to understand why it lies in each file.

**43. B.** Learn the subtleties of these system files.

**44. B.** The exam stresses the locations, contents, and purposes of the system files.

**45. A.** The 486 and the 586 still use EMM386.EXE.

**46. A, B, D.** Smartdrive is used for caching. DOS uses it. However, Windows 95, with its 32-bit environment, replaces the program and opts for real mode disk caching.

**47. A, E.** RN is not a DOS command. ATTRIB will not rename a file. Memorize all the pertinent DOS commands and their switches.

**48. B.** The -R command in the ATTRIB gets rid of the read-only attribute.

**49. A, C, E.** DIR /A:H /S will show the hidden files for your whole drive. CHKDSK will show the presence of hidden files, and ATTRIB without any switches will show you the hidden files in a directory.

**50.** B, C, D and E. Answer E is the same as /S and /E combined. The /H switch will copy all the hidden and system files as well. If you do not have the /H, then the hidden files will not be moved. /C continues copying even if errors occur. /Y prompts you before overwriting files. /W prompts you to press a key before copying.

**51.** A. This program is hidden on the last tab on the add /remove software applet. Most people usually make the boot disks when the operating system is installed. Answer B is very close to being right. If it was SYS A: instead of SYS C: then it would have been wrong. Answers C, D, E are not right. This command is often forgotten and is usually the cause of people spending much time trying to figure out why they can't get things to boot.

**52.** B. These are found in the CONFIG.SYS, usually near the beginning.

**53.** B, C, D, E. Answer A would have been right had it been MSDOS.SYS. Pay careful attention to the extensions of files.

**54.** D. It is used in the AUTOEXEC.BAT file. Also realize that SYS.INI is not a system file.

**55.** D. The WIN.INI holds all of the settings for the desktop, such as wallpaper, screen savers, and colors. WIN.INI holds many software settings, as well as settings for printers.

**56.** B, E. SYSTEM.DAT and USER.DAT. Windows 95 is trying to organize these files. After studying these, I think you can see why. The old way is just not centralized or organized well enough to be acceptable.

**57.** A, B. The other choices simply will not get you to this screen. This screen, incidentally, will let you configure multiple settings for multiple users.

**58.** **B.** A LNK extension is short for Link. These links are stored in subdirectories of the Windows directory. You can create a shortcut like this by dragging from Explorer with the right mouse button. You can right-click the desktop and choose New Shortcut. You can right-click the mouse and drag and drop from the Start menu. This is an example of the extreme versatility of Windows 95.

**59.** **A, C.** The main functions of an operating system are to define input and output devices and to provide instructions for the CPU to operate on data. Without this, we would have to compute in all 1s and 0s. Of course that would make for a very simple keyboard with only two keys, but it would take a long time to enter a copy file command!

**60.** **B, D.** DOS consists of two types of commands, internal and external. Internal commands are part of the operating kernel COMMAND.COM. External commands are all of the .EXE and .COM files located in the \DOS directory.

**61.** **B, D.** The Macintosh is based on the Motorola family of processors known as the 680XX series. This processor is also known as a RISC or Reduced Instruction Set. This processor actually has fewer low-level (binary) commands than the Intel 80x86 processor.

**62.** **C.** With the development of the **80386** chip, the processor and system memory were able to read and write 32 bits of data per clock cycle. This was the beginning of breaking the DOS 16-bit barrier. At least the hardware was ready at that point.

**63.** **B, C.** The file attribute +R (Read Only permission) will prevent a file from being deleted or overwritten. The file attribute +S (system file) will also protect a file from being overwritten or deleted. MSDOS.SYS and IO.SYS have this protective attribute. COMMAND.COM does not, although you could set it that way yourself to protect it from accidental deletion.

WINDOWS/DOS ANSWERS

**64. B, C.** Examples of internal DOS commands are DIR and COPY. These commands are compiled into COMMAND.COM and are therefore considered internal commands.

**65. B, D.** HIMEM.SYS and AUTOEXEC.BAT are not required for system startup in DOS. You won't be able to run Windows 3.*x* without HIMEM.SYS, and without several commands in AUTOEXEC.BAT, you will most likely be unable to use many hardware devices such as your CD-ROM, which normally has the MSCDEX.EXE command loaded automatically loaded in that configuration file.

**66. B, D.** The WIN.INI is similar in nature to the AUTOEXEC.BAT file in that it loads environment variables used by the Windows 3.*x* system. The SYSTEM.INI loads special device drivers for Windows 3.*x*, as CONFIG.SYS loads device drivers for DOS. Both of these files are ASCII based, and can be modified with a text editor. Many of their settings can also be modified indirectly through Control Panel. This is generally the preferred method for the less experienced user. Caution: Incorrectly modifying these files could render Windows inoperable!

**67. B.** The SYSTEM.INI file configures specific hardware devices and their associated settings in a manner similar to the way the CONFIG.SYS file configures device drivers for DOS.

**68. C, D.** The WIN.INI and the SYSTEM.INI remain in Windows 95 to maintain backwards compatibility with 16-bit Windows applications. Most new 32-bit Windows 95 applications create entries in the Registry for proper program configuration.

**69. B.** The MSDOS.SYS file remains with Windows 95 for backwards compatibility with DOS based programs and contains special settings for the operating system. Included there is a path statement. This file must always be >1024 bytes to remain backwards compatible. To safely view its contents, at the C:\ prompt type **MSDOS.SYS | MORE**.

**70.** **C.** If you are unable to run Windows 3.*x* in standard mode, chances are that DOSX.EXE is missing or corrupted. This executable portion of the kernel is essential if you are running Windows 3.*x* on a 286 PC.

**71.** **B.** To restore missing icons to the standard Windows Program Manager groups, you should click File Run and enter **SETUP /P**, then click OK. This will restore the default program groups to the way they would be after a fresh install of Windows 3.1. You may loose other icons that were placed in these groups, so you should probably copy them to another group before doing this procedure.

**72.** **B.** A little-known feature of the FDISK utility is that you can use the command line switch /MBR. Entering FDISK /MBR will restore the master boot record from the backup FAT table. This little trick has made heroes out of many of us over the years. This command syntax is very effective and non-verbose by its nature.

**73.** **B.** The FDISK command, not intended for the faint of heart, is for setting up partition tables on the fixed DISK. FDISK a drive with data on it and it's toast. This is the utility that will create the partitioning scheme for your hard disk.

**74.** **A, C.** To have Windows 3.*x* start automatically on boot-up, you should have the two lines PATH C:\DOS;C:\WINDOWS and WIN located in the AUTOEXEC.BAT file. The PATH statement should be first. WIN should be the last line of the file.

**75.** **A, C.** Windows 3.*x* Print Manager spools jobs to the location specified by the SET variable TEMP. You must have enough free space on the drive that supports the physical directory as specified in that variable. By default MS-DOS specifies the TEMP variable to be C:\MSDOS. The unfortunate result of that is that the DOS directory can get loaded up with stale print jobs. Create a new directory located at D:\TEMP and edit the AUTOEXEC.BAT file so the line SET TEMP=D:\TEMP replaces the old TEMP variable line.

**76.** **D.** The correct command and syntax would be XCOPY A:\*.* /S /E C:\LANCARD:\. The /S switch means copy the entire directory tree structure and the /E switch means include empty directories. You will be prompted regarding the creation of the LANCARD directory if it does not yet exist.

**77.** **B.** To protect a file from being overwritten in error, you should use the command and syntax ATTRIB +R <filename>. If this file is in a directory other than where your prompt was showing, you would have to include the path to the <filename>.

**78.** **A.** The Repeat Delay is the time that the keyboard port takes to begin responding when you hold down a key. The settings in this applet are especially helpful if you have a disabled customer who needs some fine-tuning on the keyboard interface.

**79.** **B.** The illustration shows the applet that starts when you click the System icon in Windows 95. Selecting the Device Manager tab will display a tree of all the devices in the system that Windows 95 recognizes.

# Memory Management

**1.** **B.** This memory area can be used a number of different ways. The first 64KB of extended memory was roped off as a control area, and labeled the high memory area (HMA).

**2. B.** By the time DOS 6.0 rolled out, DOS could also load a portion of itself in the high memory area. Originally, use of the HMA was reserved for only a single application.

**3. C.** The reserved 384KB of the first 1024 of memory became known as "upper memory." In order to take advantage of unused upper memory, memory managers, such as EMM386.EXE, were created.

**4. B.** These pages could be moved, one at a time, from the reserved area to either extended memory or the hard disk, when needed. The processor neither knew nor cared about where it got its code from.

**5. A, D.** EMM386.EXE performs two major functions. It enables and controls EMS, if desired, and enables the use of upper memory as system memory.

**6. A.** You can force EMM386 to use specific regions of upper memory by using the INCLUDE switch on the command line, where it is enabled in CONFIG.SYS. Conversely, exclude specific regions using the EXCLUDE switch.

**7. C.** Using the /C switch gives you quite a bit more to work with, including the information concerning which drivers are using conventional or upper memory, and the amount of memory they are taking.

**8. C.** Don't assume hardware first when you receive an Illegal Operation error. These errors are nearly always caused by an application error. Processors are designed not to process these operations, and therefore send an error.

**9. A.** Although it appears EMM386.EXE is an acronym for extended memory manager, HIMEM.SYS is the actual extended memory manager.

**10. D.** There is no such command as MEMINFO. To find out about which drivers are being loaded into memory, and how much memory they are taking, use the MEM /C command.

**11. B.** In order for EMM386.EXE to be loaded correctly, it must be loaded after HIMEM.SYS. EMM386.EXE is required if you would like to enable the use of upper memory as system memory.

**12. B, C.** HIMEM.SYS is the extended memory manager, and can also take the first 64KB of this extended memory area and convert it into the HMA. HIMEM.SYS is also required in order to load EMM386.EXE.

**13. C.** Both the hidden and system attributes for a file hide the file. These files do not appear when you do a DIR of a directory, and therefore lead you to believe you have more space on your hard disk than you do.

**14. C.** If you have a compressed drive using DoubleSpace, SCANDISK can be used to detect and correct errors on this drive as if it were not compressed, which CHKDSK cannot do.

**15. D.** EMM386.EXE is the expanded memory manager that is responsible for swapping pages of memory in and out of the reserved memory area. Expanded memory is basically no longer used.

**16. B.** A TSR is a Terminate and Stay Resident program that will remain in memory even though it is not being executed. These TSRs wait in memory until they are called upon, many times by a keyboard shortcut sequence.

**17. B.** Virtual memory is the process of simulating RAM by swapping information from the hard disk to memory when needed. If you have only 8MB of RAM, but you specified a 30MB swap file, you would have 38MB of memory, although the hard disk is considerably slower than RAM.

18. **D.** The AUTOEXEC.BAT does little for optimizing memory for use by applications. The AUTOEXEC.BAT is mostly used to configure the DOS environment, not configure memory-related drivers.

19. **A.** Conventional memory is the first 640KB of memory. The next 384KB is upper memory. The memory above 1MB is extended memory. The first 64KB of extended memory is the High Memory Area.

20. **C.** SIMM modules have a notch on one end of the pins. Memory chips had a notch in one end of the chip to align the chip. DIMM modules have a notch in the middle of the pins.

21. **C.** DIMM modules have 168 pins. SIMM modules have 30 or 72 pins. DRAM (DIP) Memory chips had 14 or 16 separate metal pins.

22. **B.** RAMDRIVE is part of the memory that is treated like another hard disk. However, information placed here must be written to the hard disk or it will be lost at power down. It basically is the opposite of virtual memory, as virtual memory uses the disk like memory, and RAMDRIVE uses memory like a disk.

23. **B.** The 386SPART.PAR file is the Windows 3.1 permanent swap file. The Windows 3.1 temporary swap file is named WIN386.SWP.

24. **A.** A permanent swap file always stays on the disk. It uses contiguous clusters of the disk and runs faster. A temporary swap file is created each time Windows starts, and does not always use contiguous clusters. The permanent swap file will run faster.

25. **C.** DIMM modules are installed by lining the module straight over the socket and pressing down. SIMM modules are installed by placing the module at a 45° angle in the socket then bringing it to a vertical position.

Memory chips were installed by lining up all the metal tabs and pressing down. Motherboards are installed by laying them in position and screwing them down.

26. **C.** The system BIOS and ROM chips are called firmware. The equipment is the hardware and the programs are the software. There is no bootware.

27. **A, B, D.** Windows NT uses virtual memory management. Windows 95, DOS, and Windows 3.1 use conventional, upper, and extended memory.

28. **A.** Memory chips were pressed by the installer into the motherboard. SIMM and DIMM modules have the chips already soldered to them, and the modules are pressed into the motherboard. ROM comes preinstalled on the motherboard.

29. **A, B, C.** SIMM modules are used in 386, 486, and Pentium machines. You will need to find out if they need 30- or 72-pin SIMMs.

30. **D.** The first thing to check for is a virus. If there is no virus, open the case and check the memory chips and modules. These quite often work loose or are not installed correctly. Then check the hard disk and power supply.

31. **B.** You can add memory to a 486 processor machine. The 486 machine uses the SIMM module. However, some models use a 30-pin module and some use the 72-pin module.

32. **D.** MEM.EXE displays various reports on the usage of memory.

33. **B.** MSD.EXE displays information about various items of the system and shows memory conflicts.

**34.** **B.** SCANDISK will fix the disk errors caused by files that were left in an open state. DEFRAG will go through and rebuild the FAT and make files contiguous. MEMMAKER will configure the memory.

**35.** **A.** CHKDSK is Microsoft's older program for fixing disk errors caused by files left in an open state.

**36.** **B.** The customer has gone to the DOS prompt via Windows and did not exit Windows. Typing EXIT will return them to Windows. You know he had Windows on the machine 60 minutes ago, so it is not likely that he erased it or that it is damaged. There is always a chance of a virus, so if EXIT does not work, check for a virus.

**37.** **A.** You should contact the vendor for patches, bug fixes, and updates. Always suspect a software problem before a hardware problem. If a 32-bit application is available for your program and you have only a 16-bit program, it is recommended that you upgrade if you are having problems.

**38.** **E.** XMS is extended memory.

**39.** **D.** EMS is expanded memory

**40.** **B.** EEPROM stands for Electronically Erasable Programmable Read Only Memory.

**41.** **A, B.** You need both of these lines in the CONFIG.SYS.

**42.** **E.** RAM has historically been three times faster than traditional ROM. RAM is faster than virtual RAM. Virtual RAM needs to be swapped on to the hard disk and read back off the hard disk, which can take a lot of time. Access times for RAM are measured in nanoseconds.

**43.** E. The EXLUDE switch resides in the CONFIG.SYS. If you wanted to force EMM386 to use a specific area in the upper memory, you would use the INCLUDE switch in the CONFIG.SYS.

**44.** E. The LIM memory specification renamed system memory to conventional memory. The standard defined additional (above 1024KB) as expanded, extended, and high.

**45.** E. This is provided so that you do not have other applications open when you are trying to run Word. Since RAM is so cheap nowadays it can be the economical solution to many problems. It just does not make sense to get a third-party memory optimizing program for $50, when you can solve the problem better with RAM for $35.

**46.** B, C. Expanded memory is controlled and enabled by EMM386.EXE. QEMM, which is the acronym for Quarterdeck Expanded Memory Manager, is very similar to EMM386.EXE. QEMM even can free up a bit more memory.

**47.** A, B, C. This will result in a cleaner FAT. While these errors can be caused by hardware, such as memory or motherboard, do not consider changing hardware until all software repairs have been exhausted.

**48.** A. Conventional memory is located at 640KB and below.

**49.** D. Extended memory is located above 1024KB.

**50.** D. Be careful not to get upper memory and HMA mixed up.

**51.** C. HMA is from 1024KB through 1088KB.

**52.** **A.** This is an easy question. The exam will expect you to know the virtual memory terminology as well as the concept of virtualizing RAM, which is defined as the act of creating virtual memory.

**53.** **E.** This is one of those questions that you either know or you don't. Since the A+ exam does not count anything off for wrong answers, never leave a question blank.

**54.** **E.** This is a very useful settings screen when you want to set the memory parameters for the program in the DOS window to run in Windows 95. The other choices simply do not get you to this screen.

**55.** **B.** This command will list out the memory use. The F switch is short for free. This shows how much free memory is left. Learn the pertinent switches: /C /D /F /M /P. These are short for classify, debug, free, module, and page, respectively.

**56.** **A, B.** Volatile memory is memory that is erased when the PC is turned off. SRAM and DRAM are both volatile memory.

**57.** **B, C.** RAM that requires a constant refresh rate is called dynamic RAM. Examples of dynamic RAM are DRAM and EDO RAM. Both of these require a high-speed refresh rate to maintain data integrity. This is because they are composed of tiny capacitors, which will lose their charge if not refreshed regularly. ROM (Read Only Memory) holds its data even during a loss of power (hopefully). An example of ROM is the BIOS settings for a PC.

**58.** **C, D.** A reprogrammable ROM could be an EPROM or FLASH RAM. FLASH RAM is reprogrammed with a software utility. EPROMs are erasable with an ultraviolet light and must be burned in a special PROM burner.

**59. B, D.** In a DOS-based PC with a 16-bit operating system, the memory is addressed using a segment address and an offset address. It was explained to me as working like the arm of a robot. The arm can only reach so far because of its length of 16 bits (segment address or neighborhood). However, you can move the whole arm to another section (neighborhood) using an offset address, and access memory there. The limitations of those forms of addressing are overcome by 32-bit operating systems that can access large amounts of memory directly.

**60. A.** The first 640KB of memory in a DOS-based PC is referred to as system memory. The additional 384KB of memory in the first megabyte is called upper memory. This is where device drivers should load when you use the DEVICEHIGH option in the CONFIG.SYS.

**61. B.** The LIM XMS memory specification was developed by Lotus, Intel, and Microsoft. Using this specification enables operating systems to access the memory in a PC above 1024KB.

**62. A.** The original 808x processor could only access up to 1024KB of memory. Who knew we would need more? A temporary scheme was worked out later, using expanded memory and swapping page frames to allow data to be temporarily stored above 1024KB, but this limitation clearly lead to the death of the 8088 processor.

**63. A.** Generally, the physical memory in a PC above 1024KB is called extended memory.

**64. C.** DOS, version 6.0 and above can load part of its operating system in that sweet little 64KB block above 1024KB. Read this section in the companion study guide over and over until it makes sense.

**65. C.** Phar-Lap developed the Virtual Control Program Interface (VCPI), which lost the battle to DPMI. Phar-Lap was acquired by Lotus.

**66. A.** The upper memory area is the neighborhood from 640KB to 1024KB. How would you like to be the mailman in a PC memory system? Just remember to check the zip code! Check the cheat chart below and try to memorize this information for the test.

| Memory Address in Decimal | Neighborhood | Usage |
|---|---|---|
| 0–640KB | Low | Conventional DOS |
| 640KB–1024KB | Upper | Device Drivers /TSRs |
| 1024KB–1088KB (64KB block) | HMA | DOS=HIGH |
| 1024KB–4294967295KB | Extended memory | May be used partially as expanded with the LIM spec and EMM386.EXE |

**67. B.** To load device drivers high you must use EMM386.EXE. This memory manager performs many different functions, and that's what makes it confusing. The key to understanding this and other memory management tools is to understand the command-line switches. Some important command-line options include /NOEMS and X=XXXX-XXXX to keep EMM386.EXE from conflicting with other devices in setting up UMBs for device drivers.

**68. A.** To enable page frame swapping in 80386 based PC, you must have both the Device-C:\HIMEM.SYS and DEVICE-C:\DOS\EMM386.EXE in your CONFIG.SYS file.

**69.** **D.** According to the display illustrated, no devices are loading high on the system, as shown by the command MEM /C.

**70.** **B.** Using the DOS=HIGH command to load part of the operating system in the HMA means that the first 64KB block above 1024KB will have part of the operating system loaded there.

**71.** **C.** Many newer network cards and other devices come with a soft set utility to allocate resources for the device. So the correct answer is to use the soft set utility disk that came with the card to set resources for that card.

**72.** **B.** When installing an EISA card of any type, you will need to use the EISA utility that came with the PC, adding the correct configuration file that came with the device to the EISA configuration settings. Most EISA cards come with a file that the EISA utility can read that will help to identify the device to the system.

**73.** **B.** PCI resources, particularly the IRQ settings, are set by the CMOS PCI Settings screen located in the CMOS Settings menu for the PC. Consult the motherboard manual that came with the PC for instructions.

# Installation, Configuration, and Upgrading

**1.** **D.** If Windows 95 detects the new device, but does not have a driver for the device, a dialog box will appear prompting you to supply a driver for the device.

**2.** **A.** The tool that is still being used to partition a hard disk is FDISK. Windows 95 did not introduce a graphical partitioning utility.

**3.** **B.** The maximum size of a partition in Windows 95 is 2GB. This limit has been overcome by Windows 95 B, also known as OSR2.

4. **D.** When it comes to DOS and loading device drivers, you are basically on your own, unless the vendor includes a setup disk that will modify the CONFIG.SYS and AUTOEXEC.BAT for you.

5. **D.** The CONFIG.SYS and AUTOEXEC.BAT files are not required for Windows 95 to start. However, you may need to load device drivers in the CONFIG.SYS, and modify environmental variables in the AUTOEXEC.BAT.

6. **C.** If you need to boot straight up into DOS mode when Windows 95 is installed, press the F8 key on system startup. From the startup menu that appears, select Command Prompt Only.

7. **B.** Windows 3.*x*, after being installed, does not start by default. Many people change to the directory that WIN.COM is in and type WIN, or else these commands are placed in the AUTOEXEC.BAT file and run every time the system starts.

8. **A, C, D.** Windows 95 Plug and Play will automatically configure the DMA channel, IRQ, and I/O address for devices. Although these devices are configured automatically, you can still modify them using Device Manager.

9. **A.** Windows 3.*x* will not load unless the extended memory manager, HIMEM.SYS, is loaded. This is unlike Windows 95, which does not require HIMEM.SYS, because Windows 95 manages its own extended memory.

10. **A, B, C, D.** All of the CONFIG.SYS settings listed are now provided by default in the IO.SYS file. You can override the IO.SYS by placing settings in the CONFIG.SYS.

11. **B.** The excerpts were taken from the MSDOS.SYS file, which you can now modify in Windows 95. This file is used for system startup, enabling you to

configure such startup events as enabling the boot menu, adjusting the boot delay, and disabling logos on startup.

**12. D.** If Windows 95 encounters a SYSTEM.INI file (which it will if you are upgrading your existing version of Windows), the file will not be renamed. Some settings will be moved to the Registry, but the SYSTEM.INI will be maintained for backward compatibility.

**13. C.** DOS and Windows 3.*x* (essentially because it requires DOS) both need to be booted from the first partition of the master hard disk. This is not the case with Windows 95, which can start from a different partition as long as FDISK has set the partition active, and the boot files have been copied to the partition.

**14. B.** The EBD.SYS utility is for making an emergency boot disk, hence the acronym of EBD. This is similar to the Windows NT rescue disk maker entitled RDISK.

**15. A.** With 386 Enhanced mode, you can have multiple applications active, both Windows applications and DOS applications. This does not apply to Windows 95, which uses protected mode.

**16. D.** The BOOTLOG.TXT contains a record of the current startup process for starting Windows 95. This is the file that is created during the installation of Windows 95, and shows the status of drivers that are loaded.

**17. B.** The PATH statement is an environmental variable that is loaded from the AUTOEXEC.BAT. This statement can be used as the order in which to search for a file when the exact directory is not specified.

**18.** **C.** The F4 key is not available for controlling the boot process for DOS 6.2 like it is for Windows 95. Remember, use F8 to specify the boot menu in Windows 95.

**19.** **B.** In the example of a custom DOS startup menu in the CONFIG.SYS, DOS will default to the WORK configuration after 10 seconds if a choice is not made. Every menu item is valid, and no errors will be produced.

**20.** **B, C.** A drive can always be made bootable; you can do a FORMAT with the /S switch. However, you will erase all the information on the disk. You can also use the SYS command to transfer the system files to the hard disk. There is no BOOT command.

**21.** **B.** You will run FDISK to partition the hard disk. You would then use FORMAT to format the drive. You would then run SETUP to install Windows 95. PARTITION is not a utility program.

**22.** **A.** In DOS, device drivers are manually added to the AUTOEXEC.BAT and/or CONFIG.SYS file.

**23.** **B.** Windows 95 automatically detects and loads the drivers for almost all devices.

**24.** **A, C, D.** When installing Windows 95, the minimum requirements are that you have at least a 386DX processor with at least 4MB of memory. A compatible processor from Cyrix (586) or AMD (K6) will work.

**25.** **A.** During the PC startup, the standard sequence of events is to attempt to boot from the floppy drive, then to attempt to boot from the hard disk.

26. **B.** Windows 95 starts in Normal Mode by default. You have the full capabilities of Windows 95. When Windows 95 starts in Safe Mode, only the VGA and mouse drivers are loaded. You can then make corrections to the configuration errors.

27. **C.** Windows 95 will set the IRQ, IO memory addresses and DMA addresses for new devices when using Plug and Play. However, Windows NT 4.0 does not support Plug and Play.

28. **A.** When a new device is installed by Windows 95 using Plug and Play, Windows 95 looks for the drivers first in its library of drivers. Then it looks on the Windows 95 source disks. Finally, it asks the user to insert the disk with the drivers.

29. **B, D.** DOS always has the device drivers in the AUTOEXEC.BAT or CONFIG.SYS files, or in both files.

30. **A.** When attaching a printer to Windows 95, you should run the Printer wizard. To install other hardware devices, run the Add New Hardware wizard. To install new software, run the Add/Remove Software wizard. The Add New Hardware wizard and Add/Remove Software wizard are run from the Control Panel.

31. **A.** The information in both the AUTOEXEC.BAT and the CONFIG.SYS files can be and often is changed by the user. You can use any text editor or word processor to change them.

32. **C.** When using DOS, Windows 95, or Windows 3.*x* the maximum size of a partition is two gigabytes.

**33. B.** The customer gave the clue of what is wrong when she said it is safe to use. Windows 95 has started in Safe Mode and the only drivers loaded are the VGA and mouse drivers. The network drivers were not loaded, so you cannot run the network card.

**34. A.** At startup DOS requires the COMMAND.COM file to be present. AUTOEXEC.BAT, CONFIG.SYS, and WIN.COM may be run at startup, but are not required.

**35. B.** When you initially start installing Windows 95, the CD key is requested. After going through copying the files, Windows 95 restarts the PC and then sets up Plug and Play devices. After the installation ends, you can edit the AUUTOEXEC.BAT and CONFIG.SYS files.

**36. B.** All software is upgraded to use in Windows 95. Although Windows 95 versions will run better, you can still use Windows 3.x software.

**37. A.** You should always back up the hard disk before making changes such as adding hardware or software, or changing operating systems. You usually do not want to format the hard disk. Your old versions of software should still work. Keep copies of the old operating system, as you may have to go backward.

**38. B, D.** Windows 3.x will either load as a command in the AUTOEXEC.BAT file or load when prompted by the user.

**39. B.** I do not know what Microsoft's rational for this is. Granted, it will run, but it will look more like it is walking. I'd hate to try to run an Access database on one of these minimal machines. As far as the exam is concerned, the 20 MHz screamer in answer B is the one to choose. In real life, unless all you intend to do is play solitaire all day, I'd recommend a better system.

**40.** C. Only Windows 95b (OSR2) can recognize FAT32.

**41.** D. The FAT32 filing system that was available on Windows 95b overcame this limitation.

**42.** D. The MSDOS.SYS is the file to edit in order to dual boot. This file resides on the active partition in the root directory of the master drive. It is recommended that you read the Windows 95 resource kit before editing this file. This file must always be greater than 1024 bytes in size.

**43.** A, C. This mode is also referred to as DOS mode and DOS Compatibility Mode. This is for Windows 95 to be backward compatible with older software. Typically this software is a game that is graphically intensive, and is trying to control the hardware in ways that Windows 95 does not allow.

**44.** E. The SYS C: command will not delete any data, whereas the FORMAT command will destroy all of your data. Always use FDISK and FORMAT with extreme caution. Also realize that you must do one of these commands to make a drive bootable.

**45.** C. The switches can be found at the DOS prompt by typing the name of the command followed by /?. As shown here, you see what happens when you type FORMAT /? at the DOS prompt.

```
MS-DOS Prompt                                                    _ 🗗 ✕
Auto        ▾ □ 🖹 🖺 ⊞  🖳🖨  A

Microsoft(R) Windows 95
    (C)Copyright Microsoft Corp 1981-1995.

C:\WINDOWS>format /?
Formats a disk for use with MS-DOS.

FORMAT drive: [/V[:label]] [/Q] [/F:size] [/B | /S] [/C]
FORMAT drive: [/V[:label]] [/Q] [/T:tracks /N:sectors] [/B | /S] [/C]
FORMAT drive: [/V[:label]] [/Q] [/1] [/4] [/B | /S] [/C]
FORMAT drive: [/Q] [/1] [/4] [/8] [/B | /S] [/C]

  /V[:label]   Specifies the volume label.
  /Q           Performs a quick format.
  /F:size      Specifies the size of the floppy disk to format (such
               as 160, 180, 320, 360, 720, 1.2, 1.44, 2.88).
  /B           Allocates space on the formatted disk for system files.
  /S           Copies system files to the formatted disk.
  /T:tracks    Specifies the number of tracks per disk side.
  /N:sectors   Specifies the number of sectors per track.
  /1           Formats a single side of a floppy disk.
  /4           Formats a 5.25-inch 360K floppy disk in a high-density drive.
  /8           Formats eight sectors per track.
  /C           Tests clusters that are currently marked "bad."

C:\WINDOWS>
```

**46.** **A, B, C, D, E.** You can edit these system files by all the methods listed. You do need to be careful, however, about the extensions that the programs may put on the end of them. For example, Microsoft Word is going to try to put the .DOC extension on the end of the filename. This could have bad effects the next time you boot. In order to make this not happen, choose Save as and put the filename and the proper extension within parentheses. SYSEDIT is a good program to edit these files with.

**47.** **A, C, D.** There are many third-party software programs that do a much better job than SYSEDIT, but at least SYSEDIT centrally locates all of these files.

**48.** **C.** You should always use the Print Troubleshooter once the obvious problems have been excluded, such as a paper jam, offline printer, or powered off printer.

**49.** **B.** SETUP is becoming the standard command for installs, where INSTALL used to be. Be aware that you can install Windows 95 over a network.

**50.** **C.** In a normal boot sequence the floppy will be tried first, then the first hard disk, and so on. Since this is the second hard disk, it will be third in line.

**51.** **D.** While E would work, D will fix your drive of errors with the F command and the /C will mark the errors. C would not work because /E is not a valid switch for SYS. A is wrong because the FORMAT and FDISK commands are in reverse order. In B the /S switch is not used to make the disk a system disk.

**52.** **C.** The three primary modes that Windows will start in are Normal Mode, Safe Mode, and DOS Mode. You can choose these by pressing F8 at the "Starting Windows 95" caption.

**53.** **D, E.** The additional thing that Windows 95 Plug and Play configures and tracks is the IRQ addresses. You can manually configure these attributes on these resources and override what Windows 95 has done. This can be done in the Device Manager.

**54.** **A.** This is a good solution. Note that Device Manager is where you see such things as IRQs.

**55.** **A, B, C, D, E.** Answer D will put the icon in the start menu, whereas all the others will put the shortcut right on the desktop.

**56.** **E.** In order to find out what the problem is you must double-click the device.

**57.** **B.** The exam may ask you quite a few questions about MSDOS.SYS. This file controls multiboot, and a few other booting options.

**58.** **D.** In order for a hard disk to be bootable it must have an Active partition. Generally, there can only be one active partition on a hard disk.

**59.** **B.** Windows 95 OSR2 will support hard disks greater than 2GB in size because it has a 32-bit FAT system. This is also known as VFAT. Savings of drive space of up to 30 percent can be realized with this system when compared to identical drive sizes using the 16-bit file systems.

**60.** **C.** To transfer the system files to a hard disk without loosing any data on it, you should use the SYS command. This will allow the disk to be bootable, providing the partition is bootable.

**61.** **C.** Most devices in a PC require a device driver. This is necessary for the operating system to communicate with the device. Device drivers are normally provided by the manufacturer, but Windows 95 comes with many device drivers included, to make the installation easier for the end user.

**62.** **A, B.** In DOS, most device drivers are loaded in the CONFIG.SYS file. A few exceptions to this are the MOUSE.COM driver and part of the CD-ROM driver interface, MSCDEX.EXE, which loads in the AUTOEXEC.BAT.

**63.** **B.** Pressing F8 when the Starting Windows 95 prompt appears will open a menu system that allows the user to temporarily modify the startup options, to aid in troubleshooting a system that is having trouble starting up.

**64.** **C.** To start DOS in interactive mode, press F8 when the Starting MS-DOS prompt appears during system bootup. This option will allow you to confirm or skip each line in the CONFIG.SYS and AUTOEXEC.BAT files, to troubleshoot system startup.

**65.** **C.** To add a new device to Windows 95 you should use the Add New Hardware applet that is located in Control Panel. This applet uses wizards to assist you in configuring resources for the device and installing the appropriate drivers.

**66.** **C.** To change configuration settings in Windows 95, you should use the Control Panel folder located in the My Computer folder on the Windows 95 desktop. This provides a graphical interface to make system and device driver changes to the PC.

**67.** **D.** Windows 95 Plug and Play system will track IRQ settings, DMA settings, and base addresses for Plug and Play-compliant devices installed in the system. This makes it easier than ever to configure hardware for PCs.

**68.** **B.** To install a new device in Windows 95, an INF file is usually provided by the device manufacturer, along with the appropriate drivers. This file describes the device to the operating system and assists the Add New Hardware wizard in setting up the device.

**69.** **B, C, D.** A device listed in Device Manager with a ! next to it means at least one of three things: The device driver failed to load properly, there is a resource conflict between that device and another one installed in the system, or the device driver is corrupted. The problem could be a combination of these, as well.

**70.** **B.** Windows 3.*x* will not run without HIMEM.SYS. Windows requires this driver to use extended memory. The use of extended memory is key to the functioning of Windows. Windows 95 loads HIMEM.SYS during bootup, even if it is not in the CONFIG.SYS.

**71. A.** The SYSEDIT utility is a multi-document text editor that automatically opens the CONFIG.SYS, AUTOEXEC.BAT, WIN.INI, and SYSTEM.INI files for editing purposes. It will also open PROTOCOL.INI and MSMAIL.INI, if they exist.

**72. C.** When modifying any of the Windows system-configurable text files, it is always better to comment out a suspect line than to delete it. This makes it easier to restore it later, if necessary.

**73. B.** The semicolon ( ; ) works as a comment in the WIN.INI and SYSTEM.INI files. This is the preferred method to temporarily disable a line within those files.

**74. C.** To format a disk and make it bootable, use the FORMAT /S command syntax. The /S means, "add the system files to this disk."

**75. D.** All three choices are possibilities. In order to run some older DOS programs in Windows 95, it may be necessary to edit the properties for the icon shortcut. This is a better method than editing the properties for the program itself. Running Windows 95 in DOS mode is for those DOS programs that insist on addressing the hardware directly. As a last resort, you could use the Run Old Version of DOS option as a dual boot between Win95 and DOS. This option could be made available by pressing F8 during the bootup sequence when the screen prompt displays Starting Windows 95.

**76. A, B.** To set up Windows 95 on a Microsoft Network, you only need to purchase a network card and the network cable. All of the software to connect to an NT server, or for a peer-to-peer network, comes with Windows 95. It even comes with a client for Novell Network.

# Diagnosing and Troubleshooting

**I.** **D.** The DOS SETVER utility is provided to trick DOS into believing that it is running files in the correct version of the operating system. With this command, you can report a different version of DOS for the specified application.

**2.** **B.** In order to remedy a situation with a corrupt swap file in Windows 3.*x*, you must go to the 386 Enhanced section in the Control Panel and set the swap file to None. Next time you reboot the computer, the corrupt swap file will be gone.

**3.** **B, C.** You will get the error if the file is actually deleted from the C:\WINDOWS\COMMAND directory, or if there is a line in CONFIG.SYS referencing another version of HIMEM.SYS. If there is such a line, simply delete it.

**4.** **C.** DOS Mode, or DOS Compatibility Mode as it is commonly known, allows execution of some older MS-DOS applications that are not capable of running in Windows 95. These applications are primarily applications that attempt to access hardware that Windows 95 controls directly.

**5.** **B.** Creating a Windows 95 boot disk is done in the Add/Remove Programs icon in the Control Panel. Select the Startup Disk tab, and then click the Create Disk button.

**6.** **D.** When you are dealing with a stalled print job, you would like to save the document that is currently printing. In order to do this, you need to click the File menu from the Printer Properties and select Restart Printing.

**7.** **A.** Whenever you see a printer printing garbled characters, especially after being installed, you should verify that you have the correct driver and/or print processor. The current processor or driver is not doing very well at translating the information.

**8.** **A, C, D.** With network problems, it is wise to first check the obvious, such as bad cable, account locked out, forgotten password. Verify the problem before you continue reinstalling and tearing apart a system.

**9.** **C.** MSD is a very quick and detailed method of obtaining system information. Although it's provided with Windows 3.1, it is not provided with Windows 95.

**10.** **B.** In the event you are infected with a virus in the boot record, you may be able to remove it by issuing the FDISK /MBR command. This command will replace the Master Boot Record with a copy.

**11.** **B.** The differences between the Windows version of SCANDISK and the DOS version of SCANDISK is that the Windows version does not need the /FIX switch to fix errors; this is enabled by default.

**12.** **B.** To adjust the amount of memory used for a DOS application, you need to make a shortcut to the application, and then modify the properties for that shortcut. This way, when the application begins, it will use the settings that you configured especially for this application.

**13.** **A.** CMOS viruses are viruses that make themselves resident in the CMOS of the computer. These viruses are the most difficult to remove. CMOS viruses frequently cause harm to the hardware of the computer.

**14. B.** The easiest and most common way to fix a startup or boot problem is to rerun the Setup program that came with the operating system. Just doing this can save hours of troubleshooting.

**15. C.** Enabling dynamic memory allocation permits Windows 95 to automatically give an application memory when it needs it and take memory away when the application is not using it.

**16. B.** The best solution to an application that frequently causes illegal operations errors is to force the application to run in MS-DOS mode. Applications can be forced to run in MS-DOS mode by clicking the Advanced button from the Program panel of the Shortcut Properties dialog box.

**17. C.** DEFRAG can reorganize files into contiguous sections so the hard disk will not have to work as much to read the files. The condition in which files are spread all over the disk is called fragmentation.

**18. A, B, C, D.** When you get a virus, maybe the virus itself won't destroy data, but the process of removing the virus may destroy data. You may need to format and partition a drive to remove a virus, in which case, you will lose data if the virus comes unexpectedly.

**19. A.** MSD is a good utility for displaying a wealth of information when it comes to troubleshooting a computer. This includes memory, disk, network, ports, and operating system details.

**20. C.** If the program will only run on Windows 95 and you are on a different version (3.*x*), the message will say "Wrong Windows version". Remember that Windows 4.0 and Windows 95 are the same thing.

21. **D.** SETVER allows you to tell DOS to tell a program that a different version of DOS is running.

22. **A, B.** You should first check if the driver is present. You will probably need to reinstall it. If it is not present and you no longer need it, fix the CONFIG.SYS file. There is no need to remove the CONFIG.SYS file.

23. **B.** HIMEM.SYS is loaded as a driver for Windows 3.1 as the first executable line in the CONFIG.SYS file.

24. **C.** When Windows 95 starts in DOS Mode, no GUI items are loaded. You have full DOS capability at the DOS prompt and you must use this to run some older DOS games.

25. **D.** The network drivers were probably not loaded by AUTOEXEC.BAT. The network card could be bad, but check the AUTOEXEC.BAT file first. Safe and Normal modes are in Windows 95, not 3.*x*.

26. **C.** ATTRIB allows you to display or set the attributes for files.

27. **C, D.** Computer viruses quite often are destructive, but that is not always the intention. Sometimes they were meant only to appear bad, and errors in coding caused them to become destructive. There are also many hoaxes or rumors of viruses that do not exist. Always run an anti-virus program, and before passing along e-mail of rumors, confirm that there really is a virus.

28. **C.** SCANDISK is Microsoft's program to check disk drives for errors and to fix them.

29. **A.** FDISK partitions a hard disk.

**30.** C. SCANDISK is Microsoft's program to check disk drives for errors and to fix them.

**31.** B. Windows 95 uses the Registry to store settings. In DOS the settings are stored in the CONFIG.SYS and AUTOEXEC.BAT files. Windows 3.1 uses SYSTEM.INI to store part of the settings.

**32.** B, C. Tell this customer that the CPU was told by a program to do something it couldn't do. Emphasize this is a program problem, not a user problem. He simply should press OK, which will end and restart the program.

**33.** A, B, C, D, E. A and B happen to have been upgraded for the Windows environment. If you use the online help you can find all of the tools that have been upgraded and added to Windows.

**34.** C. The correct syntax for this command is SETVER [drive:path] filename n.nn (where n.nn is the version that you want to change it to). D and Q are the only switches with this command. These probably will not be tested, though. Just knowing the syntax and the fact that you should use SETVER when you get an incorrect DOS version should suffice for the exam.

**35.** A, C. The Windows directory is the same as saying C:\WINDOWS\. This file is needed in order to run Windows 3.1.

**36.** A, C, E. The power cord and the hard disk cable may be loose. This is a problem that occurs more than one might think. The setup disk can be helpful, too. This disk contains utilities to revive the operating system. Take the time to figure out all of the ways to make a startup disk and make one. Examine all of the files on it, since you may be tested on this.

**37.** **C, D, E.** You should first reboot by pressing F8 when Starting Windows 95 appears. You should then run SCANDISK. If this does not work, you should then run the setup disk. This error occurs when the system is unable to initialize the driver that controls the file system on the drive.

**38.** **A, E.** If you search for startup disk in the help it will direct you on how to make one in their online interactive tutorials.

**39.** **C.** The Registry should not be tampered with unless you have no alternative. Answer C is the best choice. Rebooting is a good technique, though. It refreshes everything and gets rid of any lingering problems since you last started your system.

**40.** **A, B, C and D.** These are the files that will be copied to the new disk.

**41.** **D.** While answers A and B may solve the problem, neither is the best solution. First of all, a bi-directional printer has many good features that you should not disable. Secondly, and more importantly, many printer companies are saying that if a bi-directional cord is not used on a printer, the printer warranty is null and void. This is because they have seen the damage that a uni-directional cable can do to a printer.

**42.** **A, D.** The Detail tab is the proper place to install a driver, if you already have the driver. You can change the port on this same screen. Many times you will need to download the driver and this is where it should be run from.

**43.** **A, B, C, D, E.** Reboot should be first. Checking the network connections can be helpful if they are running the program off of an application server. In this case the connection or the server may be to blame. Try running the program with another computer hooked up to the same server. A re-install is tedious in that you just can't install over what is there. You need to completely uninstall the old one and save the user's macros, settings, and other items. Then you can re-install and piece everything back together.

44. **B.** Backing up your data is the most important thing to remember, although all the other answer options are valid as well. Backing up data is repeatedly stressed on the A+ exam.

45. **A.** SCANDISK can wreck long file names if you are using the 16-bit version, and DEFRAG can hinder undeletion. Note the filing system and the operating system that are being used when determining if these programs should be run.

46. **A.** Conflict Troubleshooter will guide you through resolving the problem, which may involve going into the Device Manager.

47. **B.** As far as the exam is concerned you should not go into the Registry without backing it up. You should choose Read Only as the mode. And if you ever do change anything, it should be because there is absolutely no alternative.

48. **A, C.** It is important to realize how viruses are spread in order to combat them effectively.

49. **C.** Dynamic Memory Allocation is a term you should memorize for the exam.

50. **A.** This screen offers a helpful way of looking at things.

51. **D.** EMF. Paying attention to the small details in an operating system is crucial to your success on the A+ exam.

**52.** **C.** The error "Incorrect DOS version" is caused when a DOS executable is launched from a directory that does not have the same version of DOS installed as the system has booted on. The version on the customer's PC is different from the one on your boot floppy. In this case you would have to figure out which version of DOS the customer has loaded on his hard disk and use the same version boot disk to continue with the repair.

**53.** **B.** The DOS environment is the area where things such as SET command parameters live in memory. Normally, DOS reserves only a small amount of memory for these variables. Many programs, such as AutoCAD, will require more environment space to run. Use the SHELL–C:\DOS\ COMMAND.COM /P /E:1024 command line in the CONFIG.SYS file to increase the environment space. In this example, the /E:1024 creates an environment size of 1024 bytes. The /P means permanent. In other words, use this and only this COMMAND.COM as the interpreter for this PC session.

**54.** **B, D.** The reason for the error message is that the operating system cannot find the command interpreter, COMMAND.COM. This is most likely because COMMAND.COM has been deleted from the hard disk root, or the SHELL command is pointing to the wrong path for COMMAND.COM.

**55.** **B, C, D.** The Windows 3.*x* permanent swap file, which is used for virtual memory, is a hidden system file. It requires contiguous space on the hard disk. It has the extension .PAR. The full name of the file is 386SPART.PAR.

**56.** **B.** To set up a permanent swap file in Windows 3.*x* you should use the Control Panel 386-enhanced applet. It looks like a little IC chip. You can select Permanent or Temporary as options, and 16-bit or 32-bit disk and file access on the later versions of Windows 3.*x*.

**57. C.** The best way to deal with this type of problem is to use the DOS-based portion of Windows setup. From the C:\WINDOWS directory prompt, enter SETUP to run this utility. Actually, in many cases you may not even get the error message, but rather a black screen with a blinking cursor following the Windows logo. Use this setup to change the display adapter type to one that will work, such as standard VGA, so you can start Windows.

**58. C, D.** The WIN.INI is similar to the AUTOEXEC.BAT in that it sets up the environment for Windows. If a line points to the wrong path for a file you will get an error generated by that line. A common cause of this is when a customer deletes a program that had modified the WIN.INI with some parameters it requires. Check for the presence of the path and file mentioned on the troublesome line and use a text editor to correct the line in WIN.INI or comment it out, if the files it calls for do not exist any longer.

**59. D.** Windows 95 will automatically load HIMEM.SYS, so it is not necessary to have any mention of it in the CONFIG.SYS file.

**60. C.** Windows will automatically start in safe mode when a critical device driver is unable to load. This is a feature, not a bug. Therefore, the correct answer for this question is that Windows cannot load a critical device driver and has automatically started in safe mode.

**61. D.** All of the items mentioned can cause the symptom of Windows reporting a bad or missing COMMAND.COM. Adding a path statement to the AUTOEXEC.BAT that does not include C:\WINDOWS\ COMMAND will cause this error. So will an incorrect COMSPEC line, or an incorrectly entered SHELL command line.

**62. C.** To create an emergency boot disk for a Windows 95 PC you can use the Add/Remove Programs applet in Control Panel. There is a tab on the next dialog box called Startup Disk. Click that, and a wizard will guide you through the process.

**63.** **C.** To troubleshoot a printing problem in Windows 95, the easiest method is the to use the Print Troubleshooting wizard. Click Start to access this, then click Help, then search for Print Troubleshooting and select Troubleshooting Printer Problems to start the wizard.

**64.** **D.** To change the port settings on a PC to enable bi-directional features, use the CMOS Settings | Peripheral Device Settings in the SETUP utility for the PC motherboard. Following this, you will need to run the Add New Hardware applet in Control Panel to update the Windows 95 system to support the bi-directional features of the printer port.

**65.** **B, C.** A grayed-out Printer icon means that Windows cannot access that printer. It could be because "Use Printer Offline" has been selected, or the network path to that printer is not available. Once you have corrected the problem, if it is a network printer, you may have to open the Printers folder, highlight that printer and click File, then uncheck the Work Offline setting in the drop-down menu.

**66.** **A.** After changing the settings for a printer port from SPP to ECP or EPP, you should use the Add New Hardware applet to update the port settings. This will ensure proper operation of all the features of the enhanced port in Windows 95.

**67.** **A.** Whenever a program does something that Windows 95 doesn't like, it creates a GPF. The wording has caused many customers to call me and ask if they have broken the law. The phrase "illegal operation" usually means that the program has tried to write to a piece of memory that Windows isn't happy with. The best thing to tell this customer is to re-boot the system and see if the problem continues.

**68.** **A, C.** If a GPF fault continues to occur within a specific application, the best thing to do is first try uninstalling and reinstalling the application. Always reboot between the uninstall and reinstall to update Registry settings properly for the system. If the problem continues after this, contact that application's technical support for assistance and possible upgrades, patches, or fixes for the problem.

69. **D.** If you suspect a hard disk is having problems, the best thing to do is to run the SCANDISK utility to check and repair the drive. SCANDISK will actually move data from bad clusters to other ones if possible during the process.

70. **D.** A handy utility to troubleshoot system resources is Microsoft Diagnostics (MSD). This will report such things as system settings, IRQ, and memory resources to aid in troubleshooting resource conflicts and other configuration problems.

# Networks

1. **A, B, C, D.** DOS, Windows 3.*x*, and Windows 95 are all capable of sharing files and printers with other users on the network. Of course, some operating systems are easier to configure than others. These operating system are also capable of joining a Windows NT domain to take advantage of the domain's resources.

2. **D.** E-mail uses what is known as "store and forward," which means e-mail can be stored on many different servers over the course of its travel. This means the source and destination do not have to maintain a connection while the e-mail is being sent.

3. **B.** The example in the question is HyperText Markup Language or HTML, which is the language in which most Web pages are written. HTML is a modular language that is fairly simple to use, and allows for special formatting to be applied to documents without a great deal of work.

**4.** **C.** These are examples of the many File Transfer Protocol (FTP) commands for downloading, uploading, navigating, and connecting to FTP servers. FTP is still very prevalent on the Internet; HTTP is mostly the front-end to the FTP server.

**5.** **B.** Domain Name Service, or DNS, is used to resolve friendly host and domain names such as comptia.com to IP addresses. Other documentation can refer to DNS as Domain Name System, or Domain Naming Service, but Microsoft generally uses Domain Name Service.

**6.** **C.** Microsoft's Internet Information Server is not required to gain access to the network when you are using modems to access the Internet. You will need to research modems, Internet Service Providers (ISPs), and web browsers, among other things.

**7.** **B.** The manual for your modem will not provide you with a valid IP address for the Internet. This is received from the Internet Service Provider, either automatically or manually, for you to configure your dial-up software with.

**8.** **B.** Although all answers are possible, the best answer when it comes to ease of installation and cost is a modem pool. You can have a modem pool of five modems that will be shared by all fifteen users, although not at one time. This eliminates the need to buy fifteen modems and configure these new modems for each workstation.

**9.** **C.** Making a default starting web page when the user opens up the web browser, especially in a company intranet, will make navigation easier for the user. This start page should have links to other sites or pages of interest.

**10.** **A, B, C, D.** When configuring an e-mail application, you are usually required to provide some information, such as the user's e-mail address, full name, password to access the mail account, and the POP3 or SMTP server. The POP3 or SMTP settings will be provided by the Internet Service Provider.

11. **B.** Binding a protocol means telling the computer that this protocol that is bound to the adapter will be used to communicate over the adapter. Since you are using IPX/SPX on the LAN, you can bind this protocol to the network adapter card, and bind TCP/IP to the modem for the Internet connection.

12. **A, B, C, D.** Just because you are using DOS doesn't mean sharing files on your workstation is any different. In addition to determining the level of access users have to folders on your computer, you can even assign passwords to resources. A user who knows the password will have access to the files.

13. **C.** You should never have to know the hardware (physical) address of your computer when troubleshooting dial-up networking. If you are using a modem to connect to the Internet, troubleshoot how the modem is configured, the phone line, and the protocol being used. Every computer on the Internet requires a unique IP address, so this may be the problem, too.

14. **D.** There can be many settings you can specify when configuring the web browser, but no web browser will ask for the Internet Service Provider's SNMP address. You often have to enter a default home or start page, and e-mail settings, such as username, password, and SMTP and/or POP3 mail settings.

15. **B.** Simple Network Management Protocol (SNMP) will most likely not be something you are using while you are accessing the Internet. It is quite possible that you will be using the File Transfer Protocol (FTP), querying a

Domain Name Service (DNS) server to resolve host names, and using Simple Mail Transfer Protocol (SMTP) for e-mail.

**16.** **B.** You do not need to configure parity for a network adapter card. A serial device such as a modem sends and receives information one bit at a time. Parity is used as error checking to make sure every bit arrived intact, just as it was on the original source computer.

**17.** **D.** None of the answers described a difference between configuring network cards in Windows 3.*x* and Windows 95. However, Windows 95 is a Plug and Play operating system, which can make the configuration of a network card much easier, although this was not an available answer.

**18.** **A, C. and D.** Of the software listed, it is highly unlikely you will need to install a driver for your serial port before you can get on the Internet. You will most likely need modem drivers, dial-up networking software, and possibly software for the new protocols, such as TCP/IP, that you may need to install.

**19.** **C.** DNS is the service used on the Internet to resolve a domain name to an IP address. Without DNS, you would have to memorize IP addresses when surfing the web, which wouldn't be very practical.

**20.** **C.** It is quite common to forget to dial the 9 to get out of the office when using a dial-up connection at work. Usually the phone will start ringing after about four numbers, or you will be informed that there is no such number. Either way, you won't be connecting.

**21.** **B, C, D.** The basic network topologies are ring, star, and bus. Ethernet is a popular architecture.

**22.** **B.** 10Base5 cable is used for ThickNet.

**23.** **A.** A collision on a network is when two computers send a message at the same time. The messages collide and must be resent. This occurs when using CSMA/CD.

**24.** **B.** NAUN is the Nearest Active Upstream Neighbor, which is the station that transmits to you.

**25.** **C.** Since the network was running at 4 Mbps and you can attach, your card and the settings must be fine. If one card on the network runs at 4 Mbps, the network runs at 4 Mbps.

**26.** **B.** A token ring network can have up to 260 nodes.

**27.** **A.** An ethernet network can have up to 500 nodes.

**28.** **B.** Listed from the bottom to the top, the seven layers of the OSI reference model are: Physical, Data Link, Network, Transport, Session, Presentation, and Application.

**29.** **C.** Telnet is the service you use to attach to a UNIX computer as a terminal.

**30.** **B.** FTP. OSI is the reference model that most networking uses.

**31.** **C.** IP addresses are 32 bits long and are broken up into four numbers, which are each 8 bits, separated by periods.

**32.** **B.** Class B addresses range from 128.0.___.___ to 191.255.___.___.

**33. B.** You can assign a temporary address using Dynamic Host Configuration Protocol. DHCP is used by most ISPs to assign IP addresses.

**34. A, B, C.** The URL for a web page includes the protocol (HTTP), domain name (for example, www.disney.com), and the path or file name (for example, index.html).

**35. A, C.** You can choose Map Network Drive by right-clicking the Network Neighborhood or choosing Tools in Windows Explorer.

**36. A, D.** Since the customer does not have any other phone problems, you can eliminate a bad phone line. If the modem does not work in your office, either the modem or the cable must be bad.

**37. B.** V.34 is the standard for 33.6 Kbps.

**38. A.** V.90 is the industry standard for 56 Kbps.

**39. C.** Although Eudora 3.0 is Y2K ready, it is written in C and is unable to handle dates greater than 2034. Correct the date.

**40. A, B, D.** The way to look at an Internet Service Provider is that it charges you money to connect to it. Answer C involves the company you work for buying the equipment, so they are not selling you anything. It does not matter how you connect to them. They are third-party suppliers of a service that they sell to the public.

**41. A, B, E.** The Internet is a Wide Area Network (WAN). It is an internetwork of computers and this is exactly how it got its name. It is public. Also keep in mind that it has been set up as a non-profit venture, and nobody owns the Internet.

**42.** C. The Internet is based on the protocol TCP/IP. The IP address is a number that has 4 numbers, separated by periods. Without getting into too much detail, the numbers have to be between 1 and 254 and may not include 127.

**43.** A, B. Domain names are the names assigned to IP addresses so that people can remember them easily.

**44.** B. Read. Generally, to share a file you highlight the file and choose Sharing from the menu. Then, depending on the system, you assign permissions to different users and you can then assign a password for them to enter to use the file. On the other end, people map a drive and choose your file and then they have whatever permissions you give them.

**45.** A, D. When you are sharing something with others you become a server. When you are connecting to a shared item you are a client. If you are doing both, you are a client and server.

**46.** A, D. A device is hardware, so a modem and a printer qualify. You can share just about any piece of hardware on a computer. The only thing to keep in mind is that the server that you are connected to must be turned on and communicating with the network, and shared with the proper permissions.

**47.** C. FTP stands for File Transfer Protocol. If you watch your browser when you download files off the WWW, you will notice that it's usually using the FTP protocol to download files from a directory located on the remote host.

**48.** **E.** The phone line being unplugged, or being in the wrong plug, is a common problem. Always heed the manufacturer's installation guidelines.

**49.** **A, B, C, D, E.** Networking has been around for quite a while and most major operating systems are capable of it, however primitive it is. LAN Manager was created for DOS and OS/2. For Windows 3.1 and 3.11 you need to have TCP/IP32 installed in order to have TCP/IP networking. Windows 95 has the client version of this software included.

**50.** **C.** The Internet Service Provider will provide you with your POP3 server and SMTP. These are just the servers that are going to handle things in your account like e-mail traffic.

**51.** **D.** The question is asking what is necessary. You could use a modem to connect to the network without network card drivers or network cable.

**52.** **A, B, E.** Going through the Internet is technically downloading files. Reading an attachment means that you have downloaded the attached file that was sent with the e-mail. A logon batch is a script that is run when you log on to a computer. This can contain a download from a server of things such as a patch for an anti-virus program.

**53.** **B, C, D.** The problem cannot be a virus, because you have not done anything to let one into your system. The printer going offline and paper jamming are always possibilities. When you go on the Internet, the pages that you visit get stored on your hard disk. If you do not limit these, they could take up a lot of room on your hard disk. If these take up the last space on your hard disk, the printer will not have a place to spool the print job. This will stall the printer.

**54.** **A.** The DNS (Domain Name Server) server resolves these names. Domain Name Servers are actually servers that are part of the Domain Name System.

55. **A, B, C, E.** HTML is a language and not a vehicle to upload. E-mail can be sent with attachments. You can upload into FTP and HTTP. A shared drive is capable of uploading, if the shared drive is on the receiving end of the computer.

56. **A, D.** You would choose the file, then Properties | Sharing. Note that this only works when you have a networking setup. If you want to share a printer, you can highlight it in the Printer folder and share it in a similar manner.

57. **B, C, D.** You will need DNS to resolve host names, and you also have to identify your machine with a host name and domain.

58. **A, B, C.** America Online is an ISP. ISPs derive income from selling the service of providing an onramp to the Internet. They are also an online service, because they provide content of their own that is non-Internet. Answer B is correct, because the connection is through phone lines. The screen is a Graphical User Interface.

59. **B.** To connect your PC to a LAN you will need a Network Interface Card. This device will provide a physical connection to the LAN with your PC.

60. **C.** A workstation uses client software to communicate with the server on a LAN. Windows 95 includes client software for many different types of LANs, including Microsoft Network and Novell Network.

61. **A, B.** To install a network card you usually need an IRQ and a base address. Some high-end network cards may also require a DMA channel.

62. **A, B, C.** To access a mail server on the Internet you need a username, password, and the mail server domain name or IP address. Actually the mail server can be anywhere on the Internet. Most ISP accounts include an

e-mail account, but you can actually maintain an e-mail account anywhere on the Internet, once you are connected.

63. **A, D.** A valid e-mail address must be in the format <username>@hostname.domain. The invalid e-mail addresses in this question are www.joesmith.com, which is the format for a web page address, and ftp.joepc.com, which is an FTP site.

64. **A.** The proper format for entering a URL for a web site is HTTP://www. microsoft.com. HTTP is the protocol for HTML pages. HTML is not a valid TCP/IP protocol.

65. **B.** Every host (PC) on the Internet must have a unique IP address. The only variance to this rule is in the case of a proxy server. In the special case of the proxy server, the IP address is provided by the proxy server to the client.

66. **B.** TCP/IP is considered a routable protocol. That is how the Internet works! To satisfy your curiosity, try typing the following in a DOS window on a Windows 95 PC when you are connected to the Internet: TRACERT www.tgsolutions.com. You should see the entire route, including all of the IP hops from your PC to my web site IP address.

67. **B.** To set up dial-up networking on a Windows 95 PC, you would first click My Computer. The Dial-up Networking applet is then accessed by clicking the Dial-up Networking icon. There is a wizard to assist you in setting up the connection. You will need several parameters from your ISP to get this going.

68. **B, C, D.** To set up dial-up networking in Windows 95 you would click Start, then Control Panel | Add Remove Software. Click the Windows Setup tab. Highlight the Communications icon. Then click Details and

check the Dialup Networking check box. Then click OK. You will be prompted for the Windows 95 CD.

69. **B.** In this illustration, you should be able to tell that some, but not all of the communications applications are installed. The grayed check box is your clue to this. You would have to click Details to see which applets are currently installed on this system.

70. **A, C.** Microsoft Internet Explorer 3.*x* can browse a web site and download from an FTP site. It cannot upload to an FTP site.

71. **B.** DHCP stands for Dynamic Host Configuration Protocol. This service makes administering a TCP/IP LAN easy on the Administrator. Most NOSs have a DHCP implementation such as Novell NetWare and Windows NT Server. It can save a lot of footwork.

72. **D.** A properly configured DHCP server can provide all of the items listed and more. It can provide an IP address, gateway address (also known as the default route), and the DNS address for Internet domain name resolution.

73. **B.** Of the choices given, the only correct choice is TCP/IP 32. IPX/SPX alone will not allow Internet access. NetBEUI isn't even a routable protocol.

74. **C.** If you connect to the Internet through a proxy server, you must let Internet Explorer know. To do this, set the properties for Internet Explorer by right-clicking the Desktop icon and left-clicking Properties on the drop-down menu. Then select the Connection tab. Check the box for Proxy Server and enter the correct parameters for the proxy server connection.

75. **A, B, C.** To enable Internet e-mail for Microsoft Exchange you will need to set up the personal folders, Internet mail, and personal address book. You need the personal folders for a place to store your e-mail locally.

**76.** **B.** The most common cause of mail returning as undeliverable is that the user has typed the e-mail address incorrectly. Answers C and D are also possible causes, but double-check the spelling of the address first.

**77.** **A, B.** To access Internet news services, you will require Internet access such as an ISP account and an account on a news server. There are many free news servers on which you can obtain an account. Some ISPs provide this service as part of your subscription package.

# Part 3

## Practice Exams

*Q & A*

# Test Yourself:
# Core Exam

PRACTICE
EXAMS

Q & A

his Practice Test will help you measure your readiness to take the A+ Core Exam. It contains the same number of questions as the exam. See if you can complete this test under "exam conditions," before you check any of the answers. Read all the choices carefully, as there may be more than one correct answer. Choose all correct answers for each question.

# Core Exam Test Yourself Questions

1. The pathway for signals to travel across the system board is called:

   A. Cache
   B. Bus
   C. ISA
   D. PCI

2. Which of the following are acceptable voltages from the power supply?

   A. + or – 5 Vdc
   B. + or – 12 Vdc
   C. + or – 120 Vac
   D. + or – 12.8 Vdc

3. When working on a computer you must ground the PC and yourself to prevent ESD from damaging parts. What is ESD?

   A. Electro Static Discharge
   B. Extra Static Damage

4. The customer complains that the letter N sticks on the keyboard. He assumes that this means he must buy a new keyboard. What should you do first?

   A. Sell him a new keyboard
   B. Clean the keyboard
   C. Check the plug
   D. Clean the N key

**5.** The customer calls and complains that the computer can not read the CD-ROM drive. What do you have the customer check?

A. CD is in right side up

B. Computer is turned on

C. Modem is plugged in

D. CD is in drive

**6.** When installing a modem, you go to check it at the end. The phone line plugged in the modem does not work and the modem gets no dial tone. What did you do wrong?

A. Bad modem

B. Bad phone line

C. Modem will not work with phone

D. Phone and line to phone company are plugged in wrong connections

**7.** When cleaning dust from computer parts, use:

A. Compressed air cans

B. Compressed air hose at a service station

C. Vacuum cleaner

D. Plain towels

**8.** When working with a monitor you should:

A. Use an ESD device

B. Keep both hands on the monitor

C. Touch wires to kill the power

D. Not use an ESD device

**9.** After using chemical solvents on a computer you should do what with them?

A. Contact the state environmental office for disposal rules

B. Put them in the trash

C. Flush them down the toilet

D. Throw them away

**10.** The Pentium Pro CPU chip has a _____ data bus.

    A. 8-bit

    B. 16- bit

    C. 32-bit

    D. 64-bit

**11.** The _____ architecture was introduced to compete with the IBM PS/2 computers.

    A. ISA

    B. EISA

    C. PCI

    D. VESA

**12.** A gigabyte is _____ bytes in the memory of a computer.

    A. 1,073,741,824

    B. 1,000,000,000

    C. 1,024

    D. 1,048,576

**13.** During the cleaning step of the electro-photographic print process:

    A. The toner is permanently bonded to the paper

    B. The photosensitive drum is cleaned and electrically erased

    C. A high voltage negative charge is applied to the drum

    D. The image is transferred to the paper

**14.** Network printers' maximum cable length is restricted to:

    A. 10 feet

    B. 25 feet

    C. The length specified by the type of network

    D. No restriction

**15.** A daisy wheel printer fails to print the letter E. What is the likely problem?

    A. Bad printer cable

    B. E broken off wheel

    C. Bad ribbon

    D. Wrong IRQ

**16.** Your customer wants a battery for her laptop computer. She is concerned about price. What is your recommendation?

    A. NiCad

    B. LiIon

    C. NiMH

    D. Alkaline

**17.** All PC cards (PCMCIA) are what size?

    A. 85.6 mm x 54 mm

    B. 3.3 mm x 5.0 mm

    C. 200 mm x 50 mm

    D. 100 mm x 50 mm

**18.** A pointing device on a portable computer that is similar to a mouse, except the ball side is up, is called:

    A. Mouse

    B. Trackball

    C. Pointing stick

    D. Touch pad

**19.** Portable computer displays can be:

    A. CRT

    B. Active matrix LCD

    C. Passive matrix LCD

    D. LED

PRACTICE EXAMS

**20.** Cable types that are referred to as BNC, ThinNet, and 10Base2 are in the general category of what type cable?

   A. Coaxial
   B. Twisted Pair
   C. STP
   D. Fiber Optic

**21.** The maximum length of a twisted pair cable is:

   A. 100 meters
   B. 180 meters
   C. no limit
   D. 6 feet

**22.** The Internet uses the _____ protocol.

   A. TCP/IP
   B. NetBEUI
   C. IPX/SPX
   D. DECnet

**23.** You have been instructed to install additional memory in all the machines. The supervisor has directed you to do this even if no one is at the desk. When you finish on a machine without the user being present, you should:

   A. Leave
   B. Leave the machine unassembled so the user knows you were there
   C. Leave a note saying what was done
   D. Leave a note concerning the messy desk

**24.** What attitude should you convey to a customer non-verbally?

   A. Calm
   B. Confident
   C. Angry
   D. Throwing items down

**25.** When making a repair to a PC, the user asks you to install a piece of software used by the company, but there is no license for that machine. The customer states that they need it and would get a license, but there is no money left in the budget.

   A. The customer is right. Install the software.

   B. Tell the user that your company policy does not allow you to install it.

   C. Tell the user that the company must get a license and you will come back when they do.

   D. Report the user to his supervisor.

**26.** You have finished installation of a new CD-ROM drive in a user's computer. When you are finished with the installation, you install the CD-ROM device drivers. Upon restarting the PC, the CD-ROM device drivers load successfully, but you don't hear any sound in Windows. What is most likely the problem?

   A. The wrong device driver has been loaded

   B. The audio cable has not been connected to the sound card

   C. You must configure the sound port

   D. The sound card is not configured to use the CD-ROM drive

**27.** What is the setting of the DIP switch shown here?

   A. 0010010

   B. 1101110

   C. 0100100

   D. 1011011

28. What is the most common cause of configuration problems when working with SCSI devices?

    A. IRQ conflicts
    B. Termination
    C. Address conflicts
    D. DMA channel conflicts

29. While you are working on a customer's computer that is experiencing video problems, you reboot the system and the mouse no longer works. You check that there are no IRQ conflicts with the mouse, but the mouse still does not work. What else could be the problem?

    A. Incorrect DMA channel
    B. I/O address conflict
    C. You may have disabled the mouse in BIOS
    D. Incorrect mouse driver

30. Which of the following will not cause a laser printer to print light or faint text?

    A. The transfer corona
    B. A worn ribbon
    C. Low toner
    D. The contrast setting

31. Which of the following error messages is usually displayed when a keyboard error is detected at system startup?

    A. 1**
    B. 2**
    C. 3**
    D. 4**

**32.** Which of the following is the best way to protect a computer system during an electrical storm?

A. Unplug the computer
B. Use a UPS
C. Use a surge suppressor
D. Turn off the computer

**33.** What is the best way to clean the drive heads in a floppy drive?

A. Cotton swab and isopropyl alcohol
B. A cleaning diskette
C. Cotton swab and denatured alcohol
D. You should not have to clean the heads in a floppy drive

**34.** Which of the following components are recyclable?

A. Monitors
B. Nickel-cadmium batteries
C. Toner cartridges
D. Hard disk drives

**35.** Which CPU contains 29,000 transistors and an 8-bit bus?

A. 8088
B. 286
C. 386
D. 486

**36.** What is the size of the address bus on a Pentium processor?

A. 64-bit
B. 32-bit
C. 16-bit
D. 24-bit

**37.** You have just installed a new 3.5-inch floppy drive into a computer that has an older AT motherboard style. The computer also has a 5.25-inch floppy drive. What will you use to configure the floppy drives?

A. Jumpers

B. SETUP

C. DIP switches

D. Cable select

**38.** What are the two modes in which a dot matrix printer can operate? (Choose all that apply.)

A. Font mode

B. Linear mode

C. Binary text mode

D. Dot-addressable mode

**39.** What happens after the charging phase in the laser printing process?

A. Cleaning

B. Writing

C. Developing

D. Transferring

**40.** What is the most common cause of speckled pages when using a laser printer?

A. Fuser assembly is not charging correctly

B. Transfer corona wire has minor defects

C. Scratch or defect in the EP drum

D. The roller assembly has incorrect tension

**41.** In laptop technology, what does LCD stand for?

A. Less Cooled Display

B. Liquid Center Display

C. Liquid Crystal Display

D. Lithium Crystal Display

**42.** Maintenance of what pointing device usually involves replacing a rubber cover?

   A. Touch pad

   B. Trackball

   C. Pointing stick

   D. Mouse

**43.** What is the most common type of connector for connecting a docking station to a laptop?

   A. Centronics

   B. ISA

   C. Serial

   D. Proprietary

**44.** Twisted pair is configured in a star topology, in which each device is connected to a central device, usually a:

   A. Router

   B. Hub

   C. MSAU

   D. Repeater

**45.** You are called out to diagnose a network that has terrible communication problems. The network is using ThinNet cabling in a bus topology, with each workstation using a BNC to connect to the backbone. 85 Ω terminators are being used on the network. The maximum network throughput is 10 Mbps. What is the problem in this situation?

   A. ThinNet cabling should not be used

   B. 50 Ω terminators should be used

   C. 72 Ω terminators should be used

   D. Nothing is wrong with the networking configuration

PRACTICE EXAMS

**46.** What would be the result in the event of a cable break on a 10BaseT network?

    A. All communication would cease

    B. Only the device connected to the cable would cease to communicate

    C. The hub would fail

    D. Nothing. A 10BaseT is not susceptible to cable failure.

**47.** Why should you be aware of users' moods when fixing their computer?

    A. Because they may call your boss

    B. So you will know when to start working on their computer

    C. So you will know how to converse with the user

    D. Because they may not understand your technical jargon

**48.** Why should you make sure your appearance is the best it can be?

    A. Because you want to impress the user with your appearance and your skill

    B. Because you may enter the office of a high-ranking employee, who makes decisions involving you and your company

    C. Because the user doesn't care if you fix the problem or not

    D. Because you never know whom you will meet

**49.** You are configuring a new printer for a user that you sense is getting a bit testy. You have taken more time than you like. What should you do in this situation?

    A. Continue working on the problem until you are done. Never leave a job incomplete

    B. Refer to the documentation

    C. Inform the user you are having difficulties and tell him you are going to refer the problem to another technician

    D. Stop working immediately

**50.** A user is complaining that his name brand computer is very annoying and has performance problems. How should you respond?

A. Don't say anything. Try not to take part in company-bashing.

B. Agree with the user

C. Ask the user if there is anything you can do about it

D. Ask why the user feels this way

**51.** What is the form in which the pins are arranged on newer computers to attach the chip to the motherboard? These are standard, and are identified as four rows of pins that surround the bottom of the chip

A. DIP

B. RGI

C. PGA

D. DIN

E. PGI

**52.** DTR is used to tell the receiver that data is ready to be sent. It's usually connected to the DSR on the receiving hardware. Its output is from the transmitting hardware's side. What is the full name for the acronym DTR?

A. Data Terminal Receive

B. Data Terminal Ready

C. Data Text Ready

D. Data Text Receive

E. Data Transmission Ready

**53.** Which combination yields a 16-bit bus with a total transfer rate of 20 Mbps?

A. Fast-Wide SCSI-2

B. Wide SCSI-2

C. Fast SCSI-2

D. SCSI-2

E. SCSI-1

**54.** A user is reporting that he can use his floppy disk in all computers but his own. What are possible problems? (Select all that apply.)

A.  The user's computer has a virus

B.  A cable is damaged

C.  A power cord is damaged

D.  The floppy disk is damaged

E.  The disk drive is damaged

**55.** You hear one beep on your computer when you boot up. What are the possible hardware problems that may exist in your system?

A.  Keyboard

B.  Internal Speaker

C.  Mouse

D.  Monitor

E.  Sound card

**56.** Demodulated data is:

A.  Binary

B.  Not null

C.  Analog

D.  Null

E.  None of the above

**57.** What two programs should you run to defragment a hard disk?

A.  CHKDSK.EXE

B.  SCANDSK.EXE

C.  DEFRAG.EXE

D.  SCANDISK.EXE

E.  SCNDSK.EXE

**58.** When you come across the sign shown here in a PC, which of the following is true?

   A. This is a hazard sign
   B. This is a caution sign
   C. By fixing what this is warning you about, you may hurt yourself
   D. By fixing what this is warning you about, you may hurt the equipment
   E. Not to worry, these are only for novices to obey

**59.** Which of the following are the hardest to dispose of environmentally?

   A. CMOS batteries
   B. Monitor
   C. Planar board
   D. Power supply boxes
   E. Styrofoam

**60.** Which two factors contribute to static electricity?

   A. Heat
   B. Cold
   C. Humidity
   D. Dryness

**61.** The _____ chip was the first to have a 32-bit register size, a 32-bit data bus, and 32-bit address bus, and which could handle 16MB of memory.

   A. 80386DX
   B. 80486SX
   C. 80486DX
   D. Pentium
   E. 80386SX

**62.** SRAM can hold how much memory per chip?

A. 256KB

B. 1024KB

C. 512KB

D. 2048KB

E. None of the above

**63.** A drive has 10 cylinders, 4 sectors, 2 heads, and the standard bytes per sector. What is its size?

A. 40

B. 20

C. 80

D. 81.92

E. 20.48

**64.** This roller contains a positively charged wire designed to pull the toner off the photosensitive drum and place it on the page.

A. Cleaning blade

B. Photosensitive drum

C. Primary corona wire

D. Transfer corona

E. Fusing rollers

**65.** You are looking at a document from an inkjet printer that a user has handed you. It is smudged. What are the possible causes?

A. The halogen lamp burned

B. The toner did not melt to the page

C. The cartridge had excess ink on it

D. The transfer corona was misaligned

E. The user handled the paper before the ink dried

**66.** A parallel cable consists of a _____ connector that plugs into the
_____ and a _____ connector that connects to the _____.

A. Female DB-25, printer, 36-pin Centronics, computer

B. Male DB-25, printer, 36-pin Centronics, computer

C. Female DB-25, computer, 36-pin Centronics, printer

D. Male DB-25, computer, 36-pin Centronics, printer

E. Male DB-25, computer, 50-pin Centronics, printer

**67.** What is the longest-lasting laptop battery?

A. NiCad

B. NiMH

C. LiIon

D. AlKln

E. DrLcl

**68.** Where in Windows 95 would you go to enable and set the length of mouse
trails on a portable computer?

A. Start | Settings | Control Panel | Mouse

B. Start | Settings | Control Panel | Mouse | Visibility

C. Start | Settings | Control Panel | Mouse | Pointers

D. Start | Settings | Control Panel | Mouse | Effects

E. Start | Settings | Control Panel | Mouse | General

**69.** A laptop pulls in either 120 or 240 volts. Say that the laptop is pulling 200
watts and is 120 volts, how many amperes is it pulling?

A. 2

B. .83

C. 1.667

D. 240

E. None of the above

PRACTICE
EXAMS

**70.** Your company has just set up a LAN, and it is set up with NetBEUI. You can communicate with people in your group by computer, but you can't cross a router. What is the problem?

    A. You need a newer router to handle NetBEUI

    B. You are using fiber optics for your connection

    C. You are using different brand network cards

    D. You are using different brand computers

    E. None of the above

**71.** What do CSMA/CD and CSMA/CA stand for?

    A. Collision Sense Multiple Access/ Carrier Avoidance

    B. Carrier Sense Multiple Access/Collision Avoidance

    C. Collision Sense Multiple Access/ Carrier Detection

    D. Carrier Sense Multiple Access/Collision Detection

    E. None of the above

**72.** The Electro-Magnet company is experiencing network problems, especially where they are testing the magnets. They hire you to fix the problem, and they say money is no object. What would you choose?

    A. Arcnet

    B. Fiber

    C. Star

    D. Token Ring

    E. StarBus

**73.** When in a corporate environment, how should you dress? (Choose one.)

    A. Like the customer

    B. Better than the customer

    C. Worse than the customer

    D. Like the other techs you know in other companies

    E. The way your boss recommends

**74.** Which is the worst situation to cause?

A. Unhappy customer

B. Unhappy boss

C. Unhappy computer

D. Unhappy tech

**75.** Building rapport is best achieved by:

A. Truly caring about the user

B. Avoiding conflict

C. Handling complaints

D. Working fast to respect their time

E. All of the above

**76.** You wish to optimize the memory in a DOS-based PC. After running the MEM /C command, you find that EMM386.EXE is reserving memory to support expanded memory. There are no programs on this system that require expanded memory. Which two lines must appear in the CONFIG.SYS to allow access to the upper memory area without support for expanded memory?

A. DOS=HIGH, UMB

B. LOAD DOS HIGH

C. DEVICE=C:\DOS\EMM386.EXE X=AAAA-FFFF

D. DEVICE=C:\DOS\EMM386.EXE NOEMS

**77.** ZIF is an acronym for

A. Zone Information File

B. Zero Insertion Force

C. Zero Indication Factor

D. Zone Indication Form

**78.** An SVGA cable uses which type of connector?

PRACTICE
EXAMS

A. DB-9
B. DB-25
C. High Density DB-15
D. Mini-Din

79. A customer has a PC with a mechanical printer A/B switch. One printer is a LaserJet type and the other one is a line printer. The customer claims that the Laser printer will print single pages only and the line printer will not print at all. You bypass the A/B switch, but the symptom remains the same. What is the most likely cause of this problem?

A. The A/B switch is bad
B. The printer drivers are corrupted
C. The power supply in the line printer is dead
D. The parallel port is bad

80. On a field service call you encounter a PC that is displaying the warning message that the CMOS battery is low. The CMOS battery is hard soldered on the System board. How can you quickly remedy the situation?

A. Remove the system board and solder in a new battery
B. Inform the customer that the PC must be taken back to the shop for repair
C. Sell the customer a newer, faster PC
D. Set the motherboard jumpers to accept an external battery, and install one in the PC

81. A hidden ESD would most likely be less than _____ volts.

A. 30,000
B. 15,000
C. 3,000
D. 50

82. To remove stubborn particles from a metal surface use:

A. A flat-blade screwdriver

B. A compressed air source

C. A rubber blade knife

D. Ultrasonic cleaning

**83.** Wearing jewelry when working on high voltage is dangerous because:

A. It will react with low humidity to cause ESD

B. It could cause a electrical arc or short if it contacts a voltage point

C. You could damage it and get in trouble

D. It can react to the heat dissipated by the high voltage supply

**84.** The ISA bus card can be used in which types of slots? (Choose all that apply.)

A. EISA

B. ISA

C. VESA

D. PCI

**85.** PCMCIA is an acronym for which of the following?

A. Personal Computing Monitor Card Industry Association

B. Personal Computer Memory Card International Association

C. Personal Computer Magnum Coalition International Association

D. Peripheral Component Memory Card Industry Association

**86.** When a hard disk is sectored, it means that:

A. The tracks are concentrically aligned

B. The cylinders are defragmented

C. It needs to be replaced

D. The tracks are divided into pie-shaped areas

**87.** Which type of printer will print a high-quality color image, but to avoid smearing you have to be careful to never allow the printed page to get wet?

    A. LaserJet

    B. Bubble Jet

    C. Dot matrix

    D. Daisy wheel

**88.** Which parts are similar in a daisy wheel printer and a dot matrix printer?

    A. The inkwell

    B. The print ribbon

    C. The impact coil

    D. The paper feeding mechanism

**89.** You have to configure a printer to be used with an operating system that does not support that particular model of printer. There are no drivers available for the operating system or the application you need to use it for. What are viable options in this case?

    A. Search the web for drivers for this printer

    B. Check the manufacturer's service manual for possible emulation settings of this printer

    C. Configure it as a serial printer

    D. Configure it as a parallel printer

**90.** If an Ink Jet printer is out of ink, what is the correct method to replace the ink supply?

    A. Re-fill the ink cartridge

    B. Replace the ink cartridge with a new one

    C. Clean the print head assembly with the built-in utility

    D. Reset the printer

**91.** NiMH stands for which type of battery?

   A. Nickel cadmium

   B. Lithium ion

   C. Nickel/metal hydride

   D. Nickel/metal hybrid

**92.** A type II PC card is manufactured to what dimensions?

   A. 85.6mm x 54.0mm x 3.3mm

   B. 85.0mm x 54.2mm x 5.0mm

   C. 85.6mm x 54.0mm x 5.0mm

   D. 85.6mm x 54.0mm x 10.5mm

**93.** The pointing device that looks like an eraser head is commonly called a:

   A. Trackball

   B. Touch Pad

   C. Pointing Stick

   D. Mouse

**94.** You receive a call from a customer who owns a UTP-based LAN. He tells you that his entire LAN is down. This customer is at least a good hour away from you. What one thing could you tell him to do that could solve the problem instantly?

   A. Check whether one of the network terminators has inadvertently been removed

   B. Check whether the network Hub had lost its power

   C. Talk him through a NIC card setup procedure

   D. Have him run a complete restore of the network server

**95.** Ethernet networks come in two speeds today. Identify the two possible speeds.

A. 4 MHz
B. 10 MHz
C. 16 MHz
D. 100 MHz

**96.** High network traffic would result in which of the following?

A. Loss of data
B. Slow delivery of data
C. Complete loss of network connectivity
D. Workstation crashing

**97.** What are some of the most important troubleshooting aids that also greatly enhance customer satisfaction? (Choose all that apply.)

A. Showing up with a full set of service manuals, and quoting procedures from them to the customer
B. Listening carefully to the customer's detailed history of the problematic PC
C. Saying confidently, "I know what the problem is...."
D. Following up a service call with a telephone contact the next day to see if everything is working properly

**98.** You encounter an angry PC user who has smashed his keyboard in frustration. What should you do? (Choose all that apply.)

A. Replace the keyboard and report the user to his supervisor
B. Chastise him for destroying the keyboard
C. Refuse to work on the problem because of his bad attitude
D. Replace the keyboard and share a similar experience of your own frustration to help diffuse his anger

**99.** When working on a project that may involve other PC-related companies (for example, network, software, or hardware specialists), it is always best to do what? (Choose all that apply.)

A. Cover your own tail first

B. Communicate in writing with the other professionals involved

C. Meet with the entire team to have a round-table discussion on the project

D. Blame the software manufacturer, because that is the easiest way out of a problem

**100.** You are running late, and as you are trying to leave, a customer asks you to take care of a Microsoft Word problem. What should be the best course of action? (Choose all that apply.)

A. Listen to the customer's explanation.

B. Politely explain that you have another appointment waiting, and schedule another appointment.

C. Call your next appointment to see if you can delay it.

D. Say, "Sorry, I've gotta run, I'll call you later."

# Core Exam Test Yourself Answers

1. **B.** The bus is the pathway for electrical signals on the system board. The cache is a temporary memory area. ISA and PCI are types of bus architectures.

2. **A, B.** The current supplied to the computer is 120 Vac. It converts the Vac to + or – 5 Vdc, and + or – 12 Vdc. The acceptable range is 8.5 –12.6 Vdc.

3. **A.** The correct answer is Electro Static Discharge. The discharge is what causes the damage.

4. **B.** Since the keyboard is sending the right keystrokes to the computer, the plug is fine. You should do a thorough cleaning of the keyboard, as the N key is probably dirty. If that does not fix the problem, then replace the key or the keyboard.

5. **A.** When the customer says the computer cannot read the CD, the assumption is the CD is in the drive. Also that the computer is operating. The modem has nothing to do with this problem. Have them describe how the CD is in the drive, as it may be upside down.

6. **D.** The first thing to check is whether you plugged the lines in the correct connectors. This is usually the problem. A bad phone line would have shown up with the phone previously. If the connectors are correct it may be a bad modem. If there is a connector for the phone, then it should work.

7. **A, C.** Compressed air cans and vacuum cleaners are best to clean computer parts from dust. Plain towels and paper towels will leave dust and lint on the surfaces. The compressed air hose at a service station does not have clean air and may put dirt or grease on parts and cause shorts.

8. **D.** Do not use an ESD device with monitors, due to the electrical charges held in monitors. Also do not produce shorts as you may encounter high voltages. Keep one hand free to keep from serving as a ground to the charge.

9. **A.** Chemical solvents are environmentally dangerous items. Contact your state environmental office for disposal rules.

10. **D.** The Pentium Pro has a 64-bit data bus.

11. **B.** The ISA (Industry Standard Architecture) was introduced with the IBM AT computers. EISA (Extended Industry Standard Architecture) was introduced by the ISA companies to compete with IBM's MCA (Micro Channel Architecture).

12. **A.** A gigabyte contains 1,073,741,824 bytes. It is thought of as containing approximately 1 billion (1,000,000,000) bytes.

13. **B.** The photosensitive drum is cleaned and electrically erased during the cleaning step.

14. **C.** Network printer connections are limited to the length allowed by the type of network.

15. **B.** The letter E is probably broken off the print wheel. A wrong IRQ would cause the printer to not print. A bad printer cable would cause wrong characters to print. A bad ribbon would affect all characters.

16. **B, C.** The LiIon would be the best choice, but costs the most. The NiMH costs less and produces less power.

**17.** **A.** PC cards (PCMCIA) are 85.6 mm x 54 mm.

**18.** **B.** A trackball is a device similar to a mouse except the ball side is up.

**19.** **B, C.** Portable computers do not use LED for the main display. Old models used CRTs. Current models use active matrix LCD or passive matrix LCD.

**20.** **A.** Coaxial cable comes in a number of varieties including BNC, ThinNet, ThickNet, and 10Base2. The other two major types of cable are twisted pair (including STP) and fiber optic.

**21.** **A.** The maximum length for twisted pair cable is 100 meters.

**22.** **A.** TCP/IP, NetBEUI, IPX/SPX, and DECnet are all network protocols. The Internet uses the TCP/IP protocol.

**23.** **C.** You should always reassemble the machine and leave a note concerning your work. You should never comment on how messy a desk is.

**24.** **A, B.** You should appear calm and confident to the customer. Wait until you are back in your office or other appropriate area to show your anger. Your customer will have more confidence in you if you appear calm and confident.

**25.** **B, C.** You should tell the user that without a license, your company does not permit you to install the software. However, when they get a license you will be glad to come back and install it. There is no need to tell the supervisor.

**26.** **B.** A CD-ROM drive has three cables that must be connected correctly: the power cable, the data ribbon cable, and the audio cable that connects to the sound card. This cable is used to transmit audio signals from the CD-ROM drive to the controller/sound board.

**27. C.** The proper setting for the DIP is 0100100, which is read from left to right, and the 0 or 1 bit is represented by the jumper's position as "off" or "on."

**28. B.** Unlike IDE devices, the SCSI device at the end of the chain needs to be terminated. The SCSI device may have a terminator built-in, or you need to configure a jumper or DIP switch to terminate the device.

**29. B.** Although you have verified that the IRQ for the mouse was not conflicting with any other devices, you still may be experiencing an I/O conflict. Since you are troubleshooting another device in the system, you may have inadvertently configured the device with the same I/O address.

**30. B.** A laser printer does not use a ribbon to print, so this is obviously not part of the problem when troubleshooting light or faint text on a laser printer. The remaining answers should all be checked when you are experiencing light or faint text.

**31. C.** Keyboard errors usually generate a 3** error code when POST runs at boot time. When troubleshooting a keyboard, there are only a few symptoms that you have to worry about, including non-functional keyboard, sporadic keys, and sticking keys.

**32. A.** Unplugging the computer from the wall adapter is your best line of defense during an electrical storm. This will guarantee electricity will not have a path to travel into your system. The other methods listed can still send a spike of power through the cables.

**33. B.** A cleaning diskette is the quickest and easiest way to clean the heads of a floppy disk drive. These cleaning diskettes have pads for isopropyl alcohol that come in contact with the surface of the drive heads.

**34. B, C.** Nickel-cadmium batteries and toner cartridges are the most common recyclable computer components today. Monitors are no longer accepted at landfills and must be disposed of properly.

**35. A.** The Intel 8088 processor contained 29,000 transistors and an 8-bit bus, and was used in the earliest IBM PCs. This chip only processed data at approximately 4.77 MHz.

**36. B.** Although the register and data bus have been increased to 64 bits, the address bus has remained at 32 bits. Since a 32-bit address bus makes for a gigantic amount of available memory addresses, an increase to 64-bit would not make a difference.

**37. B.** On an AT motherboard, and basically any other motherboard type, the floppy drives are configured in CMOS setup. Here is where you tell the system what type of floppy drive is present, and how many there are.

**38. A, D.** In Font mode on a dot matrix printer, the printer already has all the pins programmed for every character in its font set. In dot-addressable mode, each printed dot requires an input. This provides for a lot of flexibility to users, because they are not limited to the fonts available in the printer's memory, only by the software they use.

**39. B.** Once the photosensitive drum has been prepared in the charging process, the writing process can begin. A laser sweeps the entire length of the drum, cycling on and off with respect to the image to be created.

**40. C.** Speckled pages may be due to a failure of the cleaning step of the EP printing process. Another cause may be a scratch or defect in the EP drum, causing toner to remain in these recesses during the cleaning step.

**41.** C. Fortunately, we now have flat liquid crystal displays (LCD) in laptop computers that are much thinner, lighter, and require much less power than the small CRTs from ten years ago.

**42.** C. Maintenance of pointing stick mice is usually limited to replacing the rubber cover. These are smaller, pencil eraser-size pieces of rubber in the center of the keyboard.

**43.** D. Almost every docking station you will find is proprietary and will only work on specific laptops, or a specific brand of laptop. Very infrequently will you find a universal docking station.

**44.** B. A hub is used as a central device for connecting many computers in a star topology. This is unlike the bus topology, which uses a cable backbone that each computer must connect to.

**45.** B. Coaxial cable is organized in a bus topology, whereby each device is connected to a T-connector, which is then connected to the cable, which should have a 50Ω terminator connected to each end.

**46.** B. Since a 10BaseT network uses twisted-pair cabling to connect devices to a central device such as a hub, a cable break would only cause a connection to fail on the device immediately connected to the cable. However, if the cable connecting the hub to another hub were to fail, every computer on that hub would fail.

**47.** C. Read cues carefully concerning what type of mood the customers are in, because those cues will indeed dictate the approach that you should use in conversing with the customer. For example, do they want to chat with you, or just want you to fix their computer and leave?

**48.** **B.** Although it is important for a number of reasons, the most important reason for a nice appearance is because you may find yourself in the office of a high-ranking official who can make or break your company. If you look professional, you are representing your company and your industry. However, it is always a good idea to act professional and be well groomed!

**49.** **C.** No one is expected to know everything. There is nothing wrong with referring a problem to another technician. This also makes the user feel that many people are tending to his needs.

**50.** **D.** If a user is complaining about a computer or device, it is wise to listen to the user's complaints, and understand why he feels that way. In many cases, you can help the user configure the system to his liking, or solve a problem that has been ailing the system for months, even years.

**51.** **C.** PGA stands for Pin Grid Array. DIP, which stands for Dual Inline Package is the older version of PGA, and is identified as two rows located on opposite sides of the chip. DIP has not been used since the early eighties.

**52.** **B.** The A+ exam will frequently expect you to know the full words for each acronym. These will usually be in the form of multiple choice and the answers will either be acronyms that you must know, or the full wording for the acronym. They will use things that sound familiar and will be off by a just letter or a word. Pay close attention to these sorts of details when you study.

**53.** **A.** Remember that Wide SCSI-2 included a 16-bit bus that enabled large data transfers to be more efficient. Fast SCSI-2 was another option that increased the data transfer rate to 10 Mbps. However, the final variant combined the features of both options to create Fast-Wide SCSI-2. This combination yielded a 16-bit bus with a total transfer rate of 20 Mbps. SCSI 1 and simple SCSI 2 were just too old to perform this quickly.

**54. A, B, C, E.** Remember that viruses can mimic hardware problems. The fact that the user could use this disk on other computers points to the fact that, by process of elimination, his computer is at fault, not the floppy. By the way, many viruses are transferred when a floppy is booted into another computer, but this does not happen with all viruses. Therefore, a virus would still be in the realm of possibilities.

**55. A, C, D, E.** The question asked what are the possible problems in your system. We can rule out only the internal speaker, since that's what sounded the beep. One beep indicates that everything tested is fine, but not everything is tested. Just because POST did not find a problem with the keyboard does not mean that a key is not dead. The same is true for the mouse; if the trackball is missing, the POST will not catch it, but it will still be broken hardware.

**56. A.** MODEM stands for Modulate/Demodulate. The process of modulating is converting the data from binary to analog. When the receiving computer receives the modulated data, it demodulates it. The data becomes binary (ones and zeros) when it is demodulated.

**57. C, D.** Check the spelling of the DOS commands. Some DOS commands have abbreviations, and others don't. Know these as well as knowing the functions of the major DOS commands.

**58. B, D.** Always heed all precautions. Every warning label is there for a good reason. If you come across any warning signs, stop what you are doing and ask yourself, "Do I know what I am doing, or should I study up on this some more?" In computers, if you throw caution to the wind, you may also be throwing your PC to the wind.

**59. B.** The monitor is the hardest to dispose of environmentally. The CMOS batteries are no picnic, either. Look for a question on the exam like this one, or one that asks how to dispose of CMOS batteries. Use common sense, and don't assume you can just throw things out without checking with your state Environmental Protection Agency.

**60. B, D.** Turn up the thermostat or get a humidifier in order to correct this. Be careful though, because too much humidity can corrode circuits.

**61. A.** This chip was released in 1985. If you don't know all these facts right off the top of your head, it is time to memorize them. You will be grilled on the exam regarding all these processors and their capabilities.

**62. A.** These were early RAM chips and at that time they could not put any more memory on these. Try to remember the order that these chips where produced. The newer they are, the more memory they can hold.

**63. A.** The formula is (#of cylinders) x (#of sectors) x (#of heads) x 0.5KB. 10 x 4 x 2 x 5 = 40. Beware of extraneous information in these types of questions. Just remember cylinder, sectors, and heads are all you are looking for. Each cylinder in a hard disk is the collection of all the cross sections of each ring on each platter.

**64. D.** The transfer corona has a positively charged wire. Learn what is positively and negatively charged in all processes of the print job.

**65. C, E.** The problem of excess ink can usually be resolved by cleaning the cartridge, as prescribed by the manufacturer.

**66. D.** You need to know the different cables' characteristics. This includes whether they are male or female, the number of pins and the sockets that they go to, what they look like, the performance and limitations of each cable, and what they are used for.

**67. C.** The Lithium Ion is the longest-lasting and the lightest battery. They generally cost more than NiCad and NiMH. A memory trick is "NiCads are for cads." These are rarely used, and the performance is dismal. NiMH is in between the two. NiMH also has derivative batteries like "Smart NiMH."

**68. B.** On a Windows 95 computer, the Visibility tab in the Mouse applet is the correct place to change these settings. Applet is the terminology that the test makers sometimes use for Control Panel programs. Don't let this throw you. In this applet you can turn the mouse effects on or off and change the length of the trail.

**69. C.** Watts divided by volts is equal to amperes. In this example $200/120 = 1.667$. Just remember W/V=A. Don't be surprised on the exam if they ask a question that involves the use of this formula.

**70. E.** NetBEUI is an acronym for NetBIOS Extended User Interface. NetBIOS defines the "instructions" that Microsoft servers and clients use to communicate. The NetBIOS instructions are encapsulated into NetBEUI, IPX/SPX, or TCP/IP packets for transmission across the network. NetBEUI was originally intended to be a broadcast-based protocol for computers on early peer-to-peer networks. The NetBEUI packet does not contain a network segment ID field, and thus routers are unable to route the packets. Being routed means going though a router(s) to reach a host on another network segment. So in terms of the exam, you cannot route either NetBIOS or NetBEUI.

**71. B, D.** Detection perceives that there is a collision and responds. Collision Avoidance preemptively prevents collisions.

**72. B.** Fiber optic will alleviate the magnetic fields that are causing this problem. Since money is no object, fiber fits the bill. Arcnet is obsolete.

**73.** **E.** Doing computer work can involve going into grimy areas and handling dirty equipment. This is no excuse to wear blue jeans if you are expected to wear a suit. Ask your boss before you go into work the first day what you are to wear. Make sure that your clothing is clean and pressed.

**74.** **A.** The customer's perceptions are the most important thing to consider. If you have to sacrifice yourself and your boss's perception of you in order to make the customer happy, so be it. If you are truly making the customers happy, then your boss will come around. As far as the unhappy computer goes, you should do your best to fix everything, but if by doing so you are inconveniencing the customer, then you need to figure out how to work around the customer's schedule.

**75.** **E.** Rapport requires all of these and more. It is building and maintaining a satisfied customer base.

**76.** **A, D.** Providing that there are no existing programs that require expanded memory, you need the DOS=UMB line to allow EMM386.EXE to manage the upper memory area for the purpose of loading devices and TSR's HIGH. This is an extra feature of EMM386.EXE that makes it useful for memory management, even if you are not running any programs that require the Lotus Intel Microsoft expanded memory specification. The NOEMS switch turns off the expanded memory page-swapping feature.

**77.** **B.** ZIF is an acronym for Zero Insertion Force. This type of connector is designed to assist us in placing chips in the socket without bending pins. The processor chip that uses this type of connector should gently slip into the socket when you raise the ZIF control handle. Once you have verified the flat corner of the processor correctly, it should drop right into the socket. If it doesn't do not apply pressure to the chip. Double-check the alignment and check for slightly bent pins.

**78.** **C.** A SVGA cable uses a high density 15-pin DB-15 connector. I wish I had a quarter for all the times I went to service a PC on which the customer had tried to force the 15-pin high density connector into a 9-pin serial mouse connector. Never force any connector on a PC. The DB-15 High Density connector is probably the most fragile of the external connectors on the PC, because the pins are thinner than the DB-9 connector.

**79.** **D.** The parallel port is bad. (The two printers use different drivers and the LaserJet prints single pages, ruling out answer B.) Most laser printers have enough memory to hold at least one page. In this question, the parallel port handshake does not get through and, although the LaserJet prints one page, the line printer has to handshake for each line, so it never gets out of the starting gate. Of course a bad printer cable can cause the same symptom, but that was not one of the choices.

**80.** **D.** Set the motherboard jumpers to accept an external battery, and install a new one in the PC. After-market batteries are available in little rectangular packages. They usually come with Velcro that can be used to fasten the battery in some out-of-the-way area inside the PC chassis. A word of caution: always make note of critical CMOS settings first. It will save you time in case the CMOS becomes corrupted during the installation of the replacement battery. Making note of the hard disk parameters is always prudent, because you may have a non-standard hard disk that isn't listed in the CMOS table.

**81.** **C.** A 3,000-volt electrostatic charge could be considered hidden, depending on the humidity and the person involved. Over 3,000 volts, the charge is definitely visible. The typical components in a PC work on 5 volts, so it really does not take more than 30 volts to damage components. CMOS components are great for saving power but are highly susceptible to ESD.

**82.** **C.** To remove stubborn particles from a metal surface, use a rubber blade knife. Never use anything metal or it will scratch the surface. No one wants an ugly scar on an expensive machine.

**83.** **B.** Wearing jewelry can be dangerous when working around high voltage, because it can cause the voltage to arc and short, because of its conductivity. Gold is a great conductor of electricity. We usually keep one hand jewelry-free for reaching into high voltage areas in our shop. It's a rule that can save lives!

**84.** **A, B, C.** The ISA card is still the most compatible card in the industry. It will work in an EISA slot, a standard ISA slot, or a VESA slot. Unfortunately, it cannot take advantage of the higher bus speed or the 32-bit data transfer options afforded by the EISA or VESA bus.

**85.** **B.** PCMCIA is an acronym for Personal Computer Memory Card International Association. Interestingly, very few modern laptops use PCMCIA memory. The industry has taken advantage of the PCMCIA bus and today you can get PCMCIA modems, network interface cards, SCSI adapters, and many other devices to use with your laptop. Most new laptops use small DIMM memory chips.

**86.** **D.** The sectoring of a hard disk refers to the way that the tracks are divided into pie-shaped areas on the surface of each platter. A typical hard disk consists of several platters and a head for each one.

**87.** **B.** A Bubble Jet printer will print high-quality color graphic images, but the ink is usually water soluble. If it gets wet it will smear and run.

**88.** **B, C.** The daisy wheel printer and the dot matrix printer share some similar technology. They both use a print ribbon and they both use an impact coil. The daisy wheel printer has a single impact coil that pushes the wheel up against the paper and ribbon to transfer the image to the paper. The dot matrix printer has a separate impact coil for each dot in the print head.

**89. B.** When no drivers are available to support a printer, the only viable choice is to check the manufacturer's service manual for possible emulation settings for that printer. Many printers will emulate industry standard formats such as the IBM pro-printer or the Epson LQ series. Searching the web for something that does not exist will not help in this case, although it is always smart to search first, to determine if one is available. You may find some service information from the manufacturer regarding emulation settings that may be of use.

**90. B.** If an Ink Jet printer is out of ink, replace the cartridge with a new one that is recommended by the manufacturer. Re-filling ink cartridges is not recommended. In many cases this will void the warranty on the print head. In a Bubble Jet or Ink Jet printer, the replacement print head can be quite expensive.

**91. C.** NiMH stands for nickel/metal hydride. This is the most popular type of battery for laptops today. It is not the most efficient, but it is an economical choice.

**92. C.** A type II PC card measures 86.6mm x 54.0mm x 5.0mm. These are usually modems and network interface cards. This is probably the most common size used today.

**93. C.** The pointing device that looks like an eraser head is called a Pointing Stick. It is found on almost all IBM ThinkPad style laptops.

**94. B.** When the entire LAN is down, common sense should tell you to look at the common denominator, the Hub. When the network Hub has lost its power, the network ceases to work. We have experienced this more than a

PRACTICE EXAMS

few times. One time someone unplugged the Hub to plug in a coffeepot. That person wasn't very popular that day!

**95. B, D.** Ethernet networks come in two speeds today, 10 Mhz and 100 Mhz. There are other differences in the configuration of these networks. The Hub for the 100Mbps network is more sophisticated and expensive than a 10Mhz Hub. Many modern NIC cards support both speeds.

**96. B.** High network traffic would result in slow delivery of data. It would not normally result in loss of data or complete loss of network connectivity. Workstation crashing is not a symptom, either. Severe collisions caused by a chattering network card could cause more serious conditions.

**97. B, D.** Listen carefully to the customer's detailed history of the problematic PC and follow up a service call with a telephone contact the next day to see if everything is working properly. Both of these actions demonstrate to the customer that you genuinely care about their PC.

**98. D.** Smashing equipment is a sign of sheer frustration and desperation. How many times have you felt like punching in the screen on a frustrating PC? Replace the keyboard and share a similar experience of your own frustration to help diffuse the anger. Reporting the damage to a supervisor is not your job. If this person has a habit of damaging company property it will eventually catch up with them.

**99. B, C.** Communicate in writing with the other professionals and, if possible, meet with the entire team to have a round-table discussion on the project. Make sure the left hand knows what the right hand is doing. This is especially important when software and hardware must be specified to work properly together.

**100. A, B, C.** If you at least take the time to listen to the problem, then the customer won't feel slighted. Sometimes your next appointment may not be ready yet, and you can take care of the additional issue on the spot, and save a return trip.

# Test Yourself: Windows/DOS Exam

PRACTICE EXAMS

*Q & A*

This Test Yourself section will help you measure your readiness to take the Windows/DOS section of the A+ Exam. It contains the same number of questions that are on the exam. See if you can complete this test under "exam conditions," before you check any of the answers. Read all the choices carefully, as there may be more than one correct answer. Choose all correct answers for each question.

# Windows/DOS Test Yourself Questions

**1.** Which of the following is not a DOS system file?

A. IO.SYS

B. COMMAND.COM

C. EMM386.SYS

D. HIMEM.SYS

**2.** What happens if someone renames the COMMAND.COM file?

A. His computer would not boot up

B. Nothing

C. Nothing would happen, as long as he used the SHELL command in the CONFIG.SYS

D. Nothing would happen, if it was still in the root directory

**3.** Which of the following is an external command?

A. MOVE

B. DEL

C. COPY

D. DIR

**4.** What does the ALT-F4 keystroke combination do in Windows?

A. Minimizes the open window

B. Maximizes the open window

C. Brings up the previous application used

D. Closes the open window

**5.** What are the two types of multitasking? (Choose all that apply.)

    A. Non-Preemptive

    B. Preemptive

    C. Linear

    D. Cooperative

**6.** Of the first megabyte of memory, how much is reserved?

    A. The entire 1024KB

    B. 640KB

    C. 384KB

    D. None

**7.** What area of memory was EMM386.EXE created to take advantage of?

    A. Extended memory

    B. Expanded memory

    C. Upper memory

    D. Conventional memory

**8.** How can you erase an EEPROM chip?

    A. Use a blue light

    B. Apply a certain voltage

    C. Use CMOS ROM registers

    D. Use concentrated laser light

**9.** Lost clusters can be found by what two programs? Choose two from the following:

    A. CHKDSK

    B. DEFRAG

    C. MSD

    D. SCANDISK

PRACTICE
EXAMS

**10.** Heather is trying to free up more memory to run an application on her system. She has already loaded HIMEM.SYS and EMM386.EXE, but still remains just a few kilobytes short of the necessary minimum. She is also loading DOS high, with UMB added. What else can she do?

A. Force DOS into the reserved memory area with EMM386.EXE

B. Force DOS into extended memory

C. Streamline the CONFIG.SYS and AUTOEXEC.BAT to load drivers in a certain order

D. Use MEM to optimize the current memory settings

**11.** What are the two methods of copying the system files to a partition? Choose two from the following.

A. Use FDISK

B. Use the FORMAT /S command

C. Use the FORMAT /P command

D. Use the SYS command

**12.** Which command can make a hard disk bootable?

A. SYSTEM

B. SYS

C. FDISK

D. SYSEDIT

**13.** You have decided to use one partition for Windows 3.x (C:\ partition) and another partition for Windows 95 (D:\ partition). You would like Windows 95 to start as the default operating system at startup. What do you need to do?

A. Make adjustments in FDISK

B. Modify the MSDOS.SYS file

C. SYS drive D

D. There is nothing you can do to accomplish this

**14.** If Windows 95 finds a CONFIG.SYS upon installation, the file will be renamed to:

    A. CONFIG.BAK

    B. CONFIG.OLD

    C. CONFIG.DOS

    D. CONFIG.001

**15.** You have been called out to do an upgrade of Windows 3.1 to Windows 95 for a user. The installation is going fine, until you realize you do not have access to the CD-ROM anymore. What is most likely the problem?

    A. Windows 95 does not use the CONFIG.SYS anymore, so the device is not being loaded.

    B. Windows 95 does not use the AUTOEXEC.BAT anymore, so the MSCDEX file is not being loaded.

    C. Windows 95 placed a REM before the MSCDEX line in the AUTOEXEC.BAT

    D. Windows 95 did not find a driver for the CD-ROM, so it was not migrated

**16.** Which of the following is not a major DOS error message?

    A. Incorrect DOS version

    B. Error in CONFIG.SYS line XX

    C. Bad or missing COMMAND.COM

    D. Cannot find boot partition

**17.** What are two ways to fix the "VFAT Initialization Failure" error in Windows 95?

    A. Uncheck the option in the System applet of the Control Panel for 32-bit disk access

    B. Run SCANDISK

    C. Reinstall Windows 95

    D. Remove the File System Driver from Device Manager and restart the computer

PRACTICE EXAMS

**18.** Steve is using an application that causes General Protection Faults every few minutes. What can he do to fix the problem? (Choose all that apply.)

A. Minimize the amount of memory needed for the application in the System tab in the Control Panel
B. Reboot the computer
C. Reinstall the application
D. Reinstall the operating system

**19.** Which file does SYSEDIT.EXE let you modify? (Choose all that apply.)

A. PROTOCOL.INI
B. CONFIG.SYS
C. MSMAIL.INI
D. WIN.INI

**20.** What should you do if you receive an "Unable to initialize display adapter" error?

A. Use Windows Setup to change the adapter type
B. Reinstall the display adapter
C. Check the settings in CMOS Setup
D. Use a different monitor

**21.** In order to access the Internet on a Windows 3.1 machine, what must be installed?

A. NetBEUI
B. Remote Access Service
C. TCP/IP
D. IPX/SPX

**22.** Which of the following is not true concerning HTTP?

    A. It can be used to encode binary e-mail links

    B. It can transfer nearly any type of file

    C. It is the most common protocol on the Internet, other than TCP/IP

    D. HTTP is capable of both downloading and uploading

**23.** If I were told by my Internet Service Provider to configure SMTP, what would I be configuring?

    A. Standard Machine Type Permission

    B. Standard Machine Transfer Protocol

    C. Simple Mail Transfer Protocol

    D. Standard Mail Transfer Protocol

**24.** You have 25 workstations that will require Internet access. However, there are five computers that are used by two people at once. The network connects to the Internet using a pool of modems. The modem pool contains five modems. Assuming that all of the available connections to the Internet are currently occupied, how many unique IP addresses are in use?

    A. 5

    B. 10

    C. 20

    D. 25

**25.** What do you think has been scratched out in the Dial-Up Networking configuration dialog box shown here?

**PRACTICE EXAMS**

A. WINS address

B. IP address

C. DNS address

D. Host address

**26.** All devices that work in Windows 3.1 will also work with:

A. Windows 95

B. Windows 98

C. Windows NT

D. Windows 3.11

**27.** In Windows 95 the startup configuration is stored in what files:

A. SYSTEM.DAT
B. USER.DAT
C. CONFIG.SYS
D. AUTOEXEC.BAT

**28.** In Windows 95, filenames are limited to a length of:

A. 255 characters
B. 8 characters
C. 8 characters period 3 characters
D. no limit

**29.** A customer calls and says he copied all of drive C to drive D using the XCOPY command. However, he cannot find any subdirectories. What happened?

A. A virus is on the disk
B. You cannot copy drive C to drive D
C. He did not use the right switch
D. He should have used COPY

**30.** The customer states that when he got the hard disk a year ago it was fast, but it has been slowing down. What can you do about the problem?

A. Run DEFRAG
B. Replace the disk
C. Run SCANDISK
D. Format the drive

**31.** The memory above 1 megabyte is referred to as:

A. Conventional memory
B. Upper memory
C. Extended memory
D. High memory area

**32.** You have bought memory to install in a Packard Bell PC. After physically installing the memory, you discover the machine does not recognize the memory. What is the problem?

A. PC needs non-parity memory and you installed parity memory
B. PC needs parity memory and you installed non-parity memory
C. You installed DIMM modules in SIMM sockets
D. You have bad modules

**33.** To install SIMM modules into the motherboard you will:

A. Place the module at a 45° angle in the socket then bring it to a vertical position
B. Line up all the metal tabs and press straight down
C. Line the module straight over the socket and press down
D. Lay the module in position and screw it down

**34.** A customer calls and says he needs some DIMM modules. What type processor should he have?

A. 486
B. 386
C. Pentium
D. Pentium Pro

**35.** The Microsoft program that determines the best configuration for memory is:

A. MEMMAKER.EXE
B. MSD.EXE
C. QEMM.EXE
D. MEM.EXE

**36.** You have a new hard disk to use with Windows 95A, DOS, or Windows 3.*x*. The hard disk is a 6GB drive. How many partitions are required at a minimum?

A. 2

B. 1

C. 3

D. 6

**37.** When Windows 3.*x* is installed, how are device drivers installed?

A. Manually adding them to AUTOEXEC.BAT and CONFIG.SYS

B. Automatically detecting and loading drivers for all devices

C. Using a setup program supplied by the device manufacturer

D. Automatically adding them to AUTOEXEC.BAT and CONFIG.SYS

**38.** During the startup of Windows 95, what mode will Windows 95 start up in to give you the full capabilities of Windows 95?

A. Safe Mode

B. Normal Mode

C. DOS Mode

D. Windows 95 Mode

**39.** Windows-designed programs that are properly installed in Windows should place a shortcut in:

A. Shortcuts are not installed automatically

B. Program Manager

C. The Desktop

D. Start Menu

**40.** When installing Windows, you run what program to start the installation?

A. SETUP.EXE

B. INSTALL.EXE

C. WIN.COM

D. INSTALL.BAT

PRACTICE EXAMS

**41.** You are trying to run an older software package. You get the message "Incorrect DOS Version." What is the problem?

    A. Program is designed to run only in DOS

    B. Program is designed to run on a different version of DOS

    C. Program will run only on Windows 95

    D. Program cannot be used on this PC

**42.** As you exit a program, you get the error "Bad or missing COMMAND.COM". What is the problem?

    A. The COMMAND.COM file is missing

    B. The CONFIG.SYS file is missing

    C. The COMSPEC in the CONFIG.SYS file points to the wrong location

    D. The COMSPEC in the AUTROEXEC.BAT file points to the wrong location

**43.** In Windows 95, what do you use to set and display the attributes for files?

    A. Properties of the file

    B. Control Panel

    C. ATTRIB

    D. MSD

**44.** When you run DEFRAG, what program does it run first?

    A. FDISK

    B. SCANDISK

    C. ATTRIB

    D. MSD

**45.** To get to the Task Manager window in Windows 95:

    A. Press ALT-CTRL-INS

    B. Press ALT-CTRL-DEL

    C. Press the ESCAPE key

    D. Press CTRL-C

**46.** Data sent across a network is broken into pieces that have headers, trailers, and other information. What are these pieces called?

A. Segments

B. Packets

C. Frames

D. Packages

**47.** When connecting multiple MAUs together on a token ring network, you connect the RO connection from one MAU to the _____ connection on the other MAU.

A. RO

B. RI

C. Bridge

D. Router

**48.** The maximum number of nodes you can put on a FDDI network is:

A. 500

B. 260

C. 1024

D. 100

**49.** Class A IP addresses range:

A. From 0.___.___.___ to 126.___.___.___

B. From 128.0.___.___ to 191.255.___.___

C. From 192.0.0.___ to 254.255.255.___

D. From 192.168.0.0 to 192.168.255.255

**50.** You are operating a fiber optic, token ring network. Suddenly you begin receiving calls that several stations are down. What probably happened?

A. Break in the fiber optic cable

B. The server is offline

C. Bad network card

D. Wrong IRQ

**51.** Which of the following files are necessary to boot Windows 95?

    A. AUTOEXEC.BAT

    B. CONFIG.SYS

    C. IO.SYS

    D. MSDOS.SYS

    E. COMMAND.COM

**52.** Where do you load the KEYBOARD.SYS?

    A. WIN.INI

    B. AUTOEXEC.BAT

    C. CONFIG.SYS

    D. SYSTEM.INI

    E. ANSI.INI

**53.** The command CD in DOS stands for:

    A. Change Directory

    B. Current Directory

    C. Command Directive

    D. Chart Directory

    E. None of the above

**54.** You want to fix all your local drives of lost clusters prompting for user confirmation. You should enter what at the DOS prompt?

    A. DEFRAG /$:\ /AUTO

    B. SCANDISK /ALL /AUTOFIX

    C. CHKDSK /LOCAL /AUTOREPAIR

    D. CHKDISK /ALL /AUTOFIX

    E. SCANDISK /C …/Z /AUTO

**55.** Which of the following is an internal DOS command?

    A. MSD

    B. MEMMAKER

    C. REN

    D. DEFRAG

    E. SCANDISK

**56.** Which of the following are volatile memory?

    A. RAM

    B. DIMM

    C. ROM

    D. EPROM

    E. SIMM

**57.** What does EDO RAM stand for?

    A. Expanded Dynamic Output Random Access Memory

    B. Expanded Data Output Random Access Memory

    C. Extended Data Output Random Access Memory

    D. Extended DOS Output Random Access Memory

    E. Extended Dynamic Output Random Access Memory

**58.** Your computer is getting a memory error and you determine that it is the DIP chips. What do you do?

    A. Buy more DIP chips and snap them in

    B. Upgrade your software

    C. Reboot until you don't get an error

    D. Replace them with DIMMs

    E. None of the above

**59.** If you install DOS and don't change anything, what part of the memory is it run in?

PRACTICE
EXAMS

A. Extended
B. Expanded
C. Conventional
D. Virtual
E. EMM386.EXE

**60.** In Windows 95, virtual RAM consists of a swap memory file called:

A. PAGEFILE.SYS
B. MEM.EXE
C. EMM386.EXE
D. WIN386.SWP
E. None of the above

**61.** Which of the following operating systems are plug and play?

A. DOS
B. Windows 3.11
C. Windows 95
D. Windows NT 4.0
E. Windows NT 5.0

**62.** If you want to boot your computer in safe mode, you must:

A. Press F1 when it says "Starting Windows 95" and choose safe mode
B. Press DELETE when it says "Starting Windows 95" and choose safe mode
C. Press F5 when it says "Starting Windows 95" and choose safe mode
D. Press F6 when it says "Starting Windows 95" and choose safe mode
E. Press F8 when it says "Starting Windows 95" and choose safe mode

**63.** What utility can you use to delete old partitions that you want to get rid of?

A. FORMAT

B. FDISK

C. DELETE

D. MSD

E. None of the above

**64.** You have installed a modem and Windows 95 has recognized it and put in the driver. Now the modem manufacturer has sent you some updated drivers to use for this modem. Where do you go to install these?

A. Start | Settings | Control Panel | Modems

B. Start | Settings | Control Panel | Modems | Properties

C. Start | Settings | Control Panel | Modems | Driver | Update

D. Hardware Manager

E. Device Manager

**65.** When setting up a computer for the first time, where do you usually set up a NIC card?

A. In the Windows 95 Setup program

B. In the Device Manager

C. In the Network applet of the Control Panel

D. In the Network Cards applet in the Control Panel

E. The setup disk that came with the card

**66.** Which of the following are DOS-based tools?

A. ATTRIB

B. SCANDISK.EXE

C. SYSEDIT.EXE

D. CALC.EXE

E. DOSPRMPT.EXE

**67.** What memory area does HIMEM.SYS allow Windows 3.*x* to access?

    A. Above 1040KB

    B. Above 640KB

    C. 1024KB through 1088KB

    D. Above 1040KB

    E. Between 640KB and 956KB

**68.** You are fixing a user's computer. He has submitted a print job in Microsoft Word 97 and the screen has frozen. Unfortunately, he has not saved this 50-page presentation yet, and it is needed in 15 minutes. What do you do?

    A. Explain to the user the virtues of Autosave

    B. Press CTRL-ALT-DEL, highlight the printer, and choose End Task

    C. Press CTRL-C to end printing

    D. Check the printer and the network and see if the error clears up

    E. Press ALT-TAB to switch to another application

**69.** You want to install Windows 95 and you want to see what hardware you need. Which program do you run?

    A. System Information

    B. The About applet in My Computer

    C. EDIT CONFIG.SYS

    D. MSD

    E. EDIT SYSTEM.INI

**70.** Which of the following are types of computer viruses?

    A. Boot Sector

    B. FAT

    C. Memory

    D. CMOS

    E. Flu

**71.** Which of the following are forms of dial-up networking?

    A. Connecting through leased digital lines to an ISP

    B. Connecting to the Internet through an ISP with a modem

    C. Connecting to a bbs with a modem

    D. Connecting to the Internet through your company's network

    E. Connecting to your friend's computer by dialing it up

**72.** What protocol does the Internet predominantly use?

    A. TCP/IP

    B. UNIX

    C. CASE

    D. NetBIOS

    E. NetBEUI

**73.** What is the most commonly used protocol to transfer information in a web browser?

    A. HTTP

    B. FTP

    C. Gopher

    D. TCP

    E. IP

**74.** Which of the following is usually needed when setting up your browser for your Internet access?

    A. SMTP server

    B. POP3 server

    C. Default startup web page

    D. E-mail address

    E. Credit card number

**75.** When you go online, how are you identified to the TCP/IP protocol?

PRACTICE EXAMS

A. Domain name

B. Host name

C. IP address

D. E-mail address

E. Full name

**76.** The latest version of MS-DOS, included in Windows 95 is:

A. 6.1

B. 6.22

C. 5.0

D. 7

**77.** An early method used to share data among multiple applications is known as _____ and _____ .

A. Cut

B. Edit

C. Paste

D. Append

**78.** Which DOS system file loads an extended character set?

A. IO.SYS

B. CONFIG.SYS

C. ANSI.SYS

D. MSDOS.SYS

**79.** What are the three functions of the file WIN.COM, in correct order?

A. Switch the PC into the correct graphics mode

B. Switch the processor into protected mode

C. Ascertain the type of processor

D. Load the Windows graphic logo

**80.** You are preparing a used PC for resale and notice that the previous customer had a sense of humor. The volume label on the hard disk is FATBOY. You wish to change that to a more generic label. Which DOS command would you use to change the volume label to VOL1.

A. FORMAT /VOL1

B. COPY FATBOY VOL1

C. LABEL C: VOL1

D. D RELABEL FATBOY VOL1


**81.** Choose from the following list all of the types of physical memory.

A. RAM

B. SRAM

C. DRAM

D. HARD DISK SPACE


**82.** DIP memory chips are normally:

A. Soldered to the motherboard

B. Located on a SIMM socket

C. Socketed on a motherboard

D. All of the above


**83.** The LIM specification renamed the memory areas to be known as _____ and _____ .

A. Basic

B. Conventional

C. High

D. Low


**84.** If you take advantage of using the upper memory area to load device drivers but you have more device drivers than will fit in that area, what will be the likely outcome?

A. Some device drivers won't load at all

B. Some device drivers will load in the HMA

C. Some device drivers will load in the low memory area

D. The PC will crash and burn

85. You install a network card that requires the use of part of the upper memory for buffering. After installation, the PC fails to boot. What should you do next?

A. Run MEM /C to see where the conflict is

B. Add LOADLO to the line in the STARTNET.BAT that loads the NIC driver

C. Remove the card, consult the manufacturer's specifications for memory usage, and try to resolve the conflict

D. Add the line DEVICE=C:\EMM386.EXE to the CONFIG.SYS file to allow use of the LIM specification for memory management

86. The basic steps to installing an operating system on a PC include which of the following? (Choose all that apply.)

A. Create a partition on the hard disk

B. Format the hard disk

C. Run the operating system setup utility

D. All of the above

87. Unlike DOS, the Windows setup utility comes with a(n) _____ setup interface to make installation easier.

A. Automatic

B. Graphical

C. Proprietary

D. None of the above.

88. If you are going to upgrade an operating system for a customer, what is the first thing you should do prior to the installation of the new operating system?

A. FDISK the hard disk
B. FORMAT the hard disk
C. Back up the hard disk
D. Run a credit check on the customer

**89.** If a Plug and Play device fails installation, what should you do before trying to re-install it? (Choose all that apply.)

A. Read the manufacturer's instructions
B. Look in the Device Manager under the ? icon for the failed device
C. Call Microsoft Tech support for help
D. All of the above

**90.** You can launch a program in Windows 95 by which of the following procedures? (Choose all that apply.)

A. Clicking the icon associated with that program
B. Clicking the desktop shortcut for that program
C. Clicking Start, then Run, and entering the executable file name
D. All of the above

**91.** A customer asks you to fix his PC problem. The complaint is that his CD-ROM is no longer functioning. Upon booting the DOS-based PC, you notice an error message that goes by the screen that states "Error in CONFIG.SYS Line 3." What are the most likely causes of the problem? (Choose all that apply.)

A. The MSCDEX line is missing from the AUTOEXEC.BAT file
B. Line 3 has a misspelled driver file name for the CD-ROM device driver
C. The location of the CD-ROM driver in line 3 (the path) is incorrect
D. Someone has accidentally deleted the CD-ROM driver from the hard disk

**92.** A PC boots but is not running properly. It is prompting you for the time and date. What would be the possible cause for this error?

A. The incorrect DOS version is installed in C:\DOS

B. The SHELL command does not have the /P command switch on that line

C. The AUTOEXEC.BAT file has been deleted

D. The CONFIG.SYS file has been infected with a virus

**93.** Referring to the illustration shown here, which tab on the System applet would you choose to modify the Windows 95 virtual memory settings?

A. General

B. Device Manager

C. Hardware Profiles

D. Performance

**94.** To test a printer in Windows 95, what procedure would you follow?

A. Click Start | Find and try to locate the printer

B. Click Network Neighborhood and look for the printer on the network

C. Call Microsoft Technical Support

D. Click My Computer | Printers, then right-click the printer in question. Select Properties and click Print Test Page

**95.** You have moved a printer from LPT1 to LPT2. What must you do to enable the printer to print correctly?

A. Install the correct printer drivers and associate them with that port

B. Run the Add New Hardware applet

C. Change the properties for that printer to the correct port

D. Edit the Registry to name the correct port for that printer

**96.** A network makes it possible to share which items?

A. Files

B. Printers

C. Passwords

D. Messaging services

**97.** Each time you load a web page you are actually _____ a file.

A. Uploading

B. Downloading

C. Crossloading

D. Reloading

**98.** To access a web page you need either the _____ or the _____.

A. IP address

B. Domain name

C. MAC address

D. RIP protocol

**99.** To view a web page using HTML you will need a:

    A. Web server

    B. Web browser

    C. DNS server

    D. NIC card

**100.** To browse the web, a Windows 95 PC must have a minimum of how much RAM?

    A. 4MB

    B. 8MB

    C. 16MB

    D. 32MB

# Windows/DOS Test Yourself Answers

1. **C.** EMM386.SYS is not a DOS system file, but EMM386.EXE is. EMM386.EXE is the Expanded Memory Manager of the DOS operating system.

2. **C.** The COMMAND.COM can be moved from the root directory, as well as be renamed, but only if you use the SHELL command in the CONFIG.SYS to redirect the operating system to find the COMMAND.COM file, or whatever you have named it to.

3. **A.** An internal command is a command that is contained within the COMMAND.COM file; no file on the hard disk exists to execute the command. The MOVE command uses an actual file on the hard disk when executed.

4. **D.** Using the ALT-F4 keystroke combination in Windows will close the active window. It can also be used multiple times to close all windows. Eventually, you will be prompted to shut down Windows when no more open windows exist.

5. **B, D.** A big change between Windows 3.x and Windows 95 pertains to the difference in their multitasking capabilities. There are two different types of multitasking, cooperative and preemptive.

6. **C.** Of the first megabyte of memory in a PC, 384KB is reserved for the hardware to use. Thus, this portion of memory is called *reserved memory*.

7. **C.** EMM386.EXE was created to take advantage of upper memory. This included ways of digging out every unused portion of the reserved area, and converting it to system memory.

**8. B.** The EEPROM (electrically erasable) chip could be erased by applying a specific voltage to the chip. This is much easier than removing an EPROM chip from your system, or using light to erase the contents of the chip.

**9. A, D.** Both CHKDSK and SCANDISK can be used to find lost clusters, as well as unlinked cluster chains and lost chains. SCANDISK, however, can perform a surface scan on the hard disk surface, whereas CHKDSK cannot.

**10. C.** Even though you have HIMEM.SYS loaded and the DOS=HIGH,UMB specified in your CONFIG.SYS file, you may need to streamline the drivers that are being loaded. You may find the right combination that uses a larger device driver in memory, and therefore frees a few more kilobytes for application use. MEMMAKER is recommended for this very purpose.

**11. B, D.** You have two options for copying system files to your hard disk: using the /S switch with the FORMAT command, and using the SYS command. FDISK doesn't copy system files to your hard disk, but marks a partition as active.

**12. B.** Although the FDISK utility can make a partition active, the SYS command will transfer system files on to the partition necessary to boot the operating system. For DOS, these system files necessary for booting are IO.SYS, MSDOS.SYS, and COMMAND.COM.

**13. B.** MSDOS.SYS needs to be modified to allow "dual booting." This can be done by installing 95 to drive D: after Windows 3.1 is installed, or by directly editing MSDOS.SYS.

**14. C.** Windows 95 does not need CONFIG.SYS or AUTOEXEC.BAT to perform correctly. However, you may need it to load legacy device drivers.

**15.** **C.** As you will soon see in situations involving upgrading to Windows 95, a REM is placed on the line that contains the MSCDEX driver, which is the driver required to access the CD-ROM drive. This driver is required, in addition to the CD-ROM driver.

**16.** **D.** There is no error for "Cannot find boot partition". When the operating system startup files cannot be found, you will see an error such as "Invalid System Disk", which is good news if you accidentally have a floppy disk in the drive.

**17.** **B, C.** If you are receiving the "VFAT Initialization Failure" error, you may need to run SCANDISK to attempt to fix any drive problems. If SCANDISK doesn't fix the problem, reinstalling Windows 95 should.

**18.** **B, C, D.** When you are receiving General Protection Faults on a regular basis, you need to reinstall the application you feel is responsible, reinstall the operating system, or reboot the computer. These errors are often difficult to resolve. An application upgrade may be the answer.

**19.** **A, B, C, D.** SYSEDIT lets you edit a number of configuration files. These include WIN.INI, SYSTEM.INI, MSMAIL.INI, PROTOCOL.INI, CONFIG.SYS, and AUTOEXEC.BAT.

**20.** **A.** If Windows gives you an "Unable to initialize display adapter" error, you should use the Windows Setup utility to change the adapter type. If you are unsure of the exact model of adapter you have, VGA should always work, although it does not produce the best results.

**21.** **C.** Since TCP/IP is the protocol of the Internet, you must be using it to communicate. You can either specify an IP address, or have an Internet provider assign you one.

**22.** **A.** HTTP was originally used to transfer HTML files to computers, but has been adapted to transfer nearly any type of file. HTTP is the most common transfer protocol on the Internet. HTTP is capable of both downloading and uploading, but is rarely used for uploading.

**23.** **C.** Simple Mail Transfer Protocol, or SMTP, is the way your computer transfers mail to the destination host across the Internet. This protocol is very widely used on the Internet, due to the popularity of e-mail these days.

**24.** **A.** A user does not require a unique IP address to access the Internet, but the machine that is accessing the Internet does require an IP address. Since there are only five modems in the pool, and all of them are accessing the Internet, there are five unique IP addresses currently in use.

**25.** **B.** You must have a unique IP address on the Internet in order to communicate. This can be received automatically from a server at your ISP, or the ISP will give you a valid IP address to manually configure your dial-up networking connection.

**26.** **A, B, D.** Devices that work with Windows 3.1 will work with Windows 95, Windows 98, and Windows 3.11. However, some devices designed for Windows 3.1 will not work with Windows NT, such as Winmodems.

**27.** **A, B.** Although Windows 95 will process the CONFIG.SYS and AUTOEXEC.BAT files, it stores configuration data in SYSTEM.DAT and USER.DAT.

**28.** **A.** Windows 95 allows file names to be 255 characters long. DOS allows file names that are no longer than eight characters before a period, and three characters after.

**29.** **C.** The customer failed to use the /S switch when copying. This is the same effect as using the COPY command. This is not a virus problem. XCOPY will copy drive C to D.

**30.** **A.** The drive has become fragmented. DEFRAG will defragment the drive and speed it up. DEFRAG runs SCANDISK first. The drive does not need replacing. Running FORMAT will erase the drive.

**31.** **C.** Conventional memory is the first 640KB of memory. The next 384KB is upper memory. The memory above 1MB is extended memory. The first 64KB of extended memory is the High Memory Area.

**32.** **B.** Most PCs use non-parity memory. However, most Packard-Bell PCs use parity memory. You have installed the non-parity modules (commonly used by other PCs) instead of parity modules.

**33.** **A.** SIMM modules are installed by placing the module at a 45° angle in the socket then bringing it to a vertical position. Memory chips were installed by lining up all the metal tabs and pressing down. DIMM modules are installed by lining the module straight over the socket and pressing down. Motherboards are installed by laying them in position and screwing them down.

**34.** **C, D.** DIMM modules are used in Pentium and Pentium Pro machines.

**35.** **A.** MEMMAKER.EXE is a Microsoft program that determines the best configuration for memory. QEMM.EXE is Quarterdeck's program that configures memory.

**36.** **C.** The hard disk when used with Windows 95, DOS, or Windows 3.*x* can have a maximum partition size of two gigabytes. So you will have to make at least three partitions, no larger than two gigabytes each.

PRACTICE
EXAMS

**37.** C. The Windows 3.x user normally installs the drivers by running a setup program supplied by the device manufacturer.

**38.** B. Windows 95 starts in Normal Mode by default. You have the full capabilities of Windows 95. When Windows 95 starts in Safe Mode, only the VGA and mouse drivers are loaded. You can then make corrections to the configuration errors.

**39.** B, C, D. Windows-designed programs that are properly installed should always install a shortcut on the desktop, or in the Program Manager in Windows 3.x, or in the Start Menu in Windows 95.

**40.** A. Installation of Windows always requires you to first run the SETUP.EXE file. WIN.COM is run to start Windows. DOS-based programs often use INSTALL.EXE or INSTALL.BAT to install programs.

**41.** B. "Incorrect DOS Version" means the program will only run on a certain version of DOS. You can put an entry in the SETVER file to fix it.

**42.** A, C. The problem is that COMSPEC in the CONFIG.SYS file points to the wrong location and/or COMMAND.COM was loaded from a floppy which was removed before exiting the program.

**43.** A. In Windows 95, right-click the file, and choose Properties.

**44.** B. DEFRAG runs SCANDISK first to check for disk errors. You should do a backup first.

**45.** B. In Windows 95, press ALT-CTRL-DEL to get to the Task Manager window. (CTRL-C will abort a program in DOS. ESCAPE will sometimes abort programs in DOS. ALT-CTRL-INS on some machines will do a warm boot.)

**46. B.** Data is sent across networks in packets.

**47. B.** The RI (Ring In) connects to the RO (Ring Out). Bridges and routers are used to connect multiple network segments.

**48. C.** An FDDI network can have up to 1024 nodes.

**49. A.** Class A addresses range from 0.___.___.___ to 126.___.___.___.

**50. A.** You can eliminate the IRQ, as it did not happen when the card was added. If the server was offline, the network would still work, but the server items would no longer be available. As a number of stations have dropped, it is not likely that you have bad network cards. However, a break in the fiber optic cable will disable the entire network.

**51. C, D, E.** The AUTOEXEC.BAT and the CONFIG.SYS are slowly becoming obsolete. The information that is stored in them is stored in the Registry. The Registry is a better organized location than these files.

**52. C.** The CONFIG.SYS is where you load the KEYBOARD.SYS.

**53. A.** You can use CD to go back a directory or CD\ to go to the root directory or CD [drive:\] path to go to a different directory. CD without any switches will show you your own directory. This is useful if you are using a system that does not show the path in the command prompt.

**54. B.** SCANDISK shows up frequently on the A+ exam. Take the time to understand SCANDISK and its switches fully.

**55. C.** REN is an internal DOS command. These reside in the COMMAND. COM. A good way to think of these internal commands is as any command you can type at the DOS prompt that is not a file in the DOS directory, or a file in any other directory. The command files in the DOS directory are all external DOS commands.

56. **A, B, E.** Volatile memory is memory that is lost when the system is powered down. Since DIMM and SIMM are a form of RAM, they can also be considered types of volatile memory. ROM, on the other hand, stays in memory once the computer is shut off. Since EPROM is a form of ROM, it still falls under the same umbrella of non-volatile memory.

57. **C.** DRAM stands for dynamic RAM. SRAM stands for Static RAM. SIMM stands for Single In-line Memory Module. DIMM stands for Dual In-line Memory Module.

58. **E.** A DIP chip is actually memory that is soldered onto the motherboard. You cannot simply remove a soldered-on component and snap in a new one. Software is not going to fix this problem. DIMMs and DIPs are not compatible.

59. **C.** Conventional memory is where it is run. Conventional memory resides at 640K and below. You can change DOS to run high. In order to do this you must load HIMEM.SYS.

60. **D.** This file is automatically created by Windows 95. You can manually change the size of this file, but it is not recommended.

61. **C, E.** Windows 95 is plug and play and so is NT 5.0. These systems were written with future not-yet-designed hardware in mind.

62. **E.** F8 is the only key that will get you to this menu.

**63. B.** FDISK can get rid of old partitions. There are several menus in FDISK that let you view the existing partitions on the active drive, change active drives, delete partitions, and create a bunch of different partitions. The only reason to use this program usually is to partition a new disk or to rebuild an old drive by completely destroying the data on it. Remember that FDISK is for partitioning.

**64. E.** The Device Manager is in charge of these drivers. The Modem applet in the Control Panel only controls the settings of the modem. A shortcut to the Device Manager is to right-click My Computer and choose Properties, which brings up System Properties, which has the Device Manager tab on it.

**65. A.** Most of the time the card is recognized, and you install it from the Setup program. The Setup program will search for drivers in the Windows drivers' directory. If these are not found, then they will ask you for the disk. You may need to know the right memory address and IRQs.

**66. A, B.** ATTRIB and SCANDISK are DOS-based tools. DOSPROMPT. EXE is a Windows-based program that lets you shell out to a DOS prompt.

**67. B.** Windows 3.*x* requires memory above 640KB to operate, and HIMEM. SYS allows this.

**68. A, D.** While pressing CTRL-ALT-DEL on Windows 95 will get you out of many bad situations, this is not one of them. Your only choice would be to talk to the user about saving work in the future. It may be that the printer is connected to a print server, and if you can make this work, the print job may go through. (In this example there is actually another solution: Reboot, since Word 97 has an auto recover feature. This will bring the document back to life, even if it was never saved.)

**PRACTICE EXAMS**

**69.** **D.** MSD is the place that will tell you more than you will ever want to know about your computer. This can be especially useful if you are preparing to upgrade to Windows 95 and you want to know what you have, so that you will know what you need.

**70.** **A, B, C, D.** Unfortunately most of us will get our virus knowledge through experience. These pesky things can insidiously get into networks and can take a while to ferret out. When you have any software or hardware problem, never rule out a virus. Keep your protection up to date.

**71.** **B, E.** Dial-up networking involves a direct connection via modem to another network. Your machine acts as a node or a host on the network, which is capable of sharing devices such as file storage or a printer. The word dial implies that you are dialing a number. This needs to be you, the client, dialing the number. If you are reaching another computer that is dialing, and you are not dialing, then it is not dial-up networking.

**72.** **A.** The IP in TCP/IP stands for Internet Protocol. This is a sophisticated, rigid set of rules and concepts that define how computers will interact.

**73.** **A.** The Hypertext Transfer Protocol is the most common. A few years ago, Gopher and FTP were popular, but they did not have the graphically intensive capacity that the WWW requires.

**74.** **A, B, C, D.** The key to this question is the word usually. The default startup page may already be set up on the browser, depending on the company. E-mail addresses may be irrelevant if you do not have e-mail as an option on your Internet account. (A credit card is probably necessary for setting up your account with the ISP, but that is not setting up the browser.)

**75.** **C.** Every computer, router, bridge, and gateway has an IP address. Many books have been written on how these are derived and the subject is beyond the scope of this book and the A+ exam. Simply knowing that you get an IP address assigned to you will suffice.

**76.** **D.** The latest version of DOS, which is included in Windows 95, is version 7. Many of the friendly DOS files are located in the \WINDOWS\ COMMAND directory. This maintains the capability to run many DOS based programs.

**77.** **A, C.** An early method used to share data among applications was known as Cut and Paste. A variation on this is Copy and Paste. The difference between the two is that the Cut command removes the data from the source and the Copy command creates another instance of the data in memory, leaving the original data intact.

**78.** **C.** Seldom used since the advent of Windows 95, the good old ANSI.SYS loads an extended character set to support characters normally not supported by DOS. These were commonly used to support DOS-based programs for menu displays and such.

**79.** **C, A, B.** WIN.COM first ascertains the type of processor, then it switches the PC into the correct graphics mode, and then displays the Microsoft commercial logo. The processor is switched into protected mode by WIN386.EXE for enhanced mode operation.

**80.** **C.** The LABEL command is just that. It is for changing the volume label on a disk drive. It will work on any disk drive, including floppy disks, provided they are not Write protected. It will not affect any of the data on the disk, just the volume label.

**81.** **A, B, C.** Physical memory includes RAM (the generic term), SRAM (Static RAM), and DRAM (dynamic RAM). Using hard disk space to simulate memory is referred to as virtual memory. This process uses a swap file to hold overflow data, and executable code that will not fit in the physical memory.

**82.** **A, C.** DIP style memory chips are usually soldered to the motherboard. Some newer motherboards have them socketed to the motherboard. SIMMs or DIMMs in newer PCs have replaced this type of memory.

**83.** **B, C.** The original LIM specification renamed the memory areas in the first 1024KB to be conventional memory. Memory above that was high, expanded, and extended. Expanded memory is accessed using the swapped page frame mode. Extended memory was addressed by 80x86 processors, using the DPMI specification.

**84.** **C.** If you specify the DEVICEHIGH= command line in CONFIG.SYS, and there is not enough room in the upper memory area, then some device drivers will load in the low memory area, leaving less room for conventional DOS applications to run.

**85.** **C.** The first thing you have to do is remove the card, consult the manufacturer's specifications for memory usage, and try to resolve the conflict. If the PC won't boot up after installing anything, remove the last thing you installed. If it won't boot, you can't run any diagnostics, can you?

**86.** **D.** The basic steps to installing an operating system include creating a partition on the hard disk, formatting the drive, and running the install utility. The installation utility program that comes with the operating system can automate most of this.

**87.** **B.** Unlike DOS, the Windows 95 setup utility comes with a graphical setup interface. This is very user friendly and includes the setup wizard to help configure the hardware drivers.

88. **C.** It is always a very good idea to back up the hard disk before doing an upgrade of an operating system on a PC. It is a good idea to back up regularly, anyway. You never know.

89. **B.** If a Plug and Play device fails on installation, it is usually a good idea to look in the Device Manager under the ? icon for the failed device. Remove the failed device and try to resolve the resource or driver conflict before trying to re-install it.

90. **D.** You can launch a program in Windows 95 by all of the options mentioned. You can also start a program from Explorer by clicking the executable file name.

91. **B, C, D.** The key to this problem is the prompting from the system regarding the error in line 3 of the CONFIG.SYS file. Chances are that the line has misspelled the driver file name, or the path to the CD-ROM driver is incorrect, or someone has accidentally deleted the CD-ROM driver files or directory. You could use the F8-enabled interactive DOS boot option to verify each line in the CONFIG.SYS and AUTOEXEC.BAT.

92. **C.** If the AUTOEXEC.BAT file has been deleted, the user will be prompted for the date and time at each bootup. The AUTOEXEC.BAT must exist for DOS to bypass the date and time prompt. For more information on the SHELL command and its optional switches, consult Microsoft TechNet or the Knowledge Base on the Microsoft web site.

93. **D.** The Performance tab on the System Properties dialog box will take you to the settings for the virtual memory settings (swap file) for Windows 95. It is usually best to use the default settings that the Install program has configured, unless there is a shortage of space on the hard disk where Windows is installed.

PRACTICE
EXAMS

**94.** **D.** Testing a printer in Windows 95 is easy. It is probably one of the nicest things built into the operating system. Simply click My Computer | Printers, then right-click the printer in question. Select Properties from the drop-down menu with the left mouse button and click Print Test Page. The test page will include the Windows 95 logo (a good little graphics test for your printer) and will list all of the printer drivers it is using.

**95.** **C.** If you change the port of a printer from LPT1 to LPT2, you must change the properties for that printer to the correct port. Clicking the printer's folder, located in My Computer, does this. Then right-click the printer and left-click Properties in the drop-down menu. Select the Details tab and change the settings to the correct port.

**96.** **A, B, D.** A network makes it possible to share files, printers, and messaging services. It is not a good idea to share your network password with anybody. Network security should be paramount in your responsibilities.

**97.** **B.** Each time you load a web page you are actually downloading a file. Actually, if the page contains graphics or sound, you are probably downloading several files.

**98.** **A, B.** To access a web page on the Internet you need the IP address or the domain name. Otherwise, the web browser will return an error stating that the URL cannot be found.

**99.** **B.** To view a web page using HTML, you need a web browser. If you want to host a web page you would need the web server. DNS is a service that matches domain names with IP addresses.

**100.** **B.** To browse the web on a Windows 95 PC, you will require a minimum of 8MB of RAM.

# A
# About the
# Web Site

Q & A

# Access Global Knowledge Network

As you know by now, Global Knowledge Network is the largest independent IT training company in the world. Just by purchasing this book, you have also secured a free subscription to the Access Global web site and its many resources. You can find it at:

http://access.globalknowledge.com

You can log in directly at the Access Global site. You will be e-mailed a new, secure password immediately upon registering.

## What You'll Find There. . .

You will find a lot of information at the Global Knowledge site, most of which can be broken down into three categories:

### Skills Gap Analysis

Global Knowledge offers several ways for you to analyze your networking skills and discover where they may be lacking. Using Global Knowledge Network's trademarked Competence Key Tool, you can do a skills gap analysis and get recommendations for where you may need to do some more studying. (Sorry, it just may not end with this book!)

### Networking

You'll also gain valuable access to another asset: people. At the Access Global site, you'll find threaded discussions as well as live discussions.

### Product Offerings

Of course, Global Knowledge also offers its products here—and you may find some valuable items for purchase: CBTs, books, courses. Browse freely and see if there's something that could help you.

# Glossary

**Access Methods**     Also known as *network access,* these are the methods by which a device communicates on a network. Network access provides a standard that all devices that wish to communicate on a network must abide by in order to eliminate communication conflicts.

**Active Matrix Display**     Active matrix displays are based on Thin Film Transistor technology. Instead of having two rows of transistors, active matrix displays have a transistor at every pixel, which enables much quicker display changes than passive matrix displays and produces display quality comparable to a CRT.

**ANSI.SYS**     ANSI.SYS is a DOS system file that is loaded by CONFIG.SYS if required. This file loads an extended character set for use by DOS and DOS applications that includes basic drawing and color capabilities. Normally used for drawing and filling different boxes for menu systems, it is seldom in use today. By default, it carries no attributes, and is not required for OS startup.

**ARCHIVE Attribute**     The ARCHIVE attribute is set automatically when a file is created or modified, and is automatically removed by back-up software when the file is backed up.

**ATTRIB.EXE**     ATTRIB.EXE is a utility that can be used to change the attributes of a file or group of files.

**AUTOEXEC.BAT**     A user-editable system file, AUTOEXEC.BAT contains commands to modify the PC environment (PATH, COMSPEC, other SET commands), and to execute applications. It can be used to create a menu system, prompt for user input, or *call* other batch files to maintain a modular structure. By default, it carries no attributes, and is not required for OS startup.

**Basic Input Output System**     See BIOS.

**Bi-Directional Print Mode**     Most common in some of the newer and more advanced printers, bi-directional print mode means that the printer is able to talk back to the computer, enabling, for example, the printer to send the user exact error messages that are displayed on the workstation. It also helps the spooler to avoid print spooler stalls.

**BIOS**    Most commonly known as BIOS, Basic Input Output System is a standard set of instructions or programs that handle boot operations. When an application needs to perform an I/O operation on a computer, the operating system makes the request to the system BIOS, which in turn translates the request into the appropriate instruction set used by the hardware device.

**Brownout**    Momentary lapses in power supply. Brownouts can cause problems with computer components that are not designed to withstand these events.

**Bus**    A bus is the actual pathway used to transmit electronic signals from one computer device to another.

**Bus Topology**    In a local area network, a bus topology has each device on the network connected to a central cable, or bus. Most common with coaxial cabling.

**Cache Memory**    Cache memory is used to store frequently used instructions and data so that they can be accessed quickly by the computer.

**Carrier Sense Multiple Access/Collision Detection**    See CSMA/CD.

**Central Processing Unit**    See CPU.

**Chip Creep**    A phenomenon whereby a computer chip becomes loose within its socket.

**Cleaning Blade**    This rubber blade inside a laser printer extends the length of the photosensitive drum. It removes excess toner after the print process has completed and deposits it into a reservoir for re-use.

**CMOS**    The Complementary Metal-Oxide Semiconductor (or CMOS) is an integrated circuit composed of a metal oxide that is located directly on the system board. The CMOS, which is similar to RAM in that data can be written to the chip, enables a computer to store essential operating parameters after the computer has been turned off, enabling a faster system boot.

**Coaxial Cable**    A high-bandwidth network cable that consists of a central wire surrounded by a screen of fine wires.

**COMMAND.COM**    COMMAND.COM is a DOS system file that is automatically executed in the ROOT directory at startup. This file contains the internal command set and error messages. By default, it carries no attributes, but is required for OS startup.

**Complementary Metal-Oxide Semiconductor**    See CMOS.

**CONFIG.SYS**    A user-editable system file that provides the ability to install device drivers. Windows 95 does not require any specific settings to be made in CONFIG.SYS.

**Cooperative Multitasking**    There are two different types of multitasking: cooperative and preemptive. Cooperative multitasking means that applications must voluntarily relinquish control of the CPU. When an application relinquishes control of the CPU, Windows then decides which application will execute next. The most common way for an application to relinquish control is by asking Windows if any messages are available.

**CPU**    The CPU (Central Processing Unit) is the operations center of a computer. Its job is to provide the devices attached to the computer with directives that retrieve, display, manipulate, and store information.

**CSMA/CD**    Most commonly found on Ethernet networks, carrier sense multiple access/collision detection (CSMA/CD) is a network communication protocol and operates in much the same way as humans communicate. With CSMA/CD, a device transmits data onto the network. The device then detects if any other devices have transmitted onto the network at the same time. If it detects that another device has transmitted data onto the network at the same time, the device then waits an unspecified random amount of time and retransmits its data.

**Defragmentation**    A process that reorganizes fragmented files back in a proper, contiguous fashion. This is done by moving several of them to an unused portion of the drive, erasing the previous locations in contiguous clusters, then rewriting the files back in proper sequence. Performed periodically, defragmentation is probably the single best operation a user can perform to maintain a high-performance system.

**Device Driver**    Device drivers are programs that translate necessary information between the operating system and the specific peripheral device for which they are configured, such as a printer.

**Dial-Up Access**    Dial-up access is defined as access provided to the Internet, a LAN, or even another computer by using a phone line and a modem. Dial-up access does not have to be a connection to any network.

**Dial-Up Networking**    Refers to the type of network in which a modem is used to connect two or more workstations.

**DIMM**    A Dual In-line Memory Module (DIMM) is very similar to a SIMM; it's a small plug-in circuit board that contains the memory chips that you need to add certain increments of RAM to your computer. Because the memory chips run along both sides of the chip, DIMM chips can hold twice as much memory as SIMM chips.

**DIP Switch**    Dual In-line Package (DIP) switches are very tiny boxes with switches embedded in them. Each switch sets a value of 0 or 1, depending on how they are set. These switches are used to provide user-accessible configuration settings for computers and peripheral devices.

**Direct Memory Access**    See DMA.

**Dirty Current**     Noise present on a power line is referred to as dirty current. This noise is caused by *electro-magnetic interference (EMI)* and can stray, or leak, from the current into nearby components. When EMI leaks from power current, it is called a magnetic field and can easily damage computer components.

**DMA**     Direct memory access (DMA) is a facility by which a peripheral can communicate directly with RAM, without intervention by the CPU.

**DNS**     Domain Name System (DNS) is the Internet-based system that resolves symbolic names to IP addresses (which are a series of numbers) that the computer is able to understand.

**Docking Station**     Docking stations allow users to add "desktop-like" capabilities, such as a mouse, monitor, or keyboard, to their portable computer by plugging these components into a docking station and connecting their portable only to the docking station, rather than to each individual component.

**Domain Name System**     See DNS.

**DOS Mode**     DOS Mode, or DOS Compatibility Mode as it is commonly known, allows execution of some older MS-DOS applications that are not capable of running in Windows 95. Applications that require use of MS-DOS mode are usually blocked from operation within Windows 95. DOS itself stands for Disk Operating System.

**Download**     Downloading refers to the process of transferring a file or files from one computer to another. Unlike uploading, the transfer is always initiated by the computer that will be receiving the file(s).

**Downtime**     Downtime is the time wasted as a result of a malfunctioning computer or network.

**DRAM**     Dynamic Random Access Memory (DRAM) chips abandoned the idea of using the unwieldy transistors and switches in favor of using the smaller capacitors that could represent 0s and 1s as an electronic charge. This resulted in the ability to store more information on a single chip, but also meant that the chip needed a constant refresh and hence more power.

**Dual In-line Memory Module**     See DIMM.

**Dual In-line Package Switch**     See DIP Switch.

**Dynamic RAM**     See DRAM.

**EBKAC Error**     A common error that most technicians face, the EBKAC error stands for Error Between Keyboard and Chair. As that implies, EBKAC errors are not technical errors, but rather errors on the part of the end user. Common EBKAC errors include power cords being unplugged, no paper in printer, and power switches being turned off.

**ECP**     ECP (Extended Capability Port) is a parallel printer interface designed to speed up data transfer rates by bypassing the processor and writing the data directly to memory.

**EDO RAM**     Extended Data Output RAM (EDO RAM) is a type of DRAM chip designed for processor access speeds of approximately 10 to 15 percent above fast-page mode memory.

**EISA**     Extended Industry Standard Architecture (EISA) is an industry standard bus architecture that allows for peripherals to utilize the 32-bit data bus that is available with 386 and 486 processors.

**Electrophotographic Printing Process**     See EP Process.

**EMM386.EXE**     EMM386.EXE is a DOS system file that, along with HIMEM.SYS, controls memory management. It is not required for system startup in pre-Windows 95 machines. Basically, this is an expanded memory emulator that performs two major functions: It enables and controls EMS, if desired, and enables the use of upper memory as system memory.

**EMS**     Meaning Expanded Memory Specification, EMS is an expanded memory standard that allows programs that recognize it to work with more than 640K of RAM.

**Enhanced Parallel Port**     See EPP.

**EP Process**     The EP (Electrophotographic Printing) process is the six-step process that a laser printer goes through to put an image on a page. The process follows these six steps: Cleaning, Charging, Writing, Developing, Transferring, and Fusing.

**EPP**     EPP (Enhanced Parallel Port) is an expansion bus that offers an extended control code set. With EPP mode, data travels both from the computer to the printer and vice versa.

**Error Between Keyboard and Chair**     See EBKAC Error.

**Exit Roller**     One of four different types of rollers found in printers, exit rollers aid in the transfer and control of the paper as it leaves the printer. Depending on the printer type, they direct the paper to a tray where it can be collated, sorted, or even stapled.

**Expanded Memory Specification**     See EMS.

**Extended Capability Port**     See ECP.

**Extended Data Output RAM**     See EDO RAM.

**Extended Industry Standard Architecture**     See EISA.

**eXtended Memory Specification**     See XMS.

**FDISK**     A DOS-based utility program used to partition a hard disk in preparation for installing an operating system.

**Feed Roller**     One of four different types of rollers found in printers. Also known as paper pickup roller, the feed roller, when activated, rotates against the top page in the paper tray and rolls it into the printer. The feed roller works together with a special rubber pad to prevent more than one sheet from being fed into the printer at a time.

**Fiber Optic Cable**     Extremely high-speed network cable that consists of glass fibers that carry light signals instead of electrical signals. Fiber optic cable is best used for transmission over long distances, and is much less susceptible to environmental difficulties, such as radiation.

**File Transfer Protocol**     See FTP.

**Flash Memory**     A faster version of ROM that, while still basically developed as ROM, can be addressed and loaded *thousands* of times.

**Fragmentation**     Because DOS writes files to the hard disk by breaking the file into cluster-sized pieces and then storing each piece in the next available cluster, as files are deleted and then rewritten, they can be written in noncontiguous clusters scattered all over the disk. This is known as file fragmentation.

**FTP**     Much older than the HTTP protocol, the File Transfer Protocol (FTP) is the protocol used to download files from an FTP server to a client computer. FTP is much faster than HTTP.

**Fully Qualified Path**     A fully qualified path is the entire path of a file, starting from the root of the file system, to the file being referenced.

**Fusing Rollers**     One of four different types of rollers found in laser printers, fusing rollers comprise the final stage of the Electrophotographic Printing (EP) process, bonding the toner particles to the page to prevent smearing. The roller on the toner side of the page has a non-stick surface that is heated to a high temperature to permanently bond the toner to the paper.

**Ghosted Image**    "Ghosting" is what occurs when a portion of an image previously printed to a page is printed again, only not as dark. One cause of this is if the erasure lamp of the laser printer sometimes fails to operate correctly, not completely erasing the previous image from the EP drum. Another cause of ghosting may be a malfunction in the cleaning blade such that it doesn't adequately scrape away the residual toner.

**Handshaking**    The process by which two connecting modems agree on the method of communication to be used.

**HIDDEN Attribute**    The Hidden attribute keeps a file from being displayed when a DIR command is issued.

**HIMEM.SYS**    HIMEM.SYS is a DOS system file that, along with EMM386.EXE, controls memory management. It is not required for system startup in pre-Windows 95 machines.

**Hot Dock**    Hot docking is the ability of a system to accept new accessories while it is plugged in.

**HTML**    Derived from the Standard General Markup Language (SGML), the Hypertext Markup Language (HTML) is the markup language that dictates the layout and design of a Web page.

**HTTP**    Hypertext Transfer Protocol (HTTP) is the TCP/IP-based protocol that is most commonly used for client/server communications on the World Wide Web.

**Hub**    Hubs are common connection points for devices in a network. Hubs contain multiple ports and are commonly used to connect segments of a LAN.

**Hypertext Markup Language**     See HTML.

**Hypertext Transfer Protocol**     See HTTP.

**Impact Printer**     Impact printers, like the name suggests, require the impact with an ink ribbon to print characters and images. An example of an impact printer is a daisy wheel.

**Industry Standard Architecture**     See ISA.

**Input Device**     Input devices take data from a user, such as the click of a mouse or the typing on a keyboard, and convert that data into electrical signals used by your computer. Several devices that provide input are: keyboards, mice, trackballs, pointing devices, digitized tablets, and touch screens.

**Internet Service Provider**     See ISP.

**Internetwork Packet Exchange/Sequenced Packet Exchange**     See IPX/SPX.

**Interrupt Request Line**     See IRQ.

**IO.SYS**     IO.SYS is a DOS system file that defines basic input/output routines for the processor. By default, it carries the hidden, system, and read-only attributes, and *is* required for OS startup.

**IPX/SPX**     Internetwork Packet Exchange/Sequenced Packet Exchange (IPX/SPX) is a very fast and highly established network protocol most commonly used with Novell NetWare.

**IRQ**     Interrupt Request (IRQ) lines are the physical lines over which system components such as modems or printers communicate directly with the CPU when the device is ready to send or receive data.

**ISA**    Industry Standard Architecture (ISA) is an industry standard bus architecture that allows for peripherals to utilize the 16-bit data bus that is available with 286 and 386 processors.

**ISP**    An Internet Service Provider (ISP), as its name suggests, is a company that provides users with access to the Internet, usually for a fee. On the other hand, a company that gives their employees Internet access through a private bank of modems is usually not considered an ISP.

**Jumper**    Jumpers, like DIP switches, are used to accomplish configuration manually. Jumpers are actually made of two separate components: a row of metal pins on the hardware itself and a small plastic cap that has a metal insert inside of it. The two parts together form a circuit that sets the configuration. This form of configuration device is only used to set one value for a feature at a time, as opposed to DIP switches, which can handle multiple configurations.

**LAN**    A local area network (LAN) is created whenever two or more computers in a limited geographic area (within about a two-mile radius) are linked by high-performance cables so that users can exchange information, share peripheral devices, or access a common server.

**Local Area Network**    See LAN.

**Material Safety Data Sheets**    See MSDS.

**MEM.EXE**    MEM.EXE is a simple command line utility that, using various command switches, can display various reports of memory usage.

**MEMMAKER.EXE**    A Microsoft utility that automatically determines the best possible configuration and load sequence for a given set of applications and drivers used. Before using MEMMAKER, the PC should be configured for normal operation (i.e., mouse driver, network operation, sound support, and so forth), including any items that are loaded from the AUTOEXEC.BAT and CONFIG.SYS files.

**Memory Address**    The memory address is used to receive commands from the processor that are destined for any device attached to a computer. Each device must have a unique memory address in order for it to function.

**Memory Bank**    A memory bank is the actual slot that memory goes into.

**Memory Effect**    When a Nickel Cadmium, or NiCad, battery is recharged before it is fully discharged, the battery loses the ability to fully recharge again, which is known as the memory effect.

**MSD.EXE**    MSD, Microsoft Diagnostics, is a DOS-based utility that provides a great deal of information about the system. It is most useful in determining what the system has installed in it, such as memory and hard drives.

**MSDOS.SYS**    MSDOS.SYS is a DOS system file that defines system file locations. By default, it carries the hidden, system, and read-only attributes, and is required for OS startup.

**MSDS**    Material Safety Data Sheets (MSDS) are white pages that contain information on any substance that is deemed hazardous, most notably cleaning solvents. The purpose of MSDS is to inform employees about the dangers inherent in hazardous materials and the proper use of these items to prevent potential injuries from occurring.

**Multi-Boot Configuration**    A system that has been configured to use more than one operating system.

**Multimeter**    A multimeter is a device that measures current, resistance, or voltage, used to determine whether certain computer components are functioning correctly based on these electrical measurements.

**NetBEUI**     The NetBIOS Extended User Interface (NetBEUI) is an extremely fast network transport protocol that is most commonly found on smaller networks.

**NetBIOS Extended User Interface**     See NetBEUI.

**Network Interface Card**     See NIC.

**Network Topology**     The arrangement of cable links in a local area network. There are three principal network topologies: bus, ring, and star.

**NIC**     A network interface card (NIC) is used to connect a PC to a network cable.

**Noise Filter**     UPSs contain a special filter, called a *noise filter*, that reduces the amount of noise present in electrical current and eliminates magnetic fields caused by noise, thus providing some protection to the components that utilize the current or are nearby.

**Non-Impact Printer**     Non-impact printers do not use an ink ribbon, and therefore do not require direct contact with the paper for printing. An example of a non-impact printer is a laser printer.

**Normal Mode**     Normal Mode is the mode in which Windows 95 is started by default, which provides full functionality of the Windows 95 Explorer.

**Null Modem Cable**     A null modem cable is a special cable that has the send and receive lines reversed on the connector. It enables you to connect two computers directly, without using a modem.

**Operating System**     See OS.

**Operator Error**     Operator error occurs when the customer inadvertently makes a configuration change.

**OS**    By definition, an Operating System (OS) is a set of computer instruction codes, usually *compiled* into executable files, whose purpose is to define input and output devices and connections, and provide instructions for the computer's central processor to operate on to retrieve and display data.

**Output Device**    Output devices take electronic signals *from* a computer and convert them into a format that the user can use. Examples of output devices include monitors and printers.

**Overlays**    Rather than put all available functions into a single huge executable file, most developers choose to modularize their applications by creating library files that include additional commands and functions. These additional executable enhancement files are usually referred to as overlays.

**Page Description Language**    See PDL.

**Parallel Port**    One of two types of communication ports found on a motherboard (the other is the serial port), the parallel port is used to connect a peripheral device (most commonly a printer for this type of port) to the computer. A parallel port allows transmission of data over eight conductors at one time. The processor socket is the actual socket used to attach the processor to the motherboard.

**Parallel Processing**    The Intel 586 (Pentium) chip combines two 486DX chips into one, called the *Dual Independent Bus Architecture*. This allows each processor inside the chip to execute instructions simultaneously and independently from each other, which is called parallel processing.

**Parity**    Parity is an error-checking mechanism that enables the device to recognize single-bit errors.

**Partition**    A section of the storage area on a computer's hard disk. A hard disk must be partitioned before an operating system can be installed.

**Passive Matrix Display**    Most common on portable systems, the passive matrix display is made from a grid of horizontal and vertical wires. At the end of each wire is a transistor. In order to light a pixel at (X, Y), a signal is sent to the X and Y transistors. In turn, these transistors then send voltage down the wire, which turns on the LCD at the intersection of the two wires.

**PC Card**    The PC Card (Personal Computer Memory Card International Association, or PCMCIA) bus was first created to expand the memory capabilities in small, hand-held computers. It is a type of bus used mostly with laptop computers that provides a convenient way to interchange PCMCIA-compatible devices. The card itself is only slightly larger than a credit card.

**PCI**    The Peripheral Component Interconnect (PCI) was designed in response to the Pentium class processor's utilization of a 64-bit bus. PCI buses are designed to be processor-independent.

**PCMCIA**    See PC Card.

**PDL**    Laser printers use a Page Description Language (PDL) to send and receive print job instructions one page at a time, rather than one dot at a time, as with other types of printers.

**Peripheral Component Interconnect**    See PCI.

**Personal Computer Memory Card International Association**    See PC Card.

**Photosensitive Drum**    This light-sensitive drum is the core of the electrophotographic process inside the laser printer. This drum is affected by the cleaning, charging, writing, and transferring processes in the six-step laser printing process.

**Plug and Play**    Introduced with Microsoft Windows 95, Plug and Play offers automatic driver installation as soon as hardware or software is "plugged in," or installed.

**Pointing Stick**    One of the three most common types of pointing devices found on portable systems, the pointing stick is a small piece of rubber the size of a pencil eraser in the center of the keyboard. The on-screen pointer is controlled by simply pushing the pointing stick in the desired direction.

**Point-to-Point Protocol**    See PPP.

**POLEDIT.EXE**    The Windows 95 System Policy feature, POLEDIT.EXE, is used to set common-denominator defaults for all network users, and add certain restrictions on a global basis if deemed necessary.

**POP**    Post Office Protocol (POP) is a system by which an Internet server lets you receive e-mail and download it from the server to your own machine.

**POST**    As its name suggests, a Power On Self Test (POST) is self test performed by the computer that occurs during boot time. It is used to diagnose system-related problems.

**Post Office Protocol**    See POP.

**Power On Self Test**    See POST.

**Power Spike**    When there is a power spike, there is a sudden, huge increase in power that lasts for a split second. Power spikes can literally burn out computer components.

**PPP**    The Point-to-Point protocol (PPP) is a serial communications protocol used to connect two computers over a phone line via a modem. SLIP is the alternate protocol that is acceptable to most browsers, though it's not as common as PPP.

**Preemptive Multitasking**     There are two different types of multitasking: cooperative and preemptive. Preemptive multitasking means that control is passed from one program to another automatically by the Windows process scheduler.

**Primary Corona Wire**     This highly negatively charged wire inside a laser printer is responsible for electrically erasing the photosensitive drum, preparing it to be written with a new image in the writing stage of the laser print process.

**Processor Socket**     The processor socket is the actual socket used to attach the processor to the motherboard.

**Protocol**     A set of communication standards between two computers on a network. Common protocols include TCP/IP, NetBEUI, and IPX/SPX.

**READ ONLY Attribute**     The READ ONLY attribute prevents a user or application from inadvertently deleting or changing a file.

**Refresh**     Refresh refers to the automatic process of constantly updating memory chips to ensure that their signals are correct. The refresh rate is the frequency by which chips are refreshed, usually about every 60 to 70 thousandths of a second.

**Registration Roller**     One of four different types of rollers found in laser printers, the registration roller synchronizes the paper movement with the writing process inside the EP cartridge. Registration rollers do not advance the paper until the EP cartridge is ready to process the next line of the image.

**Ring Topology**     In a local area network, a ring topology has each device arranged around a closed-loop cable. This is most commonly used  with fiber optic cabling.

**Rollers**     Rollers are located inside a printer to aid in the movement of paper through the printer. There are four main types of rollers: feed, registration, fuser, and exit.

**Safe Mode**　　Safe Mode is a special diagnostic mode of Windows 95 that starts the operating system without any network, CD-ROM, and printer drivers. This special mode allows you to change an incorrect setting, which will in most cases allow you to return an abnormally functioning system to its correct operation.

**Serial Port**　　One of two types of communication ports found on a motherboard (the other is the parallel port), the serial port connects to a serial line that leads to a computer peripheral—the type used most commonly with modems and mice. The serial port transmits data sequentially, bit by bit over a single conductor.

**SIMD**　　Single Instruction Multiple Data (SIMD) works by allowing a single instruction to operate on multiple pieces of data when an application is performing a repetitive loop.

**SIMM**　　A Single In-line Memory Module (SIMM) is a small plug-in circuit board that contains the memory chips that you need to add certain increments of RAM to your computer. The chips are positioned along one side of the board.

**Simple Mail Transfer Protocol**　　See SMTP.

**Single In-line Memory Module**　　See SIMM.

**Single Instruction Multiple Data**　　See SIMD.

**Slack**　　Slack is the space left between the end of a file and the end of the cluster in which the file resides.

**SLIP**　　The Serial Line Interface Protocol (SLIP) is a protocol used to manage telecommunications between a client and a server over a phone line. PPP is the alternate protocol that is acceptable to most browsers, and is in fact the most common.

**SMTP**    Simple Mail Transfer Protocol (SMTP) is the underlying protocol for Internet-based e-mail.

**Socket Services**    Socket Services is a layer of BIOS-level software that isolates PC Card software from the computer hardware and detects the insertion or removal of PC Cards.

**Solenoid**    The solenoid is a resistive coil found in dot matrix and daisy wheel printers. When the solenoid is energized, the pin is forced away from the printhead and impacts the printer ribbon and ultimately the paper, thus impressing the image on the page.

**SRAM**    Unlike DRAM, Static RAM (SRAM) retains its value as long as power is supplied. It is not constantly refreshed. However, SRAM does require a periodic update and tends to use excessive amounts of power when it does so.

**Star Topology**    In a local area network, a star topology has each device on the network connected to a central processor, usually a hub. This is most commonly used with twisted pair cabling.

**Static RAM**    See SRAM.

**Stylus**    Shaped like a pen, a stylus is used to select menu options and the like on a monitor screen or to draw line art on a graphics tablet.

**Sync Frequency**    Monitors use a *sync frequency* to control the refresh rate, which is the rate at which the display device is repainted. If this setting is incorrect, you get symptoms such as: a "dead" monitor, lines running through the display, a flickering screen, and a reduced or enlarged image.

**SYSTEM Attribute**    The SYSTEM attribute is usually set by DOS or Windows, and cannot be modified using standard DOS or Windows commands, including the ATTRIB command or File Manager.

**SYSTEM.INI**    SYSTEM.INI is a Windows system file that configures Windows to address specific hardware devices and their associated settings. Errors in this file can and do cause Windows to fail to start, or crash unexpectedly.

**TCP/IP**    The most common protocol in use today, Transmission Control Protocol/Internet Protocol (TCP/IP) is the protocol upon which the Internet was built. It refers to the communication standards for data transmission over the Internet.

**Time Slicing**    The process of the CPU dividing up time between applications for preemptive multitasking is called time slicing.

**Token Passing**    Token passing is a network communication protocol by which a token is passed from device to device around a virtual (and frequently physical) ring on a network. Whenever a device receives the token, it is then allowed to transmit onto the network.

**Toner**    Toner is comprised of finely divided particles of plastic resin and organic compounds bonded to iron particles. It is naturally negatively charged, which aids in attracting it to the written areas of the photosensitive drum during the transfer step of the laser printing process.

**Touch Pad**    A touch pad is a stationary pointing device commonly used on laptop computers in replace of a mouse or trackball. They are pads that have either thin wires running through them, or specialized surfaces that can sense the pressure of your finger on them. You slide your finger across the touchpad to control the pointer or cursor on the screen.

**Trackball**    Most commonly, trackballs are used in older portable computers to replace a mouse. Trackballs are built the same way as an opto-mechanical mouse, except upside down with the ball on top.

**Transfer Corona**    This roller inside a laser printer contains a positively charged wire designed to pull the toner off of the photosensitive drum and place it on the page.

**Transistor**    A transistor is the most fundamental component of electronic circuits. A CPU chip, for example, contains thousands to millions of transistors, which are used to process information in the form of electronic signals. The more transistors a CPU has, the faster it can process data.

**Transmission Control Protocol/Internet Protocol**    See TCP/IP.

**Twisted Pair**    By far the most common type of network cable, twisted pair consists of two insulated wires wrapped around each other to help avoid interference from other wires.

**Uninterruptible Power Supply**    See UPS.

**Upload**    Uploading is the process of transferring files from one computer to another. Unlike downloading, uploading is always initiated from the computer that is sending the files.

**UPS**    The uninterruptible power supply (UPS) is a device that was designed to protect your computer and its components from possible injury from the problems that are inherent with today's existing power supply structure.

**VESA Local Bus**    See VL-Bus.

**Virtual Memory**    Virtual memory is memory that the processor borrows from the hard drive as if it were actual physical RAM.

**Virus**    Any program that is written with the intent of doing harm to a computer. Viruses have the ability to replicate themselves by attaching themselves to programs or documents. They range in activity from extreme data loss to an annoying message that pops up every few minutes.

**VL-Bus**    Originally created to address performance issues, the VESA Local Bus (VL-Bus) was meant to enable earlier bus designs to handle a maximum clock speed equivalent to that of processors.

**WAN**    A wide area network (WAN) is created whenever two or more computers are linked by long-distance communication lines that traverse distances greater than those supported by LANs (or, greater than about two miles).

**Wide Area Network**    See WAN.

**WIN.INI**    WIN.INI is a dynamic Windows system file that contains configuration information for Windows applications. Errors made in this file seldom have global implications to Window's operation, but can cripple specific applications or features. Printing is also controlled by settings in this file.

**Windows Accelerator Card RAM**    See WRAM.

**WINFILE.INI**    In pre-Windows 95 systems, this is the configuration file that stores the names of the directories that File Manager displays when starting.

**WRAM**    The Windows Accelerator Card was introduced into the market out of a need to assist some environments with running Microsoft Windows. WRAM utilizes memory that resides on the card itself to perform the Windows-specific functions, and therefore speeds up the OS.

**XMS**    Meaning eXtended Memory Specification, XMS is a set of standards that allows applications to access extended memory.

**Zoomed Video**    See ZV.

**ZV**    Zoomed Video (ZV) is a direct data connection between a PC Card and host system that allows a PC Card to write video data directly to the video controller.

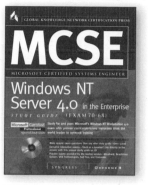